THE
U. S. PRESIDENCY
IN CRISIS
A Comparative Perspective

COLIN CAMPBELL

New York   Oxford
OXFORD UNIVERSITY PRESS
1998

To
Moya and Ben

Oxford University Press

Oxford   New York
Athens   Auckland   Bangkok   Bogota   Bombay
Buenos Aires   Calcutta   Cape Town   Dar es Salaam
Delhi   Florence   Hong Kong   Istanbul   Karachi
Kuala Lumpur   Madras   Madrid   Melbourne
Mexico City   Nairobi   Paris   Singapore
Taipei   Tokyo   Toronto   Warsaw
and associated companies in
Berlin   Ibadan

Copyright © 1998 by Oxford University Press, Inc.

Published by Oxford University Press, Inc.,
198 Madison Avenue, New York, New York 10016

Library of Congress Cataloging-in-Publication Data
Campbell, Colin, 1943-
The U.S. presidency in crisis: a comparative
perspective / Colin Campbell.
p.   cm.
Includes bibliographical references (p.) and index.
ISBN 0-19-509143-4 (cl). —ISBN 0-19-509144-2 (pb)
1. Presidents—United States.   2. Executive power—Great Britain.
3. Executive power—Canada.   4. Executive power—Australia.
I. Title.
JK516.C36   1998
352.23'0973—dc21   97-27332

9 8 7 6 5 4 3 2 1
Printed in the United States of America
on acid-free paper

Contents

Acknowledgments

This book stems from work on the US presidency and executive leadership in the United Kingdom, Canada and Australia spanning more than twenty years. In that period, I have conducted nearly 700 interviews with senior government officials in the respective countries. My methodological approach is more fully described in Campbell and Szablowski (1979), Campbell (1983), Campbell (1986), Campbell and Halligan (1992) and Campbell and Wilson (1995). The development of my thoughts and work over the years also owes a great debt to my previous co-authors—George J. Szablowski, John Halligan and Graham K. Wilson.

My earlier books on executive leadership have mentioned over twenty research assistants who helped me in previous projects. To these I add ten students who worked on this current book—namely, Maria Gonzalez-Asis, Peggy Kim, Jose Antonio Mejia, Juan-Carlos Mendoza, Matthew Michael, Xuan Nguyen, Cory Porter, Stephen Shannon, John Joseph Smith and Lin Xia. I am immensely grateful for their dedication and diligence. Of course, very warm thanks go to my assistant Nancy Farley who has served as ringmaster for my projects since 1989.

I have derived immense satisfaction and counsel from testing out the ideas found in this book with a marvelous group of colleagues and friends including Joel D. Aberbach, Peter Aucoin, Jonathan Boston, Harvey Feigenbaum, Peter Hennessy, Charles O. Jones, George W. Jones, William Keegan, Anthony King, Gillian Peele, B. Guy Peters, John Power, Paul J. Quirk, A. James Reichley, Bert A. Rockman, Byron E. Shafer, Norman C. Thomas, Elaine Thompson, R. Kent Weaver, and the late Aaron Wildavsky.

Very special thanks go to the faculty, staff and students of Campion Hall and Nuffield College at Oxford where I developed my preliminary ideas for this book while presenting the Martin D'Arcy lectures during Hilary term in 1993. I am especially grateful to Joseph Munitiz, SJ,

Norman Tanner, SJ, and Byron Shafer, of the respective institutions, for arranging for joint sponsorship of the six-part series.

My editors at Oxford, especially David Roll who signed the book and Nancy Lane who brought it in for a landing, proved immensely helpful throughout this project. As well, the work greatly benefitted from the critiques of anonymous referees, both of the original proposal and the final manuscript.

Finally, I dedicate this book to my wife Moya Langtry, who could not be a better partner in the executive leadership of our little family, and my stepson Ben Sullivan, who displays great patience and understanding when his mother and I try to micromanage his never-dull life as a twentysomething.

1

Putting the U.S. Presidency in a Wider Context

As the saying goes, "If it isn't broken, don't fix it." Applying this to the U.S. presidency, we find good news and bad news. The latter is that the presidency is indeed broken. The good news is that it has good company. Chief executives have encountered much greater difficulty in leading advanced democracies than they did in the two decades immediately following WWII. To be sure, some of their problems have taken root in structural defects stemming from constitutional frameworks. Yet, executive leadership has proven extremely difficult regardless of institutional settings.

To get the presidency on the road to recovery we have to take it out of the isolation ward. There observers have focused excessively on the exceptionality of the American case. Sometimes people will say that something is "extremely unique." When we hear this we know that we have encountered something that is not in fact unique. Rather it represents an extreme on some sort of continuum. We might well conclude in this book that the US presidency is extremely broken. But this will not ipso facto make it unique.

The issue of executive leadership is a huge topic. However, it appears to be an especially urgent one these days. This clearly is the case in countries such as Italy and Japan. There concerns about ossification and corruption—almost overnight—demolished the political viability of parties that had established themselves as the natural government in the entire postwar epoch. Considering the other established democracies in the world, we would likely conclude that four Anglo-American democracies—the United States, United Kingdom, Canada, and Australia—comprise the next most challenged of troubled regimes. (New Zealand ostensibly belongs to this category. However, it has embraced such radical reforms since 1984 that caution counsels against its inclusion in this book.)

A distemper of sorts has arisen in these very old democracies. Part of the problem rests in a sea change in public assent to the role of the state in their lives. And each of these countries has found itself in a less competitive economic situation in the last twenty years than it did in the immediate postwar era. Perhaps more fundamentally, the dynamics of the relationship between executive leaders and voters have changed almost entirely in the new electronic era of politics. Almost Messianic expectations emerge around certain figures—often relatively unseasoned—who manage to obtain power. However, lynch law often sets in when these individuals seem to compromise principle to pragmatic considerations. Publics also appear not to consider honest mistakes as forgivable. If Anglo-American voters instituted a three-strikes-and-you're-out policy, most hapless chief executives would heave a sigh of relief.

If the crisis of executive leadership in Anglo-American democracies were a linear phenomenon, then it might not be that interesting to examine in detail. In fact, it has served up a number of inconsistencies and ironies. This makes the topic inherently engaging. Even looking for a moment at the immediate landscape, imagine the richness of what presents itself. In the United States, voters rebuked Bill Clinton by throwing Democrats out of power in the Senate and the House of Representatives. For a year, the action significantly marginalized the presidency while turning Newt Gingrich into a quasi prime minister. Then the public turned on Gingrich. And Bill Clinton romped to victory in the 1996 presidential election.

In the United Kingdom, John Major retained power in a 1992 election even though voters liked him much less than his predecessor, Margaret Thatcher, and he ran a poor campaign (Newton 1993; Butler and Kavanagh 1992, 247–268). Voters shied from going back to Labour. They immediately turned on Major—especially after the collapse of the pound in September 1992. This backlash turned Major's second term into a torment. The Labour Party seized power in the May 1997 general election.

From 1984 to 1993, Canada experienced nine years of rule by a man, Brian Mulroney, who interpreted voter unhappiness with the Liberal Party as a mandate to redefine the Canadian state. In the 1993 election, two new parties emerged which brought Mulroneyism to its logical conclusions—the Reform, which embodied the rugged individualism of the Western provinces, and Bloc Quebecois, which brought committed separatists to the federal Parliament. These two vehicles for those unhappy with the nature of the Canadian state struck voters as much slicker streetcars than the Progressive Conservatives. Canada's first party of government ended up with two seats in the House of Commons, less than required to be considered a party at all.

Australia has attracted international attention for its pursuit of market-oriented economic policies. Interestingly, Labor governments pressed the core reforms during the mid-1980s. Labor lost power in 1996 under an acerbic and not-loved Paul Keating. At the time of its passing, the Keating government bore all the marks of a cadre which had run out of steam.

Anglo-American systems, thus, share the experience of passing through especially difficult times for executive leadership. Beyond this point, however, this book considers the crisis of the U.S. presidency along with that of other Anglo-American systems for four reasons. First, all share similar constitutional legacies—although, of course, the United States is presidential as against parliamentary; the United Kingdom is unitary rather than federal; and the United Kingdom is without a written constitution, while it and Australia do not have a written bill of rights.

Second, elites in the four systems tend to refer to the practices of one another when adapting to change. Here U.S. and U.K. elites make much of the "special relationship." Canadian traditionalists tend to stress British practice in preference to U.S. because of deep concern about the erosion of the integrity of the Canadian system in relation to the allure of the U.S. presidential system. Australians have proven immensely eclectic—adopting innovations from the various systems without deep concerns about whether they fit within the "presidential" or "parliamentary" traditions. Indeed, their approach has become manifest in the debate over whether the country should become a republic.

Third, all four countries considered themselves "victors" after WWII. They went through two decades of relative economic prosperity. The upbeat view of democracy and sense of well-being fueled in all four systems unprecedented inventiveness and expansiveness in governance. By the 1970s, all four countries—especially in the face of two energy shocks, disillusionment with democracy, and sharp declines of relative economic advantage—began to wake up to the fact that they had in some respects perhaps lost WWII.

Fourth, and very important, all systems maintain fairly sharp distinctions between the vocations of the political leadership and permanent government officials. This does not suggest a greater salience in these countries of the distinction between policy and administration—far from it. However, even in the United States—with the immense importance of political appointees—a line is drawn between what is proper for political executives and for career bureaucrats. In most continental bureaucracies and in Japan, on the other hand, permanent officials must now identify with one or other partisan group to insure their advancement. Differences in the executive-bureaucratic cultures of the Anglo-American systems and those of other advanced democracies mean that the former make symbiosis between politicians and bureaucrats less attainable. In turn, this constrains the degree of policy coherence that these systems might achieve.

How the crisis of executive leadership has worked its effects in Anglo-American countries since the late 1970s suggests strong commonality for three reasons. All have made a sharp diversion to minimalist government, which has worked wrenching effects on the functions and performance of the state. The resulting building-down of government has borne serious consequences for infrastructure, the balance between regulation and markets in the operation of the economy, and the social well-being of citizenries. Finally, with the emphasis on minimalism and disengagement of leaders from the state apparatus, political executives have stressed style at the expense of substance. This has resulted in an overuse of direct appeals to the public with little regard to the standing political-bureaucratic complex—a practice which makes systems error-prone. It also has encouraged presidents and prime ministers to resort to crisis inflation to galvanize political support. Both practices undermine the capacity for democratic institutions to deliberate and self-correct.

The rest of this chapter treats in detail the points of commonality between Anglo-American systems and the elements of their shared crises.

THE ANGLO-AMERICAN LEGACY

Constitutional and Historical Factors

Common language bespeaks a similar heritage. The principles associated with rule of law (Jowell 1989) and a balance of power between the elements of government—with the convention of parliamentary "supremacy"—first took root in Britain (Bradley 1989). Regarding the latter, Montesquieu's conception of a separation of powers—which played such an important role in the development of the American Constitution—derived originally from his analysis of structural reasons explaining why Britain had attained much greater liberty than had France. To be sure, the United States emerged from a revolution which repudiated British rule. But this rupture did not extend to every dimension of the British form of governance (Diamond 1975; McDonald 1985, 12, 144, 209–213).

The leadership problem as it manifested itself at the time of the American Revolution stemmed from the nonresponsiveness and incompetence of the German family that had assumed the British crown early in the eighteenth century (Mackintosh 1977, 51, 67). The initial American experiment tried to pursue rule without strong executive authority of any kind, even at the state level (Wood 1969, 136). This effort collapsed. The resulting constitutional discussions attempted a delicate balancing act. They sought to provide enough executive authority to enable the government to perform coherently (Ketcham 1984, 5–7). Yet, they also tried to insure that no head of state could rule impetuously.

In its 200-plus years, the resulting arrangement has frequently facilitated coherent rule (Mayhew 1991; Jones 1994). This is no small achievement in an especially fragmented society. However, the Constitution also has produced its moments of near-imperial governance, on one extreme (Neustadt 1976, 27–34), and it has on occasion slumped into paralytic gridlock, on the other (Campbell 1991). And some Americans, at least, still glance longingly at the British system with responsible party government and unity between the executive and legislative branches (Sundquist 1986; 1988–89).

On occasion, parliaments can work relatively swiftly at holding the government of the day to account for gross misdeeds (Turpin 1989, 74–79). However, in some countries and cases the evidence is ambiguous (Campbell and Wilson 1995, 255–259; Finn 1993, 136–137). Watergate presents itself as one incident in which a parliamentary system would likely have facilitated a more rapid transfer of authority than allowed for in the cumbersome impeachment process. But parliaments adapt even more readily when chief executives have simply become nonresponsive. As Margaret Thatcher found, parliaments conveniently can shed a leader who has worn out her welcome without removing an entire administration.

Perhaps more enticingly, parliamentary systems provide a framework in which a government can actually deliver upon its programmatic commitments. Those on the right and left in the United States have found this characteristic especially appealing. Westminster systems remain important to the American political consciousness because they work a fairly positive demonstration effect—an aptitude for getting things done.

Links between Leaders

The elites of political systems make up a very exclusive club. The normal run of international engagements and transactions involves a phenomenal amount of interaction. Political leaders and top officials usually cannot resist the temptation on such occasions to compare notes on how they conduct their business. In fact, entire units in international organizations such as the World Bank, the Organization for Economic Development and Cooperation, and the International Monetary Fund take as their function cross-fertilization of the best practices for governance.

A bias emerges here among the Anglo-American systems. No other four countries claim similar commonality. History and language make communication and understanding much simpler than proves the case between other constellations of countries. As a result, the Anglo-American systems mimic one another a great deal. Look at the development of market-oriented, neo-liberalism during the 1980s (Niskanen 1973a; Roberts 1984; Aucoin 1990; Pusey 1991). It spread like wildfire through Anglo-American systems in a period when most other nations clung to postwar paradigms focused on planning and state intervention.

Anglo-American systems differ greatly in their proclivities for organic views of society. Still, historically they all have placed great value in the autonomy of the individual. For instance, the U.S. Declaration of Independence states that it seeks "life liberty and the pursuit of happiness." The preamble of Canada's constitution, on the other hand, enshrines "peace, order and good government." Yet both countries give great weight to similar principles of the rule of law. For instance, in each system an individual charged with a crime is assumed to be innocent until proven guilty—a principle that does not pertain in most of continental Europe. And each has basic documents—for the United States the Bill of Rights and for Canada the Charter of Rights and Freedoms—in the respective constitutions which place a premium on the protection of the individual from arbitrary governmental actions. Only through a tortuous process culminating in a constitutional amendment in 1982 did Canada adopt this approach (Tarnopolsky 1983). In the United Kingdom and Australia, the courts do not find recourse to written constitutional documents when judging whether the executive or the legislative branches have failed to adhere to rule of law.

Anyone who monitors developments in executive leadership between Anglo-American systems finds a tremendous amount of copycat behavior. When Robert McNamara developed the Planning-Programming-Budgeting System under President John F. Kennedy, variants of the device soon cropped up, albeit with considerable modification, in the United Kingdom and Canada (Kaufmann 1964, 21–23, 28–32; Wildavsky 1974, Ch. 6; Heclo and Wildavsky 1974, 272; Doern 1971, 87–88). Public choice emerged in the United States in the late 1960s as a prescription for fighting budgetary logrolling and the tendency for bureaucrats to engage in institutional (and, by extension, self-) aggrandizement (Buchanan and Tullock 1962). Political leaders did not take public choice theory to heart until stagflation struck in the late 1970s. To many, it became clear that the circumstances required shock treatment. This would involve automatization of budget decisions forcing public sector organizations to go cold turkey on bureaucratic aggrandizement (Niskanen 1971; 1973b). Top analysts saw this new emphasis as comporting with the tendency to downplay programmatic approaches to budgeting in times of fiscal constraint (Schick 1981, 94–95; Wildavsky 1983, 181). Its adherents achieved much greater success in the United Kingdom and Australia than they did in the United States and Canada (Keegan 1984, 107–182; Keating and Dixon 1989). In the latter cases, the fragmented nature of the respective policy arenas made automatization of budget cuts too difficult to achieve with any consistency (Peterson and Rom 1988; Pierson 1994, 176–178; Carmichael 1988).

Personalities enter into the equation as well. To begin, Britain and the United States are supposed to sustain a "special relationship" (Bartlett 1992). This informal concord built upon the partnership forged between the two nations during WWII. The fact that the two nations initially stood as the only nuclear powers resisting Russian imperialism certainly deepened the psychological bond (Taylor 1990, 58–59). In 1946, Winston Churchill employed the term "Iron Curtain" for the first time on American soil. He had already confected the term "special relationship" in 1943. Facing a new hegemony, Britons had played up intangible cultural factors as a means of keeping the attention of the United States (Dimbleby and Reynolds 1989, 95–96).

The special relationship requires comity between actual incumbents. Harold Macmillan and John F. Kennedy worked out an arduous but difficult agreement in 1962 after the Pentagon's cancellation of the Skybolt nuclear weapons system left the British without a modernized deterrent. Although the crisis did some damage to Macmillan's political viability, the two leaders concluded their negotiations without their relationship having been damaged (Fisher 1982, 300–304). Ronald Reagan attempted the role of mediator when the Falklands crisis broke out in 1982. In fact, even before the hostilities began, he saw to it that Britain received intelligence, logistical support, and supplies—which many say made the difference in this extravagantly risky venture (Freedman 1988, 44, 72). Mrs. Thatcher bucked up George Bush in the immediate aftermath of the Iraqi invasion of Kuwait (Thatcher 1993, 816–822). Some say that had she not been conferring with Bush in Colorado precisely as he was crafting his response, the United States might never have concocted the scheme which resulted in Desert Shield (Gordon and Trainor 1995, 36–37).

Relations between U.S. presidents and Canadian prime ministers have worked less well. Kennedy and John Diefenbaker—the Canadian prime minister from 1957 to 1963—became deeply antagonistic toward one another. One slight—real or just perceived—seemed to follow upon the other until, as perceived by Diefenbaker, any basis for personal friendship had completely dissipated (Bothwell, Drummond, and English 1981, 232). Lester B. Pearson—prime minister between 1963 and 1968—dared to utter publicly qualms about the war in Vietnam (Pearson 1975, 138–139). For this affront, he faced the ire of Lyndon Johnson. When the two men next met, Johnson grabbed Pearson by the lapels of his jacket as he underscored his displeasure with the prime minister (Bothwell, Drummond, and English 1981, 277).

Pierre Elliott Trudeau's term in office spanned the Nixon, Ford, Carter, and Reagan administrations—beginning in 1968 and ending in

1984 (with nine months off in 1979–80 during the brief government of Joe Clark). This imposing figure—perhaps the greatest intellect to serve since WWII as a chief executive in any Anglo-American country (Radwanski 1978, 119–20, 347)—often encountered difficulty with presidents. Trudeau's facial expressions and body language frequently betrayed his inability to suffer fools gladly—as became evident the first time he met Ronald Reagan (Granatstein and Bothwell 1990, 321). Occupancy of the most powerful office in the world did not exempt American presidents from Trudeau's aura of superiority. Trudeau did not even warm to Jimmy Carter—who at least was a great mind if not a true intellectual (ibid. 99–100). United States–Canadian relations became extremely strained during the Trudeau years. Brian Mulroney's calls for a more conciliatory attitude toward the Americans contributed to voters' support of the Progressive Conservatives in the 1984 election. Mulroney and Ronald Reagan—both misty-eyed Celts—became exceptionally fond of each other (Jeffrey 1992, 205–220; Martin 1993, 57). Right-of-center parties now held power simultaneously in the United States, United Kingdom, and Canada for the first time since 1960. Reagan, Thatcher, and Mulroney began to see themselves as a triumvirate—spreading the neo-liberal gospel in the English-speaking world. The North Atlantic was finally safe and sound for capitalism. In time, any vestiges of the overweening welfare state would disappear.

Not so easy in Canada: the Canadian publics' broad support of the welfare state made it difficult for Mulroney to keep up with Reagan and Thatcher in the realm of domestic policy. Discretion being the better part of valor, he pressed the neo-liberal line by stealth (Jeffrey 1992, 228–229). As well, tensions between Quebec and Ottawa diverted much of his attention and energy from the neo-liberal agenda. Mulroney knew that Canadians' view of the minimum safety net would cost more than the American variant. Even hints of dismantling programs met with howls of protest—forcing the Conservatives time and again to take political cover.

Mulroney made up for his domestic lapses in neo-liberal observance. He set Canada on course for a Free Trade Agreement with the United States—notwithstanding the fact that polls indicated that public support for this initiative remained very soft (Doern and Tomlin 1991, 294–295). The adverse consequences of the agreement contributed to public aversion to the Conservatives and their virtual annihilation in the 1993 federal election.

The bonhomie between Mulroney and Reagan offers an instance when a leader adopted an untenable position in order to please a "friend." Jean Chrétien—Canadian prime minister since October 1993—made it clear that he would seek a balance between Trudeau's confrontational style and Mulroney's desire to accommodate. In a pointed comment after the federal election, Chrétien noted that he would refrain from singing for Bill Clinton. He was alluding to Brian Mulroney's winning rendition of "When Irish Eyes Are Smiling," which so pleased Ronald Reagan when the two met at the 1985 Quebec Summit.

The same type of bonhomie even struck Australia's Bob Hawke (prime minister from 1983 to 1991)—though he was the head of a left-of-center party. Hawke long displayed a love of the Americans. Indeed, he used his unstinting support of Americans on defense issues as a means of undermining the more skeptical positions of Bill Hayden, his predecessor as leader of the Labor Party (Kelly 1984, 117, 186). Indeed, some observers attribute Hawke's rapid rise in the Labor Party to CIA support (Pilger 1992, 250–252, 362–364). Whatever, Hawke considered himself quite a mate of key Republicans, such as Reagan's secretary of state George Shultz with whom he liked to golf. His own memoirs speak in fawning terms of this relationship (Hawke 1994, 208). During the 1988 U.S. election, he told one interviewer that he wanted George Bush to win for the simple reason that he knew Bush and his people so well that he could readily represent Australia's interests to them. The memoirs make it appear as if he actively coached Bush on how to win the election (ibid. 427–428). In the wake of the 1990 Iraqi invasion of Kuwait, Hawke contributed a small naval force when George Bush passed the plate around to the "allies."

The Age of Interventionist Governance

Each of the Anglo-American nations played a role in pioneering liberal democracy in this century. In the first third, attention focused on extension of suffrage. Interestingly, Australia—not the United States—led the pack in this process. The fact that the country took shape as a nation at the turn of the century meant that they were writing on clean slates. Reformers could implement liberal ideals espoused in nineteenth century British political philosophy with relatively little entrenched resistance (Thompson 1994, 13–14).

In the middle third of this century, Anglo-American systems shifted their attention to how governance might attain both a high degree of democracy and social security. The collapse of the world economy in the late 1920s had spawned both the Great Depression and the rise of fascism and nazism in Europe. The view emerged that governments must do more to protect individuals from economic downturns and to redistribute wealth (Hennessy 1992). In the immediate postwar period, the increased attractiveness of communism in some western states worried leaders of Anglo-American democracies. All four grappled with the need to provide workers with tangible signs of the benefits of the liberal tradition. Unlike many of the recovering democracies in continental Europe, none of the Anglo-American systems had developed strong "statist" traditions—at least within the fields of domestic policy (King 1986, 38–39; Rockman 1984, 49). That is, they all shared a high degree of skepticism about the role of the state in guiding the economy and/or safeguarding the well-being of citizens (Esping-Andersen 1990, 31). For instance, the Germans under Bismarck had pioneered the concept of the welfare state (Pierson 1991, 104–105)—albeit one which relied upon societal stratification (Esping-Andersen 1990, 24). And the French had throughout the century drawn upon a strong tradition of harmonization between state policy and private enterprise (Feigenbaum 1985).

In so far as it had existed at all, statism in Anglo-American democracies tended to derive from the ability to mobilize civilian armies. Occurrences such as the American Civil War, the Boer War in South Africa, the Spanish American War, and the two World Wars all tended to work strong rally effects. These stemmed from a mixture of imperial aspirations and indignation over the perceived lack of democracy among antagonists.

The extension of statism to the domestic arena involved a complicated process. Political leaders would have to hone skills which would take them beyond the relatively negative task of fanning contempt for "inferior" societies. They would have to motivate citizens toward the construction and maintenance of state capacities for economic and social intervention.

In none of our systems did this prove an easy process. However, each greatly enhanced—especially in the late 1930s, in the immediate postwar period, and the mid-1960s—the role of the state in domestic affairs. The successive iterations in the process placed a high premium upon the expansiveness and inventiveness of political leadership. In turn, the leaders of the time, especially the likes of Roosevelt, Kennedy, and Johnson—in the United States, Atlee and Wilson—in the United Kindgom, King, Pearson, and Trudeau—in Canada, and Curtin, Chifley, and Whitlam—in Australia—inspired many young, able, and idealistic men and women to choose public- over private-sector careers.

To be sure, consolidators emerged in this period—Truman, Eisenhower, and Nixon; Churchill, Macmillan, Eden, Hume, and Heath; St. Laurent and Diefenbaker; and Menzies, Gorton, and Fraser. And not every system achieved the same level of state intervention. Yet the epoch marked one of the most explosive phases of governmental adaptation yet experienced. The fact that it bucked a decided Anglo skepticism of the state made it all that more remarkable. On the other hand, the Anglo-American states reaped the benefits of one feature which distinguished them from many continental European nations. The Anglo-American countries enjoyed the relative absence of deep sectarian divisions over the roles of the state and church in social provision. This paved the way for the former to advance the welfare state with little or no religiously based opposition. That is, the classic struggle between Catholicism and socialism—which has dominated politics in much of Western Europe—played relatively small roles in the Anglo-American democracies (Castles and Mitchell 1992, 16–17). In fact, the Labor Party in Australia actually drew the bulk of its support in the first half of this century from Catholics—the main sources of cleavage being state support of Catholic schools and conscription during WWI (Aitkin 1985, 219–221; Thompson 1994, 64–65). Only the Canadian province of Quebec presented—until the "Quiet Revolution" associated with secularization during the 1960s—an instance where the Roman Catholic Church stood as a bulwark against the expansion of the state (McRoberts and Posgate 1980, 30).

Just as a similar dream propelled our societies in the middle third of this century, a shared sense of disillusionment began to set in during the 1960s. This became especially manifest in the restlessness of youths and intellectuals. It reached pronounced levels in the mid-1960s and persisted into the early 1970s. Such skepticism focused on the slowed or halted momentum in building up the state's capacity for intervention. It felt acutely the systemic obstacles to more thoroughgoing pursuit of the welfare state.

By the late 1960s, every one of our nations began to experience severe pressures on available resources for government intervention. In the United States, Johnson's simultaneous pursuit of the Vietnam War and the War on Poverty overheated the economy. The damage left the United States sputtering at the most crucial phase of economic globalization. Britain began to face the consequences of the loss of its Empire. As well, it had done a poor job of retooling for the postindustrial era. It found itself one of the least well equipped major European powers to contend with the loss of markets resulting from the explosion of Asian enterprise. And its late entry into the European Community would delay the process whereby it could gain access to continental markets.

Canada's economy always follows closely the fortunes of that of the United States. Thus it slipped into stagflation in the early 1970s—just as the U.S. economy had. The energy crises of 1973 and 1979 placed an added burden upon Canada. The eastern part of the country relied heavily upon imported oil. As Britain oriented its future toward the European Community, Australia began to suffer serious losses in markets for agricultural products. In addition, sluggish global economic performances beginning in the early 1970s meant that demand for minerals became unstable. Australia began its struggle with diversification from an economy based on the farm and the quarry.

The Great Depression had sparked support for an interventionist state in our four countries. However, the chilling excesses of fascism and nazism, followed by the postwar threat of communism, had deepened the demands upon leaders to secure liberal democracies. Most saw more equitable distribution of resources as key to this process. And this reflex had a strong run throughout the 1950s and 1960s. However, in most advanced democracies less auspicious economic circumstances began to constrict the social democratic vision in the 1970s (Rose and Peters 1978; Arndt 1978).

The explosion and then retrenchment of state intervention followed similar lines in our four countries. However, some notable differences revealed themselves. Britain faced the constraints of decline even at the outset of its construction of the welfare state (Hennessy 1992). This owed both to the gargantuan task of recovering from World War II—for instance, the government did not end rationing until 1954—and adjustments associated with the relentless decline of the Empire. Even though Britain's social programs achieved comprehensiveness long before those of our other nations, they ran on relatively scant resources. In this respect, Britain was no Sweden. As well, a scarcity syndrome prevailed whereby even the Conservatives embraced economic planning and some state ownership of the means of production.

In the United States and Canada, social programs generally received relatively generous resourcing. However, their adoption and implementation became somewhat uneven. In both countries, the federal government negotiated patchworks of funding and administration arrangements with state/provincial governments. Therefore, programs and benefits varied widely between jurisdictions. Even Canada's celebrated universal health care system is actually ten systems which differ considerably between provinces. Each of the welfare states stalled short of "cradle to grave" coverage. For instance, Medicare—provision for the elderly—and Medicaid—health care for the poor—proved the best that the United States could achieve.

The slow progress of the United States owed to the states rights movement in the 1950s and 1960s and the separation of powers in the federal government. In Canada, much of the delay stemmed from the country's highly decentralized federal system. The constant claims on the part of Quebec for special arrangements exacerbated this difficulty. As noted earlier, the Quebec case offers the only exception to the assertion that sectarian struggles worked little effect on expansion of the welfare state in our four countries.

In Australia, the right-of-center Liberal Party dominated federal politics through most of the period in which the welfare state rose in Anglo-American democracies. This meant that Australia moved cautiously toward social intervention. When the political will congealed, however, the actual mechanics of the process went much more smoothly than in the United States or Canada. Three factors entered this equation. First, Australians share a relatively egalitarian societal view which facilitated the adoption of redistributive policies (Castles and Mitchell 1992, 18). Second, the society lacks the depth of regional and sectarian attachments which might have slowed the advancement of the welfare state. Third, the federal system in Australia clearly favors the Commonwealth Government—especially with regard to taxation. Thus once the federal government embraced one or other element of the welfare state it enjoyed both the resources and the leverage to establish programs and monitor their implementation.

The Emergence of Neo-Liberalism

As noted earlier, the emphasis on the individual accorded by liberal democracy connects our four systems more than anything else. Unlike continental European advanced political systems, none of our nations places a high value on organic views of society. None of our systems fosters in citizens strong notions that the sum of the parts of society exceeds that of its individual components. Nor do religious movements within our societies exert sufficient sway so that the perceived interconnectedness of the community of believers begins to impinge upon the relationship between the state and the individual.

There is some variation here. The U.S. system gives greater deference to the individual than do the others—although Canada's 1982 Charter of Rights and Freedoms quickly has introduced a similar emphasis in that nation. Still the political leadership and publics of our four countries generally have enlisted pragmatic argumentation in support of greater state intervention—eschewing grand ideologies. As well, they normally have avoided divisions based on sentiments about the prerogatives of religious communities.

A climate of economic growth and prosperity prevailed during the 1950s and 1960s. Under the circumstances, the publics of our respective countries viewed benignly the gradual expansion of social programs. It proved relatively easy for political leaders to stir sentiments supportive of individuals' responsibility toward society—especially the less advantaged. The residual effects of the Great Depression generalized the salience of such appeals. Many of those who enjoyed the benefits of prosperity had suffered during the 1930s. They recognized that social safety nets served a function in society.

In time, the perilous years of the Great Depression began to fade in the public memory. As well, declining economic growth began to constrict support of government spending. During the period of expansion, government programs actually helped fan the economy and produce tangible improvements in individual standards of living. As decline began to work its effects, social expenditure began to function as a drag on the economy. New programs gave very little appreciable value-added to living circumstances.

By the mid-1960s, significant questions arose about the continued expansion of the welfare state. Initially, these focused on issues associated with the effectiveness and efficiency of programs. Analysts looked at the margins of expenditure to see how resources could be used more wisely. As conditions worsened during the 1970s, questions got increasingly hard. Ultimately, analysts began to grapple with the most fundamental issue—should government involve itself at all in myriad areas?

In the 1960s, a school of economics called public choice developed (Buchanan and Tullock 1962). Critics of this approach have argued that it has fostered a minimalist view of what government should do (Self 1993), often on the basis of scant or dubious empirical grounding (Green and Shapiro 1994, 11–12; Blais and Dion 1991; Campbell and Naulls 1991). For instance, it holds that governments breed programs far beyond what the public expect or require. This stems from the desire of government officials to devise ways to build their own empires (Niskanen 1971). Empires require resources. And one must exert great entrepreneurial skills in devising and expanding programs which can command ever-expanding resources. Public choice theorists urged electorates to select representatives who would clip the wings of government officials. Such representatives would apply automatic devices for eliminating programs and cutting expenditures—that is, methods which would proscribe special pleading from bureaucrats.

The Anglo-American systems ran through the entire decade of economic decline in the 1970s before political leaders advocating views akin to public choice—or its political manifestation, neo-liberalism—took power (Self 1993, 64–68). Margaret Thatcher came first, forming a government in Britain in 1979. Joe Clark soon followed in Canada. However, he lacked a majority and lost power in 1980. Ronald Reagan installed a strong neo-liberal administration in that same year. Bob Hawke—though head of a left-of-center party—seized control from the conservative coalition in Australia in 1983. Labor had successfully co-opted the neo-liberal appeal. Finally, Brian Mulroney brought Canada's Progressive Conservatives back to office in 1984. From that time until Bill Clinton's inauguration in 1993, neo-liberalism dominated the Anglo-American political scene. In fact, neo-liberalism proved highly resilient in all of our countries except Canada.

In Britain, John Major plied essentially the same course as did Margaret Thatcher. The 1992 general election indicated that British voters—whatever their qualms about Thatcherism—remained loath to return Labour to power. In Australia, many believed that Bob Hawke's successor—Paul Keating—would not be able to renew Labor's mandate against a Liberal Party which finally had staked out a strong neo-liberal agenda. In the 1993 election, however, the Liberal Party's message struck many voters as too strident. As well, Labor had since 1987 become adept at presenting itself as a government which has embraced a form of neo-liberalism which retained a social conscience. In January

1994, even the president of the Australian Liberal Party publicly praised Labor for attaining such balance. Of course, Labor fell off the high wire in 1996 in an election in which the Liberal Party brilliantly underplayed its true neo-liberal self.

The Clinton administration—though hardly neo-liberal at its core—had from the outset to acknowledge the sway that the approach enjoyed both in Congress and in the populace (Jones 1996; Quirk and Hinchliffe 1996). It eschewed the introduction of tax increases as part of its deficit reduction initiatives. Its failed health care reform package went through Rube Goldberg–like contortions to make itself look like a private-sector solution to a public crisis. The administration even enshrined a neo-liberal icon—the North American Free Trade Agreement—much to the chagrin of bedrock Democratic Party supporters such as unions and voters in the industrial Northeast and Midwest. All of this proved to be too little too late and the Congress swung radically onto the neo-liberal side of the ledger in the November 1994 elections (Burnham 1996). The Republican Congress, however, got ahead of the people. This allowed Bill Clinton to position himself as a centrist defending America from the extremes of its neo-liberal "contract."

In Canada, the federal Progressive Conservative's variant of neo-liberalism received a stinging rebuke in the October 1993 federal election. As prime minister, Brian Mulroney, had deeply antagonized voters by playing footloose and fancy-free with the viability of Canada as a nation. Whatever its appeal as an economic theory, the free trade agreement with the United States seemed to have decimated the Canadian manufacturing sector. As well, Mulroney's willingness to cede federal functions to the province of Quebec—along with the funds necessary to run related programs—struck voters as cavalier in the extreme. The repudiation—which was directed at the Progressive Conservatives under Mulroney's hapless successor, Kim Campbell—went beyond electoral defeat of a neo-liberal regime. The collapse of the PCs to two seats in the 1993 election resulted in their defrocking as a parliamentary party. Ironically, the Liberals' budgets have made many tough, neo-liberal choices that the Progressive Conservatives—notwithstanding all of the lightning and thunder—never could bring themselves to. In this respect, Jean Chrétien's government has tried to replicate what the "economic rationalists" of Bob Hawke's Labor government accomplished in Australia during the mid-1980s. They have presented themselves as neo-liberals with heart.

We have seen—especially in the last few years—that neo-liberalism is not a panacea. To an extent, voters continue to embrace it because they have yet to return to political leaders who articulate more positive views of the function of the state. It has even become clear that neo-liberal politicians must make their appeals more palatable. Thus George Bush spoke of a kinder and gentler America, John Major pushed the concept of a Citizens Charter, and the Australian Labor government had stressed the importance of equity as it pursued "economic rationalism."

THE CRISIS OF EXECUTIVE LEADERSHIP

Neo-liberalism took hold much more pervasively in all Anglo-American systems than it did anywhere in continental Europe. This speaks volumes about the susceptibility of the Anglo-American mind to argumentation based on individual-centered versus organic views of society. However, neo-liberalism—and the minimalist governance that has stemmed from it—has come at a cost. Voters have begun to experience the pain of excessive retrenchment of government. However, they remain very chary of supporting parties which provided administrations during the most traumatic phase of economic malaise—the late 1970s and early 1980s.

Thus a type of electoral schizophrenia has emerged. If voters renew the mandates of neo-liberal administrations, they do so grudgingly. This has been the case in Britain and Australia where ambiguous mandates led to a cacophony of voices in previously tidy neo-liberal regimes. If on the other hand, voters decide to embrace a former governing party which fell into disrepute during the economic crisis of the late 1970s, they do so reservedly. Certainly, this pertained in the United States where many voters lodged their protest by selecting Ross Perot—thereby denying Bill Clinton a strong mandate. In November 1994, they compounded the confusion by voting in a Republican Congress. A similar process has functioned in Canada. There English-speaking Canadians of all stripes swamped the Liberal Party in the eleventh hour. They recognized that a minority government in a Parliament whose official opposition was the separatist Bloc Quebecois would becalm the ship of state.

At the end of the heyday of the welfare state, problems with the implementation of social legislation—due to irreconcilable pulls of government organizations and special interests—proved the bread and butter of analysts (Lowi 1969; Pressman and Wildavsky 1973). The cumulative evidence of contradictions in policy outcomes and unintended consequences helped lay the groundwork for neo-liberalism. Even those broadly committed to the social agenda began to note a crisis in faith (Heclo 1981) about the governability of the complex welfare state (King 1975). We, of course, can assume that what is good for the goose is good for the gander. However, neo-liberalism—perhaps because it has become the flavor of the month and has only recently taken shape in actual policies—has so far received relatively light treatment. Many observers have challenged it only around the fringes. Few have made frontal attacks of the order of those aimed at the welfare state in the 1970s. However, works both by columnists (for instance, Phillips 1990; Keegan 1992) and scholars (Donahue 1989; Marmor, Mashaw, and Harvey 1990; Durant 1992; Self 1993; Savoie 1994; Henig 1994) suggest ways in which neo-liberalism has served up its own contradictions and worked unintended consequences. These include the danger of building-down of the state below what is required to sustain society and the apparent emergence of an insidious process whereby style has supplanted substance in governance.

The Unintended Consequences of Build-Down

In the aftermath of the Cold War, we have seen that military leaders have adopted a fairly predictable strategy in order to protect their prized programs. They have offered sacrificial lambs for slaughter on the altar of economy. However, they also have accentuated the uncertainties that surround what nations will require in the form of defense establishments. Given these imponderables, they argue, prudence dictates that a certain level of expenditure be maintained so that numerous possible scenarios might be anticipated. They are saying—with some effectiveness—that political leaders who cut defense expenditure to the bone might find that they lack the wherewithal to respond sufficiently to crises in an unstable global environment.

In many respects, the type of build-down so feared by the military establishments of Western nations, has already occurred in the physical and social infrastructures of Anglo-American systems. Some of the resulting decay has raised questions about the viability of these societies as liberal democracies.

All of this would present acute challenges even if these systems were running in place. They might be able to cope if they functioned in stable circumstances. In fact, they do not. The relative competitive positions of Anglo-American democracies in the world economy have declined notably in the past thirty years. As well, the social mores of each have changed considerably with the rise of the electronic era and the decline of the family. Further, environmental dangers hover over each in ways which suggest that future development will have to follow fundamentally different contours than in more innocent epochs.

Each society shoulders a considerable burden in integrating immigrant groups into the mainstream. Britain continues to struggle with the seemingly insuperable obstacles to the resolution of the crisis in Northern Ireland. The other nations all must contend with an entirely new order of claims on the part of aboriginal peoples. Globalization has made Americans and Canadians think of themselves as North Americans, Britons to consider themselves Europeans, and Australians to ponder whether their futures rest in being "Asian."

In all these circumstances, the publics of these countries are slowly coming to the realization that the hegemony of Anglo-Saxons—or, as they are referred to in Australia, "Anglo-Celts"—is quickly drawing to a close. These societies no longer can view themselves and one another as tall, slim, fair-haired, and light-eyed. This change constitutes a main element of the crisis. Ethnocentrism provided no small amount of propulsion for our societies during the period when they flirted with organic views of individual obligations toward the wider community (Lind 1995). Now we see huge debates over immigration. In the United States, Congress has even considered whether the benefits usually accorded U.S. citizens should be extended to those who attained this status through naturalization.

We already know that "white flight" can gut urban schools in the United States—both in regard to parents' willingness to expose their children to diversity and taxpayers' support of public schools. Already, huge segments of the United States—sometimes, as is the case with Detroit, entire cities—convey a sense of abandonment to visible minorities. Some observers see in this growing phenomenon the beginnings of an underclass. And recent developments associated with the poor employment prospects of white youths suggest that the decline will not confine itself to visible minorities. For instance, thousands of white youths from the north of England sleep "rough" on London streets. Many completed school but left their home towns in a futile search for work. Society has found them dispensable.

Neglect—even of services essential to commerce—has become the hallmark of the neo-liberal era. Physical infrastructure in all of our countries has taken a sharp turn for the worse (Webley 1985; Munnell (ed.) 1991; Bureau of Industry Economics 1994). Look at highways. In the United States, it takes as long to bypass large cities on hugely overburdened freeways as it did to go right through them on arterials in the 1950s. In Britain, one rarely travels on motorways more than fifty miles without running into road works and huge delays. The Trans Canada Highway—built as a symbol of national unity in the 1960s—has begun to crumble. In Australia, a trip which takes a little more than an hour by air—for instance, between Sydney and Brisbane—requires at least two days by car. The carnage on the highways—many of which are run-down, two-lane roads with narrow bridges—has reached the point where many Australians simply refuse to drive "interstate."

Health has emerged as a crisis in all of our countries. As probably the worst case, the District of Columbia has attained third-world levels of infant mortality. AIDS and, more recently, drug-resistant strains of tuberculosis have raised the specter of uncontrolled and lethal epidemics. Economy has prompted political leaders and legislators to cut back funds for immunization of children. This has caused a public health nightmare in the United States. However, slippage has occurred in the other countries even though they boast universal health care programs. For instance, Australia has stopped immunizing boys against measles. The result: large proportions of Australian schoolboys test rubella-positive. Health care costs are an acute drag on the U.S. economy. However, at the very time that the Clinton administration groped for some affordable approach to universal health care provision, those countries with state-run, single-payer systems were struggling mightily to adapt them to the age of stringent financial circumstances (White 1995).

The privatization and deregulation binge of the 1980s has left its wreckage strewn all over the place. Countless investors in all four countries saw their life earnings disappear in shady deals by con-artists who called themselves bankers. The collapse of insured savings corporations put immense pressure on governments—especially in the United States, where the Savings and Loan Crisis gobbled up hundreds of billions of public funds. The May 1996 crash of a ValuJet DC-9 in the Florida Everglades revealed the consequences of putting profits before safety in the airline industry. ValuJet had "outsourced" maintenance of its aircraft to so many small companies that it made a mockery of the concept of "self-regulation."

The wholesale privatization of natural monopolies in Britain has necessitated the erection of regulatory organizations. However, these alleged guardians of the public interest as often as not became the dogsbodies of the Conservative government. As an extreme instance, the head of the commission regulating private water companies proclaimed in summer 1993 that he saw no reason why these corporations should have to provide a product which came up to European Union standards. What would one expect a former deputy chief economist of Her Majesty's Treasury to say?

In Canada, deregulation of the airline industry, followed by privatization of the former national carrier—Air Canada—has produced bedlam (Goldenberg 1994; Skene 1994). Two airlines—Air Canada and Pacific Western (the latter now styled Canadian Airlines International Ltd.)—quickly consumed the others and embarked on a predatory effort to gain a complete monopoly. Air Canada piled up huge debts though the government wrote off much of its debt at the time of its privatization. Canadian—run by supposedly rough-and-ready Albertan entrepreneurs—limps along on loan guarantees patched together by the federal and provincial governments. The "economic rationalism" guiding policies in response to the ongoing crisis concerns more than anything else the unwillingness of many Western Canadians to use an airline whose headquarters is in Montreal. Canadian airline deregulation and privatization has accomplished exactly nothing and cost taxpayers and travelers billions.

In Executive Leadership, Style Supplants Substance

In Anglo-American systems other than the United States, observers have become increasingly absorbed with the issue of "presidentialization" (Weller 1983; Jones 1983; 1991). This concern has emerged whenever prime ministers make appeals directly to the public—attempting to bypass opponents in cabinet. In Britain, Canada, and Australia this approach is seen by some observers as a threat to the integrity of the constitutional system. Strong conventions in all three systems prescribe that prime ministers consult with their cabinets before committing their governments to a course of action.

The term *presidentialization* implies that prime ministers who "go public" and outflank opposition in cabinet have followed a strategy which comports more with the U.S. Constitution than with parliamentary government. In reality, very serious concerns have arisen in the United States about the tendency of U.S. presidents to go public (Kernell 1986; Rose 1991). In such cases, incumbents have tried to override the counsel of both cabinet colleagues and members of Congress who oppose a proposal. Through speeches, campaignlike tours, endorsements, and well-placed leaks, they have employed the immense power of media attention to turn public opinion against their opponents. President Clinton's 1993 campaign to gain approval of the North American Free Trade Agreement against stiff opposition from the leadership of his own party in the House of Representatives serves as a classic instance of going public. In fact, the encounter between Vice President Al Gore and Ross Perot on *Larry King Live* brought the art form to new heights. Styling going public among prime ministers as presidentialization misses the point. The new era of electronics affords executive leaders of any type immense capacity for bypassing constitutional institutions and making policy directly with the people (Seymour-Ure 1991).

The dysfunctions of this approach apply across systems—regardless of whether we are assessing the performance of a president or a prime minister (Campbell 1993, 394–398). First, executive leaders who go public run the risk of not sufficiently drawing upon the constructive contribution potentially made by other institutions in the constitutional system. Second, such leaders can undermine the legitimacy of institutions—the bureaucracy, cabinet, legislators, and public interest organizations—which form the building blocks of liberal democracy. In other words, each instance of going public—especially circuslike events such as the Gore-Perot debate—pushes the system toward populism and a-institutional approaches to resolving disputes within the body politic. Third, executive leaders can do themselves a great deal of harm by going public more than the public can bear. The approach can be easier than dealing with institutions—remember George Bush's lament in 1990 that he would rather deal with Saddam Hussein than with Congress. However, it is not always the smart way to proceed (Jones 1996).

Executive leaders in all four of our countries increasingly have become products and exploiters of electronic appeals. That Ross Perot—utterly unencumbered by institutional buttresses—bought his way into a strong third-place performance in the 1992 presidential election suggests the proportions of the problem in the United States.

Kim Campbell's rise and fall in Canada gives us a view of how a-institutionalism might develop in parliamentary systems (Dobbin 1993). Campbell caught the eye of Brian Mulroney soon after her election to the House of Commons in 1988. He rapidly promoted her to justice minister and then the defense minister. She became his heir apparent and this made her a media darling. Once leader of the Progressive Conservatives and prime minister in summer 1993, she spent virtually all her time nurturing her relationship with the electorate—attending an endless succession of festivals and fairs to the delight of the fawning media. She did not convene parliament and she rarely met with cabinet. She completely reorganized the bureaucracy—actually, she mostly rubber-stamped a plan worked out by Mulroney and his top mandarins—and then absented herself from the tough work of implementing the reforms.

This approach held together until the real campaign started in the fall. Then the press and public began to question Campbell's ability to engage herself as an executive leader. Time and again, she stumbled in public utterances about her policies. She became detached even from her organization—speaking only occasionally to her campaign manager. In a colossal gaffe, she asserted that she could not discuss how she would cut the deficit. She implied that such issues went beyond the ken of the electorate—adding that she would decide them privately when she became prime minister.

The Campbell experience points up two things. First, political leaders in parliamentary systems can establish themselves through electronic means with facility close to that of presidential aspirants and incumbents. Second, there still might be a threshold for a-institutional appeals. In this regard, the electorate's chagrin over Ross Perot's performance in the NAFTA debate might help us locate the fault line in the United States. Voters might tolerate a demagogic style in a presidential campaign. However, they might expect a certain respect for office when a private citizen engages an incumbent vice president in a TV debate.

APPLES AND ORANGES, BUT WITH SOME HYBRIDIZATION

Any effort at comparative politics must deal to some degree with the issue of apples and oranges. This involves the question as to whether the various subjects for analysis differ in structural ways which make comparison forced. The prior discussion highlighted the commonality between the United States and the other Anglo-American systems. This has ranged from shared political cultures and traditions to similar encounters with expansive governance in the first three decades of the postwar period and the constrictive experience of neo-liberalism since the early 1980s.

Notwithstanding the commonality, some structural features sharply distinguish Anglo-American systems. However, two important points immediately emerge from any inventory of these differences. First, the divergence does not always fall neatly along a United States/other dichotomy. Second, our four systems show some signs of behavioral—if not structural—convergence.

Two Key Structural Differences

Many readers might at this point focus on the structural feature which distinguishes the United States from Britain, Canada, and Australia. This is, of course, that the former system is presidential. Some readers might have missed entirely the other key difference. The United States, Canada, and Australia are all federal systems, whereas the United Kingdom is unitary. The second distinguishing feature reduces the importance of the first in defining the context of this analysis.

We should not underestimate the relevance of the presidency in differentiating the United States from the other systems. Incumbency to the presidency brings with it one immense advantage and one huge disability. The advantage is the entire monocratic framework of the U.S. executive branch. The Constitution does not even mention cabinet. It lamely suggests that the president might occasionally request written advice from named cabinet secretaries. As a result, all executive authority lodges in the president. Any consultation with cabinet collectively is simply a courtesy. And while the media and the public might blame the president or individual cabinet secretaries for ineptitude or malfeasance, cabinet as a collective noun scarcely even registers on the consciousness of the nation. All of this gives presidents immense leverage. The downside, of course, is that they usually catch the bulk of the flak when things go wrong.

The disadvantage is that the president and his men and women usually are strangers in their own government (Heclo 1977). The separation of powers generates a situation in which presidents must deal with "divided government." Functionally, this often is even the case when their own party controls both houses of Congress. To make matters worse, the bureaucracy serves myriad masters. This practice departs radically from our other systems. There, permanent civil servants still grit their teeth and say, "Yes, Prime Minister" when given express orders by the chief executive. They do this even though they generally bring to their work greater astuteness about the executive-bureaucratic arena than do either appointees or career officials in the United States (Campbell and Szablowski 1979; Campbell 1983; Campbell and Halligan 1992; Campbell and Wilson 1995).

The American permanent bureaucracy almost totally lacks coherence. Its actions respond to congressional mandates almost as much as they do to orders from the president. The people whom the president appoints to give some semblance of direction to permanent officialdom as frequently as not "go native." That is, they end up defending their departments and agencies from direction by the White House and, on occasion, the president himself.

The division of powers still only partially serves to differentiate our systems from the standpoint of structure. Canada and Australia—as well the United States—have embraced federalism. Indeed, with the decline of the states rights movement in the United States since the 1960s—a trend which seems now to be reversing itself—one might even have argued that these two systems are more federal than the United States. This is with the caution that Australia operates a form of federalism which sustains a high degree of fiscal centralization (Henderson 1990).

Canadian provinces and Australian states loom much larger in the consciousness of their citizens than the fifty states do in the United States. In Canada, one province—Quebec—even styles itself a "nation." Alberta embodies, in high-proof form, the frontier, Western, rugged individualism of several "mountain states" in the United States. We saw earlier the lengths the elite of that province has gone to retain its own "national" airline. The next province to the east—Saskatchewan—has chosen socialist governments as often as not since WWII. It was the first jurisdiction in North America to embrace universal, state-run medical provision.

Virtually every service that an Australian sees on a day-to-day basis occurs under the auspices of the state rather than the federal government or local authorities. Even in cities such as Sydney and Melbourne— each with over three million inhabitants—the police cars, fire engines, and ambulances which rush down the streets all bear the name "New South Wales" or "Victoria."

Apart from their relevance to the establishment and maintenance of differences in political culture, Canadian provinces and Australian states find themselves beneficiaries of added negotiation power. Making a large number of regions into states debases the currency. Rationing the number of players to ten—as is the case in Canada—and six—the case in Australia—greatly increases the leverage of each unit. Each commands greater areas, populations, and resources than it would otherwise. Perhaps more important, they can more readily form coalitions for or against action on the part of the federal government. Thus if we construe federalism as a variant of separation of powers, having fewer units makes Canada and Australia at least as prone to divided government as the United States.

For instance, the leverage of Canadian provinces vis-à-vis the federal government cancels out many of the potential benefits of the parliamentary system as against U.S. separation of powers. The federal government must enter into tortuous negotiations with provinces in any area where the powers of the two overlap (Simeon 1972). The entire process requires a byzantine array of ministerial and civil service committees. Indeed, an entire subfield within Canadian government and politics centers on "federal-provincial diplomacy." Australia had eschewed such formalization of commonwealth-state relations. However, recurrent fiscal crises in the past several years have exacerbated the difficulty of co-ordinating policies between levels. This has provoked the beginnings of a Canadian-style approach.

Part of the difficulty of federal-province/state relations in Canada and Australia stems from the parliamentary system itself. This imposes a much stronger convention of party discipline on the elected representatives of the people than found in the United States. The approach functions reasonably well in Britain. However, the fact that the United Kingdom embodies a relatively homogeneous population takes us some way in explaining its apparent effectiveness there. On the other hand, Canada and Australia each encompass relatively heterogeneous populations—although the former struggles with much greater difficulties than does the latter. Strong party discipline impinges upon the ability of elected representatives to vent regional frustrations with the federal government.

Importantly, discipline in the Canadian House of Commons—the only elective branch of Parliament—has proven exceedingly rigid. Increasingly in the British lower house, party leaders have tolerated fairly substantial backbench revolts—just so long as they do not threaten the life of the government of the day. In Australia, caucuses exert great influence over the positions that party leaderships assume. Indeed, when Labor was in government, its caucus elected cabinet members and ran its own committee system for legislative review.

The ossification of party discipline in Canada seems to exacerbate rather than ameliorate fragmentation in the society generally. A pattern has emerged whereby provincial electorates turn completely away from the party which holds power in Ottawa. For instance, only Alberta retained a Progressive Conservative government at the end of the Mulroney era. The dramatic swing of Ontario in June 1995 to a strongly neo-liberal variant of the PCs suggested a continuation of this pattern. A similar—although less pronounced—pattern emerged in Australia during the Labor hegemony in the Commonwealth that extended from 1983 to 1996.

Regional protest often flows over to segmentation of parliamentary delegations from provinces or states. Pierre Trudeau—whose primeministership spanned 1968–84—frequently encountered difficulty gaining seats in Western Canada. This made cabinet formation very difficult. A strong representational imperative bears down on Canadian prime ministers. Voters will more likely tolerate the suppression of regional grievances by government caucus members if they know that these will receive full amplification in secret cabinet discussions. Trudeau found it difficult to say that Western views played a role in policy making. Most of his cabinets limped along with only a few Westerners. The fact that these often were members of the appointive Senate—seconded for duty in the cabinet due to a lack of elected representatives—did not help matters. Again, difficulties on the Australian scene fall short of this depth of dysfunction.

Points of Convergence

This book focuses on the crisis of executive leadership in the United States within the wider context of Anglo-American democracy. We have seen in the prior section that more than the United States' adherence to a separation of power differentiates these systems. In addition, whether they are federal plays a role. More important, all of the systems have been grappling with immense changes in the context of executive leadership. Many of these transcend national boundaries. The explosion of electronic links between politics and the public has radically transformed both campaigning and incumbency. As well, all of our countries underwent a radical retreat from the interventionist state since the early 1980s.

To gain power, executive leaders have virtually all presented themselves as neo-liberals bent on building-down the state. This device can pave the way to gaining office. However, it eventually can become an albatross. Problems that require some sort of public attention still emerge. Voters expect leaders to respond. However, they have been fed the line that taxes can be cut. They expect leaders to solve problems with ever-shrinking resources.

Changes in the conditions of governance have spawned a convergence of executive leadership in Anglo-American states that—to a degree—functions independently of structural factors. The various dimension of this convergence include: a shift from selecting "insiders" as chief executives to one of choosing "outsiders"; a decreased salience of collective means for decision making within the executive branch; and a preference for preservation of political viability over solving problems.

THE RISE OF OUTSIDER POLITICS?

Over the years, the U.S. system has frequently produced presidents with no experience in elective federal office. Our three parliamentary systems, however, had until the early 1980s normally yielded prime ministers with considerable experience in elective office at the national level.

Presidential candidates play to a constituency taking in the entire country—beginning with state-level primaries and ending with the national election (Wattenberg 1991). This has allowed some figures with little or no experience in Washington nonetheless to attract a national following. Prime ministers, on the other hand, still must hold a seat in the national Parliament. As well, leadership selection processes still fall far short of the openness of U.S. primaries and presidential elections. Still, available evidence suggests that voters' opinions of individual leaders in Westminster systems have greater effects on their views of parties than vice versa (Graetz and McAllister 1987). This leaves more room for the emergence of "outsiders" as chief executives in these countries.

That the Westminster systems have begun to depart from the insider-only pattern becomes clear when we look at party leadership over the past few years. The shift toward outsiders began in Canada in 1968 when Pierre Trudeau became leader of the Liberals and prime minister. Trudeau had only gained a parliamentary seat three years earlier and had served in only one cabinet post. The Progressive Conservatives started their departure from insiders with the selection of Robert Stanfield—a former premier of Nova Scotia—in 1967. They replaced Stanfield with Joe Clark in 1976. Clark had only served in Parliament for four years. He became prime minister in 1979 without ever holding a cabinet position. Brian Mulroney succeeded Clark as leader of the PCs in 1983. At the time, he did not have a seat in Parliament. Kim Campbell came to Parliament in 1988. She served in two cabinet posts. However, some observers would say that this reflected a deliberate grooming process which—in the end—proved illusory.

Margaret Thatcher might strike readers as the "insider" par excellence. In fact, she assumed the primeministership with relatively little experience—having only served as secretary for education and science in Edward Heath's 1970–74 government. John Major entered Parliament on the coattails of the 1979 Thatcher landslide. Before that he had held a public relations position in a merchant bank. He did not assume a cabinet post until four years before he became prime minister. Bob Hawke did not even belong to the Australian House of Representatives until three years before becoming leader of the Labor Party and prime minister. He had previously served as president of the Australian Council of Trade Unions.

The politics of the 1980s suggested, thus, that electorates in Anglo-American parliamentary democracies embraced parties whose leaders brought with them relatively little experience in the national policy arena. The shift toward this pattern might reflect simply the volatile mood of the decade. Voters had developed a decided aversion to politics as usual. They sought leaders who promised to sweep with a new broom. On the other hand, the enhanced significance of electronic approaches to building appeal—both among elites and the electorate—has probably played a role as well. The electronic revolution has allowed chief executives to lead with direct pitches to the public. These often short-circuit institutional channels. Politicians who show promise in garnering public support in this way enhance their image as someone who can govern in an age of institutional intransigence. They might, therefore, find that they can leapfrog over more conventional aspirants to leadership positions whose career paths have followed traditional institutional lines.

We might be seeing a return to Parliament-centered politics in these systems. In Australia, Paul Keating—though a strong campaigner—also brought to his primeministership a reputation as one of Australia's most experienced and effective parliamentary scrappers. He had also served as Treasurer in the Hawke government for eight years. John Howard first won election to the House of Representatives in 1974. He brings to the primeministership nine years of ministerial experience including five years as Treasurer. Canada's Jean Chrétien first served in Parliament in 1963 and has occupied virtually every significant cabinet portfolio in the federal government.

THE TENDENCY TOWARD MONOCRATIC LEADERSHIP

An extensive literature has developed on the presidentialization of Anglo-American parliamentary systems. The view has emerged among several scholars that prime ministers increasingly devise ways of bypassing full cabinet discussion of government policies. Usually, they do this simply by confining consultation to inner circles of colleagues upon whose support they can almost invariably rely. In more extreme cases, they actually decide matters and present them as a fait accompli to their cabinet colleagues.

A great deal of bickering has developed among political scientists over the proper term for the tendency among some recent prime ministers to limit cabinet consultation. Some see it as prime ministers arrogating to themselves the prerogatives normally associated with presidents. The U.S. Constitution concentrates executive authority entirely in the hands of the president. It nowhere stipulates that he must confer with cabinet officers before acting. Of course, only constitutional convention sustains cabinet consultation in the parliamentary systems.

Britain lacks a written constitution. Further, none of the basic laws of the Westminster countries specifically prescribes cabinet consultation. Still, observers who see reduced utilization of cabinet as a sharp departure from convention will likely style it "presidentialization." Others who see it simply as a greater emphasis of central guidance and coordination will term the trend "primeministerialization." Still others maintain that prime ministers—not even exceptionally determined leaders such as Mrs. Thatcher—could not depart from the convention of cabinet consultation to any significant degree (Jones 1991). These observers maintain that cabinets willingly go along with strong primeministerial leadership and jettison the offending leaders the moment they become political liabilities. Those in this camp construe Mrs. Thatcher's 1990 ouster as validation of this perspective.

In essence, the participants in this debate have ensnarled themselves almost completely in semantics. Even in the United States, concerns have arisen over presidents' increasing tendency to make decisions without the counsel of their cabinet colleagues (Porter 1980; Hess 1988, 230–233; Shoemaker 1991). Of course, in the United States an instrumental imperative—rather than a constitutional convention—bears down on presidents (Campbell 1986). Presidents can avoid error by roundtabling issues. This way cabinet secretaries can point up the pitfalls of various courses of action.

Any examination of the U.S. system soon brings home an important point that observers in other Anglo-American systems should bear in mind. Prime ministers who behave "presidentially" have simply imbibed the headier wine of executive leadership in the electronic era. This gives a huge advantage to political leaders—be they presidents or prime ministers—who occupy center stage in the political arena. The hunger of the media for soundbites and events entices chief executives into making direct appeals to the public over the heads of Cabinet colleagues and legislatures. When they connect, modern chief executives begin to believe that they can manipulate the core themes that will rivet the public consciousness.

For most such leaders, a high degree of acuity in directly rallying public support ultimately will lead to monocratic behavior. Only the most disciplined leader recognizes that even an effective device can be used once too often. Most go blithely on with little regard to the hostility building among cabinet members and legislators over their preemption from the most critical initiatives of the administration. As well, most chief executives do not recognize that the public gives about the same run to an average political spellbinder as it does to most TV series.

RESPONSIVE COMPETENCE OVERSHADOWS POLICY COMPETENCE

Over the years, the tendency for the United States to run a hybrid bureaucracy has occasioned a great deal of commentary suggesting that only this system exposes itself to "politicization" (RIPA 1987; Van Loon 1985; Campbell and Halligan 1992, 201–203). In the United States, political appointees occupy the top four or five layers of departments. Theoretically, this distances career public servants from policy issues. It also allegedly enhances the capacity of the president to direct the bureaucracy toward fulfilling his agenda.

Some American observers have raised cautions about the introduction of further layers between cabinet secretaries and permanent public servants (Heclo 1977, 68–78; Berman 1979, 118–119). They have argued that this separates the former from "neutral competence"—that is, the expert advice of professionals with a great deal of subject-matter expertise and institutional memory. Others have asserted that presidents require this distance in order to prevent themselves and their Cabinet-level appointees from becoming inundated by the ongoing agenda of the Washington establishment (Moe 1985, 239). They argue that they must pursue responsive competence—that is, a weather eye for actions and stances which will sustain their support among the electorate. This book will take the view that presidents should seek a mix of responsive and neutral competence.

Whereas some have styled this an American problem, it has reared its head in the parliamentary systems as well. Each has seen an erosion of the boundary between the political leadership and the permanent bureaucracy. This, in turn, has meant career public servants have experienced new constraints in the policy content of their work. They also have found it more difficult to convey to their political masters caveats about various courses of action.

Such difficulties do not by any means owe to the extension of political appointments in parliamentary systems—although this has been an issue. In fact, one can argue that political executives can benefit much more from the advice of professionals deeply steeped in the folk ways of the policy village than from appointees with varying degrees of exposure to the system. Rather the problems stem from a secular change in approaches to leadership in all of the democracies considered in this book. Currently, the incentives have favored the deinstitutionalization of politics.

We have already seen that this has meant that chief executives bring to their work less experience in the national policy arena and that they rely less on their cabinets for counsel. We should not, thus, view the declining role of permanent bureaucracies as especially surprising. It serves, rather, as another sign of the immense power of electronics in imparting to chief executives the option of governing more according to short- and medium-term exigencies than considerations of caveats registered by those who purport to have a highly developed grasp of long-range concerns.

THE PLAN FOR THIS BOOK

The rest of this book is divided into six chapters. Chapter 2 starts by probing the peculiarly American elements of "divided government." The chapter stresses the fact that the dysfunctions of the system link directly to the separation of powers—a constitutional principle which still enjoys considerable legitimacy. However, a tendency has arisen in the past decade for analysts to ascribe too much importance to divided government as a factor in the nonperformance of political executives. Some of the blame rests on the shoulders of presidents who have failed to optimize the art of the possible—that is, to lead. The result has been a debilitating spiral which has undermined public confidence in U.S. governmental institutions. Chapter 3 examines Bill Clinton's struggle with the broken presidency.

Chapter 4 begins the work of canvassing other Anglo-American systems for models of leadership in the era of electronic politics. The chapter focuses on the United Kingdom with special emphasis on Margaret Thatcher, her legacy, and the performance of John Major. It essentially asks whether Thatcher went too far. It first suggests that the conditions that emerged under Labour in the late 1970s proved no worse than those which had developed in other Anglo-American democracies. It also asserts that Labour played by the book in addressing the crises of the period—ultimately embracing monetarism, wage controls, and fiscal constraint (especially cash-limited expenditure).

Over time, Thatcher began to style her accomplishments as if the post-Winter-of-Discontent crossbar was at eight feet rather than simply four feet. The added hubris resulting from her Falklands War victory raised the bar once again to something in the order of twelve feet. In the process, Thatcher turned herself into an icon. She began to view her continued rule as essential to the redefinition and survival of the British nation. Many heaved a sigh of relief when John Major succeeded Thatcher. Even on good days, he found it difficult to clear four feet. Further, he wrestled with a paradox. The icon left, but the cadre of young MPs who defined themselves during the rise of Thatcherism came into their own, both in Major's cabinet and in the House of Commons. Icons can cover a multitude of lapses in governance. However, they prove to be very tough acts to follow.

Chapter 5 offers us an opportunity to probe a central issue in the book. As noted earlier, the book argues that executive leaders should strive for policy competence—that is, a blend of attentiveness to (re)electability and engagement of the state apparatus. They will become error-prone if they neglect the latter and run the risk of alienating voters if they give insufficient regard to the former. Pierre Trudeau and Brian Mulroney both pursued highly personalized leadership and each failed to achieve policy competence. Trudeau pursued a sort of designer neutral competence which involved waves of bureaucratic reforms that attempted to reshape the permanent civil service according to his own image and likeness. The cumulative effect produced a deep electoral antipathy toward the Liberal Party and a public service so bulked up with innovative systems that it could scarcely move. Mulroney, on the other hand, accomplished little by way of simplifying the Trudeau system and injected an element of demoralization through his practice of truncated collective decision making with deals worked out in private with only a few ministers. Mulroney's successor, Kim Campbell, took Mulroney's approach to extremes and drove her party into the ground (two Progressive Conservatives survived the 1993 federal election). In the aftermath, Jean Chrétien, even though mildly rebuked in the 1997 election, demonstrated that voters—his approval ratings once rose higher than any previous Canadian prime minister since the beginning of polls—admire a blended policy competence approach when they see one.

Chapter 6 looks at executive leadership in Australia. This case offers an instance of leaders that proved apt for the circumstances. Facing many of the conditions experienced by the other Anglo-American systems, the Labor administration began its run at governance—which extended into five terms—with a less than viable blend of political responsiveness and neutral competence. However, the severity of Australia's vulnerability in the global economy sunk in dramatically in 1986. Spurred on by Paul Keating—then the treasurer—Bob Hawke co-opted the forces for economic rationalism by wrapping Labor's appeal in radical neo-liberal language. Yet this evolved into market economics with a difference. A symbiosis arose between the political leadership and the permanent bureaucracy which allowed Labor to implement its reforms with a high degree of engagement of the state apparatus. As well, the alliance between Labor and the national union leadership in seeking reforms provided an environment in which affected groups accepted a degree of sacrifice. The chapter assesses how the Hawke legacy fared under Paul Keating.

Chapter 7 distills the main points from the previous chapters and applies these lessons to the modern presidency. It stresses the fact that individual presidents will function in unique ways. However, they should invest a great deal more time and care in discerning their strengths and weaknesses and sculpting their management styles and the institutions through which they will work accordingly. In Anglo-American systems since the early 1980s, the tremendous adaptations brought on by the politics of constraint have exacerbated the difficulty of this task. Leaders have tended to take various paths of least resistance—disengagement from institutions, personalization, and even self-mythologization. All of these strategies have come at a cost—the bloated deficits of the United States and Canada, all four systems' banking upon service-sector expansion while allowing manufacturing to atrophy, the emergence of racial and regional underclasses in the United States and the United Kingdom, and the exhaustion of the Canadian spirit through prolonged constitutional brinkmanship. The time has passed when placebos and grand gestures can count as leadership. Presidents find themselves as much subject to this reality as do prime ministers.

2

Reagan, Bush, and the Emergence of the Gridlocked System

This chapter focuses on the U. S. democratic system and the central issue of the recent presidency—gridlock. What do we mean by gridlock?
If historians go back years from now and look at the 1992 presidential
election, they are going to be tempted to call it the gridlock election. It
certainly was one of the first elections in memory where a central theme
had to do with the nature of the system, yet went beyond bashing the
civil service. The public had twigged to the question: "Who should be
blamed for the increasing distemper in the policy arena?"

There were those who faulted the Democratic Congress. George Bush
pushed this interpretation. If voters would only elect a Republican Congress all of the problems would go away. Then there were people who
said that George Bush had caused gridlock. If the election produced a
Democratic president, finally the nation could address its ills. More significantly, a fairly substantial segment of the population had abandoned
hope in either the Republicans or the Democrats. This mood swing
proved especially intense in the 1992 election. The degree to which people had become concerned about general paralysis within the system
gave an unprecedented profile to the dysfunctions of divided government. People had become greatly concerned with the constant struggle
between the president and Congress (Baker 1993, 57–59; Pomper 1993,

142). Their anxieties focused on the incapacity of the system to handle many of the key problems facing America at the time.

From fears about gridlock there emerged what many observers viewed as a fanciful and dangerous idea. Many ordinary voters began to see the way around gridlock as going directly to the people—through the type of electronic "town-hall" democracy which Ross Perot utilized so effectively (McWilliams 1993, 199).

We might ask, "Why not go to electronic voter participation in specific decisions?" Presidency scholars had written about a postmodern presidency—less reliant upon links to institutional power bases among interest groups and Congress—for at least a decade (Rose 1991). And incumbents increasingly were going "public" with direct appeals to voters—going over the heads of traditional loci of power (Kernell 1986). Modern technology brought radically different modes of governance into the realm of the possible.

Yet the Perot approach sent chills down the spines of those concerned with the integrity of the American democratic system. Perhaps Perot himself was too successful by half in executing his campaign. His appeal—based as it was on oversimplification of issues, populist meanderings, and a seemingly unlimited supply of cash—flew in the face of a constitutional heritage which for over 200 years had deliberately eschewed majoritarianism and populism.

Chapter 3 summons a number of reasons why Bill Clinton as president has failed to eliminate gridlock. Ross Perot's ultimate impact in the 1992 election was to draw so many votes away from Bush and Clinton that neither could emerge with an absolute majority. Bill Clinton, thus, had to govern during the first term with a 43% plurality—a mandate whose weakness seemed constantly to revisit the president. Further, Clinton came to Washington as an outsider. He lacked strong ties to the Democratic establishment in Congress. He appointed a great many people with little or no experience in Washington to White House and executive-branch offices. Perhaps more important, Clinton—from early on—fell into the trap of blaming gridlock whenever he encountered difficulties with advancing his program. This provided a golden opportunity for the Republicans. They could go to the electorate—as they did in the 1994 midterm elections—and argue that—even with control of the White House and both houses of Congress—the Democrats were incapable of solving the ills which plague the nation.

Even before the Republican sweep in the 1994 midterm elections, most analysts believed that demographic shifts along with gradual movement of the electorate to more conservative views would produce Republican majorities in the Senate and the House of Representatives before the turn of the century (perhaps as early as 1996). They expected these majorities, unlike those the Republicans enjoyed in the Senate between 1981 and 1987, to reflect a realignment. That is, they would not depend so much on the popularity of a given Republican incumbent president or candidate for president. They would approximate the stability of Democratic Party majorities in Congress since 1954 (Burnham 1996).

Would the Republicans actually achieve greater coherence between the executive and legislative branches if they had the presidency and majorities in each house of Congress? We should not hold our breath in anticipation of the end of gridlock. Recent research has not lent much support for those maintaining that majorities in both houses actually improve presidents' ability to press forward coherent and consistent programs (Mayhew 1991; Jones 1994). In fact, Jones maintains that we misinterpret the intent of the founding fathers if we ascribe to them the desire to make presidents progenitors of responsible party government. More fundamentally, no one who has observed the diversity of views warring within the Republican Party would remain unguardedly optimistic about its ability to sustain unified governance.

This takes us back to basics. Divided government links to the separation of powers. It is an old and recurrent theme in American politics. It might not loom large in every election. However, we should not view it as an aberration. Much of the political science discipline in the United States would go out of business if it lacked the division of powers and its consequences. For instance, congressional studies would become a sleepy backwater—much like parliamentary studies have always been in the United Kingdom, Canada, and Australia.

Certainly, we can understand how some members of the general electorate would find presidential leadership based on specific electronic mandates appealing. Many voters have despaired of the capacity for politicians to solve the nation's problems. However, we should keep in mind that even scholars have in various epochs proposed a streamlining of the system. The most dramatic intervention—from that of the contributions of various individuals—occurred in 1950. In that year, the American Political Science Association Committee Report on Political

Parties called for a responsible two-party system in the United States. Such a system, the authors believed, would allow parties to set out their programmatic goals and then maintain sufficient cohesion—while in government—actually to deliver upon these.

Many have subsequently questioned the appropriateness of these ideas for the American system. After all, the founding fathers embraced a totally different type of constitutional context from those eventually to prevail in parliamentary systems and did so quite deliberately. However, the debate over the shape of the American Constitution has never reached complete resolution. Many Americans find the British system very alluring. From afar it appears much more amenable to change-oriented politics.

In the middle part of this century, the British system attracted a following among members of the intellectual community in the United States with a commitment for greater state intervention in pursuit of social welfare. Advocates of the welfare state encountered considerable frustration as they observed the slow progress of social legislation in the United States. However, the 1980s ushered in a period in which neo-liberals began to look longingly across the Atlantic at Margaret Thatcher. Here a chief executive could actually implement the top-down, command-oriented leadership deemed necessary for the right to stanch deficits' depletion of national wealth and turn the state apparatus into an agent of enterprise.

Ronald Reagan had talked very much like Mrs. Thatcher. In his first term, he identified goals similar to hers—easing the tax burdens of the wealthy, cutting social programs, and reenshrining the military as an expenditure sacred cow. Yet notwithstanding a strong start, he eventually found himself thwarted by dissension in his administration and the resistance of Congress (Roberts 1984; Stockman 1986). Bush, of course, lost his mandate because he kept the neo-liberal policy coordinates of Reagan even though the nation gradually had swung back toward the center (McWilliams 1993, 194).

Some observers have actually positioned themselves as constitutional consulting engineers—arguing that, wherever you sit on the ideological spectrum, strong parties would help the system work better. Thus, some figures, such as James Sundquist, have employed the strong-party argument both during the candy-store period of state intervention and the current age of stringency. Notwithstanding its appeal, we have to ask how practical and realistic this type of option is (Sundquist 1988–89).

We also have to take into consideration the fact that divided government does not confine itself to situations where one party controls the presidency and another party dominates Congress. This argument appeared in 1963 in a book which has become the classic work on this theme: James MacGregor Burns's *Deadlock of Democracy*. Burns maintained that the U. S. system effectively runs with four parties. There are congressional and presidential Democrats and the congressional and presidential Republicans. All four groups seek and maintain markedly different clienteles. Even if the Democrats or the Republicans control the White House and both houses of Congress, this does not necessarily—in fact, it probably will not—add up to a unity of governance approximating that which usually prevails in parliamentary systems.

The Burns thesis, of course, bore itself out most recently in the aftermath of the 1992 election. This produced for the first time since 1969 both a Democratic administration and Congress. For many reasons, the circumstances did not add up to more coherent governance. Ross Perot's third-party candidacy robbed Clinton of an absolute majority, thereby weakening his mandate. Clinton attempted to wrap himself in the centrist garb of a "New Democrat." However, the Democratic contingents in both houses of Congress persisted with policy stances considerably to the left of the president's. The resulting internal tensions in the Democratic camp did nothing to assuage public fears of gridlock. They also set up the Republicans for a golden opportunity. Under the leadership of Newt Gingrich, the Republicans presented themselves as an administration-in-waiting. Their Contract with America offered to many the prospect of coherent governance emerging from the sheer force of newly minted Republican majorities in the Senate and the House of Representatives. As the mixed record of the Republicans during the 104th Congress suggested, however, Gingrich and Co. encountered problems of their own with the separation of powers.

PLURALISM, PUBLIC CHOICE, AND SHIFTING VIEWS OF THE PRESIDENCY

Of course, Burns's concerns—emerging as they did in an age of government interventionism—contrast sharply with recent preoccupations—focusing on the seemingly insuperable difficulties with the deficit and management of the inevitable shrinking of government. In the 1960s, reform, a word very much at the left of center, meant pushing forward the interventionist agenda. Reformers in the 1960s became anxious that—even though the Democrats controlled the presidency and both houses of Congress—they encountered an apparent incapacity to move forward rapidly in policy areas crying out for timely and comprehensive treatment (Lowi 1969; Walker 1966; 1969). These included civil rights, social policy, and foreign policy.

In the mid-1960s, worries about divided government seemed less warranted than before. For one thing, Lyndon Johnson appeared to have broken the impasse between the presidency and Congress. He managed to push through sweeping civil rights and social legislation and engaged Congress in aggressive pursuit of the Vietnam War. Even among students of politics, a new generation emerged. Increasingly, the most prominent scholars had developed a strong sense of the inherent limitations of the U. S. Constitution. The pluralist view of American politics began to assert itself as the strongest influence on thinking about the Constitution. The view focused on the "is" of American politics rather than the "ought" (Lindblom 1965; Dahl 1971). Since the prospect of responsible two-party government seemed to fit squarely under the latter column, it attracted much less attention than earlier.

In fact, two groups emerged in the 1960s which positively repudiated the responsible two-party option. The first of these was the pluralists. They held the view that the checks-and-balances within the American system reflected and accommodated the inherently fragmented and fractious nature of American society. No constitutional system can impose greater coherence than a society can yield. Thus, strong party responsibility would—even if it were desirable—remain elusive within the American context.

Anyone acquainted with highly diverse societies that have tried to exist with strict parliamentary government—Canada being an especially notable example—certainly will be able to grasp the intuitive appeal of the pluralist view (Lijphart 1977, 118–129; Lijphart, Rogowski, and Weaver 1993). Interestingly enough, Australia—like the United States and Canada, a federal system—does not embody a comparable degree of diversity and actually does function pretty well with strict party discipline and relatively centralized commonwealth-state relations (Campbell and Halligan 1992). Of course, the Australian Parliament provides the escape valve of an elected Senate with considerably more clout than the Canadian counterpart (Weller 1985, 175–176).

The Canadian and Australian cases seem to sustain the view that— in devising constitutions—drafters should begin by examining the nature of the society and the appropriateness of particular structure to its peculiar circumstances. The pluralists quite rightly said, "Look, the best you can expect out of this system is incremental decisions. These will always prevail over any type of comprehensive rationality." However, the notion persisted that societies, like Britain, proved capable of comprehensive rationality and the types of decisions that built upon that aptitude.

As noted, another group—which would eventually rival the pluralists—emerged in the 1960s. However, there was quite a lag before it had any type of influence on mainstream thought about the nature of American politics. It consisted of what we now call the public choice theorists—including researchers such as James Buchanan and Gordon Tullock (1962), and William Niskanen (1971). These scholars had received their training in economics. They attempted to study politics as an economic phenomenon. They focused on what they called principal-agent relationships. In democracy, they argued, the principal is the citizen. He or she engages services of an agent, that is the politician. Elections serve as the core mechanism which sustains the relationships.

Consistent with the centrality of the principal-agent relations, the view emerged that, in fact, party discipline short-circuits the connection between the citizen and the politician. Individual politicians find their accountability diminished if they feel themselves beholden to an entity beyond their ultimate principals.

Notwithstanding the lag in its effects upon thinking about American politics, by the late 1970s and, certainly, throughout the 1980s public choice theory has worked a very strong effect upon mainstream views and now pervades contemporary approaches to the study of politics (Miller 1993, 286; Moe 1993, 354–355). Public choice has revealed a bias toward examining those things which are amenable to mathematical expression. This constitutes a distinct matter from whether a subdiscipline proves amenable to critical analysis. Indeed, public choice has often gotten ahead of the discipline by theorizing beyond what empirical analysis might reasonably be expected to sustain (Green and Shapiro 1994).

The rise of public choice has meant that a different breed of cat has dominated scholarship on American politics, and by extension, the definition of the core issues surrounding leadership within the context of the separation of powers. The 1960s-style pluralists became absorbed with the theory and practice of empirical analysis; 1980s-style public choice theorists became enamored of elegant formal expression. The empiricism of the pluralists constricted students of the presidency (Edwards, Kessel, and Rockman 1993). The institution did not present many cases of presidents. Unlike medieval popes, none of these served contemporaneously. Even those working for the president as cabinet secretaries and advisers often operate behind a veil of secrecy that few scholars have readily pierced. These obstacles to full membership in the empirical community inclined presidency scholars toward a focus on variations in incumbents' personality, style, and power.

Public choice theorists interested in the presidency found it no easier than pluralists to do mainstream work. Interviews with individuals served as the building blocks for pluralists. Votes functioned as the sine qua non for public choice analysts—hence their early focus on congressional behavior. Presidential vetoes—potential surrogates for votes—make pretty slim pickings for empirical work.

On the other hand, myriad executive branch agencies have budgets. The ability of "bureaus" to defend and augment their resources—as recorded in budgets—became the focus of public choice analysis concerned with the presidency. From this emphasis, the view that only maximizing their budgets motivates bureaucrats took hold (Niskanen 1971). Relatedly, analysis became focused on the gearbox between administrations and the standing bureaucracy (Moe 1985). This emphasis flowed naturally from the public choice epistemology. The crucial gauge of a presidency became the ability of politicians to exert principalship over bureaucrats (their agents).

It was not by accident that public choice supplanted pluralism during the late 1970s and early 1980s. This period corresponded with the emergence of the age of constraint, which had worked profound effects on the art of the possible in every liberal democracy (Rose and Peters 1978). In the expansive period of governance—a time of the candy store of possibilities—debate among students of politics about their assumptions centered on the potential responsible party government as against pluralist incrementalism. Responsible party advocates believed that pluralists simply provided a rationalization for the incapacity of the system to make fundamental choices. Yet the realpolitik that prevailed among most students of American politics in the 1960s made sense: "Don't be in such a rush; the system was designed to be incremental. Ultimately, the commitments will be made and the options selected."

The age of constraint brought us to a sharply different context. Government became a culprit. It was robbing the populace of its economic future. Bureaucratic self-promotion stood at the heart of the problem, control of the promoters of "big government" became the core imperative of political leadership. The fit between the development of this neo-liberal perspective and the emerging epistemology of public choice was almost one-to-one (Campbell 1993).

In the past decade, neo-liberal governments dominated Anglo-American democracies. With varying degrees of specificity, these embraced the principal-agent theory of governance. Neo-liberals ask first not "What should you do for your country?" but "How can you move toward getting it off your back by eliminating functions—especially social ones?" It determines whether a function should be performed at all, it then moves to the issue of whether government should involve itself. Even if the answer is yes, it then counsels marketlike arrangements—like contracting out and commercialization—as surrogates for customer-supplier relationships.

Such an emphasis shifts the focus of accountability onto the clearly transactional dimensions of political leadership. Through its strong association with fiscal conservatism, public choice also packages itself as a means for controlling the aggregate size of government—although its actual follow-through has proven patchy at best—certainly in the United States and Canada and—under Major—in Britain, too (Savoie 1994; Campbell and Wilson 1994). It has failed most clearly at the connecting points in political leadership—where macro meets micro, where policy and administration become intertwined. One finds clear-cutting, boutique forestry and nothing in between.

An irony emerges if we compare the actual effects of public choice in the United States to those in other liberal democracies. The two strategies—disaggregated governance and automatized budgeting—have encountered considerable success in Britain and Australia (Aucoin 1990). During the 1984 to 1993 rule of the Progressive Conservatives they achieved virtually nothing in Canada even though that country labored under a larger deficit problem than the United States.

What explains the different experiences of Britain and Australia, on the one hand, and Canada and the United States on the other? One possible answer comes to mind immediately. Both Canada and the United

States function within the context of divided government. In each case, the ambivalence of the respective founding fathers has carried over to our present epoch. For Canada, this concerns fears of an overpowerful federal government vis-à-vis provincial, ethnic, religious, and regional interests. For the United States, it relates to deep suspicions of executive authority. In each instance, divided government has impeded the pursuit of public choice options as much as it impaired the process of expanding the welfare state during the candy-store phase of politics.

In the age of constraint, U. S. presidents deal with essentially the same fragmented bureaucracy that hobbled their predecessors during the era of expansive governance. They have achieved virtually nothing to make the bureaucracy more managerial. They lack a coherent government to reinvent (Heclo 1977; Hansen and Levine 1988). It has become a banality to say that gridlock stood at the root of the deficit. And through it all, presidents bravely had to assert that America competes with economies that have spurted ahead of the United States precisely because of the aggregate governance. That is, they plan. They have not disaggregated governance; they maintain a structured coherence—a capacity to relate all of the parts to the whole (Olson 1982). Japan serves as the archetype of coherent governance (Pempel 1982). Continental European systems—Germany and France—also plan. An old saw says that these nations' success came at the cost of true democracy. However, recent research suggests that the matter is not that simple (Feigenbaum, Samuels, and Weaver 1993). And the simple fact remains, the U.S., as well as other fragmented systems such as Canada, took a long time learning how to cope with the age of constraint.

The rise of neo-liberalism in the United States has ushered in a neo-institutionalistic view of the presidency. Expectations for presidents to lead increasingly take a back seat to indulgence of nonperformance due to the institutional straitjacket of divided government. Obeisance to the view that presidents can do little covers a multitude of sins of omission. Because of the focus on institutions and the linkage between administrations and the permanent bureaucracy, the discipline has not advanced analysis of the relationship between personality, management style, and presidential performance during the past twenty years.

In illustration, this point proved the standard assessment of George Bush that prevailed in the discipline until about twelve months before his defeat in the 1992 election—even among observers not especially identified with neo-institutionalism (for instance, Jones 1991; Sinclair

1991; Edwards 1991). Allegedly, the public did not expect him to be addressing domestic problems. They perceived him as someone whose strong suit was foreign policy. Voters did not see him as capable, institutionally, of advancing a domestic agenda. Is it problematic to give so much credence to institutional factors? Did this obscure from analysts very serious dysfunctions in the administration which, ultimately, would lead to trouble?

Any president must master the engagement of two, not one, gearboxes. Neo-institutionalism, as associated with neo-liberalism, has almost completely ignored one of these. The first gearbox deals with the relationship between the administration and the rest of the bureaucracy—which neo-institutionalists say went just fine under neo-liberalism because the public service received one heck of a bashing. However, neo-institutionalists assumed that neo-liberals had taken care of the second gearbox issue. This concerns the relationship between the president and his team.

In fact, the Reagan administration had led the neo-institutionalists down the garden path. The view developed that there had been a quantum change in the relationship between a regime and the standing bureaucracy (Moe 1985). But neo-institutionalists had overinterpreted the results. Too anxious to proclaim victory for public choice, they discerned an irreversible, linear process in which the standing bureaucracy was declining and the presidency rising. More fundamentally, they assumed a coherence within administrations which would allow presidents to sustain strong central direction. Actual events provided something quite different.

We saw in the second Reagan term a weakening of the direction coming from the administration vis-à-vis the bureaucracy (Campbell 1986). A notable decline in teamwork accompanied this shift. Both of these developments became much more severe in the Bush administration (Campbell 1991).

In the early 1970s, James David Barber's work raised a debate in the United States about the role of personality in the presidency (1972). Barber introduced a paradigm which postulates four types of presidents: active-positive, active-negative, passive-positive, and passive-negative. All of this makes for an iffy theoretical framework. It is very difficult to establish who fits into which of the quadrants. Yet the paradigm is strongly evocative. What can be done with it to enhance its salience for presidential studies?

Let us assume that all presidents start off being pretty active and pretty positive about their job. The question remains: "Active and positive about what?" History certainly serves up "new order" presidents who wanted to do great things; we conventionally put the acronym presidents here—FDR, JFK, and LBJ. Then we find exceedingly active and positive presidents who view themselves as gifted at running things and making them more efficient. Such "executive" presidents have an appetite for detail and a passion for finding how things actually run. Jimmy Carter stands as a perfect illustration of this kind of president. Because of his resume, many analysts expected George Bush to fit this mold. He did not.

We also have had "being there" presidents. What these presidents are active and positive about is massive engagement of themselves in the symbolic dimensions of office. Ronald Reagan serves as a very strong illustration—if not the archetype—of this sort of president. Finally, there is a "let's deal" president. He is a very pragmatic leader who is very finicky about tackling seemingly intractable problems. If he takes on an issue he will want fairly rapid outcomes. He will deploy his energy and concentration within a very short time-frame.

George Bush was that type of president. His approach achieved what was deemed success in foreign affairs. It failed on the domestic front. Clinton, too, is a "let's deal" president. The emergence of two of this type of leader in immediate succession should prompt us to ask whether something has happened to the system that favors this leadership style?

The rest of this chapter examines precisely this point. It will probe two issues. Did the Reagan presidency function as a harbinger for dysfunctions in two gearboxes—that between an administration and the standing bureaucracy and that between the president and his administration? If so, is the "let's deal" presidency a symptom of these dysfunctions, an art-of-the-possible method for addressing them, or both? Thus, we focus in this chapter on how Reagan and Bush coped under pressures which might have transformed the presidency. These pressures include not only the age of economic decline and acute fiscal constraint, but, more fundamentally, exacerbation of the intractability of the system which we now term gridlock. However, before looking at these two presidents and their administrations let us first examine elements of the two gearboxes which seem to persist independently of who takes charge of the apparatus.

THE TWO GEARBOXES IN THE UNITED STATES

The arrangement of our two gearboxes appropriate to a given administration in a specific country at a particular time will vary greatly (Campbell 1988). However, even the most astute leader advised by the finest institutional engineers available would fail to overcome completely the clear limitations in the U. S. system to coherence and consistency. All presidents—even those fortunate enough to belong to parties which control both houses of Congress—face daily the realities of the separation of powers. In myriad ways, this means that presidents and their advisers face unparalleled limits—at least in comparison to chief executives in other Anglo-American nations—on the art of the possible for administrations seeking integrative policies.

The U. S. executive branch comes across as extremely fragmented in comparison to other executive-bureaucratic complexes. This might strike some as ironic, because of the monocratic status of the president. He labors under no tradition of collective responsibility. Indeed, those who exercise the authority of the administration do so in the president's name. Cabinet does not act as an executive agent (Fenno 1959). This means straight away that the president must fight a two-front war in directing his administration. The first, centering on the first gearbox, relates to how he might give some direction to the ongoing bureaucratic apparatus. The second, focusing on the second gearbox, concerns keeping his cabinet and closest advisers marching in time. To be sure, prime ministers in our other Anglo-American countries cannot take the second gearbox for granted. However, the institutional and cultural biases of the executive-bureaucratic arenas in these countries flow in the direction of relative harmony based on teamwork.

The monotonic nature of the U. S. executive branch—focused as it is on the president—greatly limits the potential benefits of cabinet dynamics toward improvement of greater coherence and consistency even when employed. Since so much of what the executive branch does requires the president's formal approval, the circuits to the Oval Office easily become overloaded (Hess 1988). With so much discretionary authority resting in one person, Congress takes every opportunity to define narrowly how agencies must respond to specific circumstances. This multiplies exponentially the requests to the president to intervene in response to special pleading, or to seek corrective legislation or regulations.

The circumstances surrounding the operation of the first gearbox in the United States also present a special case. In some of our systems, a strong view has developed that the career bureaucracy has aligned itself with the usual party of government. This means that members of the usual party of opposition might develop the view that they will encounter problems with the bureaucracy if and when they assume power. However, it goes further than that. Usual parties of government—such as the Liberals in Canada and the Conservatives in the United Kingdom—have a tendency to ossify over the lives of administrations. Eventually, the rank and file of these parties realize that their leaders must adopt dramatically new positions if they want to succeed in future electoral tests. However, pressing for such adaptation might prove futile if the party executive has developed a symbiosis with the bureaucracy. Such a relationship might lead to only conventional proposals emerging from the cozy "group think" of the political leadership and the top bureaucracy.

The United States lacks a unified civil service system (Heclo 1977). This means that administrations rarely achieve anything close to group think with the permanent bureaucracy. However, it also means that a new administration must contend with iron triangles—tight alliances of the bureaucracy, Congress and interest groups (Aberbach, Putnam, and Rockman 1981, 90–100). These alliances prove somewhat more formidable than the symbioses which emerge in Westminster systems between the political executive and the permanent bureaucracy. Iron triangles build upon relatively autonomous bureaucratic cultures which sustain themselves through the astute modulation of congressional and interest-group support. They certainly benefit from the indulgence of the political appointees assigned to supervise bureaucrats' work.

Departments employ widely different means of recruiting and training their personnel. Career officials move from unit to unit within agencies relatively infrequently, much less transfer from department to department. They often develop narrow foci in highly specialized policy fields. Their networks will include congressional staffers, scholars, members of think tanks, lobbyists, and public interest organization representatives as much as fellow civil servants. All presidents encounter difficulty with their appointees going native—that is, succumbing to the insularity of their departments or units within these.

Cabinet rarely operates as a collective decision-making body. In fact, confusion abounds as to exactly what "cabinet government" might mean. Jimmy Carter, for instance, frequently employed the term. However, he viewed cabinet as a collection of chief operating officers in a conglomerate of subsidiaries (Campbell 1986, 59–64). He did not expect them to have group dynamics. He preferred, instead, that they run their organizations as much as possible without reference to the White House or to one another. The Carter approach led to a steady stream of domestic policy fiascos (Lynn and Whitman 1981). This owed in part to the fact that cabinet secretaries did not coordinate with one another. More fundamentally, it stemmed from the fact that Carter did not hold up his part of the bargain. He found it extremely difficult to stay out of detailed policy issues once these broke through the barriers and crashed into the Oval Office.

Whenever presidents and their advisers have tried to inch the American cabinet system toward more formalized consultation they have encountered a seemingly intractable difficulty. Unlike the other systems covered here, the United States cannot draw upon a constitutional convention which would legitimize collective decision making. Those arguing for more routinized cabinet deliberations must base their appeals on the potential instrumental utility of a regularized cabinet system. This compounds the difficulty of successfully implementing reforms.

Although its performance has proven uneven at best, the National Security Council (NSC) constituted a significant step (Nelson 1981; Destler 1982). Instituted by congressional mandate at the request of Harry Truman, the NSC emerged as a significant force in the immediate postwar years. In fact, it—and the secretariat which supported it—became strongly institutionalized during the Eisenhower administration. The Treasury Board in Canada is the only cabinet committee among the Westminster systems which enjoys a statutory base. However, in the U. S. instance, the NCS's being legitimized with a legislative instrument does not prevent presidents from using it highly selectively. Kennedy virtually ignored the NSC. He believed that Eisenhower's institutional approach to foreign policy overcooked issues. Johnson and Nixon exploited the NSC staff. They placed little value on collective deliberations—preferring to run foreign policy from the White House.

Ford and Carter demonstrated greater respect for their cabinet officers in the foreign policy field. The NSC process actually came back to life under Carter. And it functioned reasonably effectively during Reagan's first term. We now know that it operated too during the second term. However, the Iran-Contra scandal suggests that ideologues in the NSC staff ultimately highjacked the collective decision-making process.

Bush's scattered attention to issues took its toll on the NSC process during his presidency (Berman and Jentleson 1991). The December 1989 Panama invasion came in the aftermath of the administration's embarrassment over its inept handling of a coup attempt earlier that year. The existing evidence suggests that the administration performed very poorly indeed in responding to the early indications that Saddam Hussein was preparing to invade Kuwait.

On the domestic side, cabinet committees have developed only very gradually. The Economic Policy Board under Ford did a pretty solid job of coordinating between economics agencies (Porter 1980). It drew upon the support of a White House secretariat which performed well as an agent of neutral brokerage. Carter instituted an Economic Policy Council. From the beginning, the group included far too many participants. Further, the assistant to the president for domestic policy—Stuart E. Eizenstat—operated more as a principal in meetings than a neutral broker. In fact, he frequently corrected public comments by W. Michael Blumenthal—the treasury secretary. This habit seriously undermined the latter's role as the U. S.'s "finance" minister.

During his first term, Reagan went further than any of his predecessors in differentiating cabinet business. He eventually created seven cabinet councils. Only two of these—Economic Affairs, and Commerce and Trade—met with any regularity. The system received some credit for defusing middle-range conflicts between departments. However, the White House—largely through the Legislative Strategy Group headed by James A. Baker III—tended to draw the really big issues into its vortex and limit participation to key players. For instance, this approach applied both to the 1981 tax measures and the 1983 Social Security reforms. The system pretty much fell apart during the second term. The president collapsed the seven cabinet councils into two—Economic Policy and Domestic Policy. Bush continued this structure but, in fact, did not operate it with any consistency. Clinton opted for a National Economic Council and a Domestic Policy Council. Neither met with any regularity. The successive heads of the NEC staff functioned more as fixers, even advocates, than neutral brokers.

Presidents have employed different strategies to compensate for the perennial deficit in the system's capacity for collective coordination. Some of these tighten up the first gearbox—the relationship between the administration and the career bureaucrats embedded in line departments. Others pertain to organization of the president's team in the White House and, therefore, focus more on the second gearbox.

Two general strategies have emerged in connection with the first gearbox. Both of these have involved top-down imposition of coherence and consistency (Nathan 1975; 1983). The first entails the use of the White House staff to shadow departments and insure that cabinet secretaries do not stray from the president's priorities and agenda. The second sees presidents reviewing very closely nominees for subcabinet political positions in departments from the standpoint of ideological tests.

Republican presidents have used these devices much more than Democrats. This probably reflects the relatively undisciplined nature of the Democratic Party. Indeed, the last third of the twentieth century has seen no fewer than three Republican chiefs of staff—H. R. "Bob" Haldeman (Nixon), Donald Regan (Reagan), and John Sununu (Bush)—who have seriously damaged the standing of their bosses by arrogating to themselves immense discretionary decision-making authority and then abusing this power. Both Nixon (second term) and Reagan (each term) enforced very strict loyalty tests on appointees. The former failed because he faced a public increasingly fearful of his "imperial" style. Reagan succeeded. Thus he greatly added to his administration's capacity for coherence and consistency—even though these strengths based themselves on hierarchical control rather than collective decision making.

The Clinton administration upheld diversity as a goal more than loyalty. That is, the president paid a great deal of attention to the degree to which his appointees reflected various segments of American society. Concern focused on appointment of greater proportions of women and racial and ethnic minorities than have pertained in previous administrations. In pursuing this approach, Clinton ran into two problems during the first term. He tended to give gray-haired, white, male members of the establishment the plum posts within the cabinet. He made nominations in the service of diversity which did not withstand Washington standards both regarding experience and political conventionality.

One important by-product of the two gearbox problems increasingly has impinged upon the operation of the presidency over the years. This has taken the form of institutional layering through the creation of career units reporting through appointive directors to the president. Here some functions most effectively performed once-removed from the president lodge themselves right within the Executive Office of the President. The process works more readily discernible long-term effects than the development of shadow bureaucracies of career appointees. Presidents may much more readily adapt the latter to specific circumstances. On the other hand, formally instituted offices within the Executive Office of the President often base their existence on congressional mandates and retain permanent staff.

The development and integration of economic policies presents one area in which layering has greatly complicated decision processes. In Westminster systems, convention normally sustains a principle whereby the prime minister and the main cabinet minister responsible for economic policy enjoy a special relationship. This usually allows the latter to develop the core economic strategy as an agent of the prime minister rather than the entire cabinet. Indeed, instances in which the trust between the two have fallen short of implicit might occasion the resignation of the minister responsible for economic policy. Such a situation emerged in the United Kingdom in 1989 over Britain's membership in the European Monetary System when the chancellor of the exchequer—Nigel Lawson—resigned from the Thatcher government.

In the United States, development and integration of an administration's core economic strategies involve both agencies responsible to the treasury secretary (the Department of the Treasury) and those directly responsible to the president (most notably, the Office of Management and Budget [OMB], Council of Economic Advisers). The Treasury undertakes the classic collection of "Finance Department" functions including international economics, monetary affairs, economic analysis, tax policy, and domestic finance. It does not, however, cover budget review—a function which was hived off from the Treasury in 1939 and put under the direct control of the president. The agency which performs this task—OMB—used to be the Bureau of the Budget (BOB).

BOB was created in 1921 (Berman 1979). Before it moved, in 1939, to the newly created Executive Office of the President, it had existed as a separate organization residing in the Treasury but reporting to the president. It obtained the name Office of Management and Budget in 1970 as a result of a Nixon administration effort to give greater focus to management within the budget review process.

The 1946 Employment Act created the Council of Economic Advisers (Porter 1991). The legislation stipulates that the CEA—supported by a small staff of professional economists—advise the president on the means necessary toward accomplishment of full employment. Currently, the council's three members—who now call upon the support of some fifteen economists, normally on secondment from academia or the think tanks—shoulder responsibility for major presidential economic statements and reports and insert themselves into administration discussions of the economic implications of various policy initiatives. Concerning the latter function, the CEA has—since the first push toward deregulation under the Carter administration—played a very substantial role in advocating market-oriented economics.

The interaction between the core players in key economic decisions normally reaches a high degree of intensity. This owes to the clash of missions and cultures between the career-staffed Treasury and OMB—each of which takes dramatically different views of the economy—and the relatively scholarly CEA. To add to the cacophony, other organizations operating out of the Executive Office of the President frequently adopt views at odds with the inner circle of economics central agencies. During the Carter administration, these organizations included the Domestic Policy Staff (DPS), the Office of the U. S. [Special] Trade Representative (STR), and the Council on Wage and Price Stability (CWPS). During the Reagan and Bush administrations, the successor to the DPS, the Office of Policy Development, played a more circumspect role in economic policy; CWPS faced disbandment—its mandate did not fit into supply-side economics; STR continued to play a substantial role in economic issues with trade implications; and the National Security Council (NSC) staff—largely through aggressive efforts to link trade issues to national security—began to play significantly in international economics.

Regarding the NSC staff role, it reached such proportions by midpoint in Reagan's first term that the administration created an NSC senior interagency group on international economic affairs chaired by the treasury secretary. The Clinton administration followed along these lines. The chairman of the National Economic Council (NEC) staff attends meetings of the NSC and the deputy head of the NSC staff covers sessions of the NEC.

The evolution of this complex array of organizations has reflected a tendency for American presidents to try to resolve problems by creating new institutions—most of which have attached themselves to the Executive Office of the President. And as indicated above, the United States has not proven adept at mitigating the dysfunctions of a multiplicity of institutional players through enhanced interagency coordination. One coordinative apparatus actually had a fairly successful run from its creation under Lyndon Johnson through to the end of the Carter administration. Called the "troika," three layers of trilateral committees—bringing together the CEA, the Treasury, and OMB—worked at reconciling differences in the three agencies' economic projections. The need for a complex of committees to negotiate forecasts highlights the extent to which even economic projections—controlled by one department in our other systems—became subject to interagency negotiations.

As has proven the case with the increased politicization of forecasting in other systems, rigorous analytic criteria have taken a back seat to political exigencies in the devising of economic projections in the United States. During the Reagan administration, this trend became especially problematic as supply-side economics gained sway. This ascendancy shifted the interagency battleground from arcane issues associated with the functioning of models to ideologically motivated debates about desirable economic targets.

Since the 1980s, with a ballooning deficit whose implications have reached global proportions, participants and observers alike rightfully registered concern about the coherence and consistency of the U. S. budgetary process and the effectiveness with which the U. S. public service is managed (Stockman 1986; Roberts 1984). However, much of the difficulty owes to the separation of powers and the resultant ability of Congress to override the executive in the appropriation of funds. As well, the context of divided government provides excellent cover both for presidents and congressional leaders who talk tough about fiscal stringency and then give special interests what they want. The separation of powers provides a perfect context for blame avoidance (Weaver 1986).

Institutionally, the central capacity for rigorous budget examination has experienced considerable erosion beginning in the 1960s (Berman 1979). Congress supported the 1921 creation of BOB within the Treasury because it recognized that the president could best monitor the budget process to insure coherence and consistency. During the implementation of the New Deal, it became obvious that the president required an agency operating directly under his control rather than at arm's length. However, the initial view of the BOB—even when it moved to the Executive Office of the President—was that it would provide "neutral" advice. In the 1920s, this largely focused on the application of sound management principles to the utilization of public resources.

Through the 1940s, 1950s, and 1960s, "neutral" gradually became hard-nosed assessment of the likely effects of new policy initiatives and the consequences of existing programs. The evolutionary process culminated in the effort during the mid-1960s to extend throughout the bureaucracy Planning, Programming and Budget Systems (PPBS), which Robert McNamara had first introduced to the Pentagon early in the Kennedy administration. Scholars and practitioners alike tend to view PPBS as prone to information overload and ill suited to the ad hoc decision processes of the U. S. bureaucracy. Nonetheless, the introduction of analytic approaches ancillary to PPBS revolutionized the capacity of the U. S. bureaucracy to back—when called upon to do so—its policy advice with rigorous assessment (Heclo 1977, 150).

Notwithstanding the Kennedy and Johnson administrations' emphasis on analytic criteria, their respective impatience with pursuit of their programmatic priorities planted the seeds for a diminution of assessment in budget decisions, which reached full growth by the 1980s. Both presidents, many of their key advisers, and many commentators on the role of BOB began to believe that "neutral" analysis had become a rearguard effort to stall the advance of New Frontier and Great Society programs (Berman 1979, Ch. 4). A consensus emerged in Washington that something had to be done to make the BOB more responsive to the timing and priorities of the president's political agenda. Richard Nixon introduced the structural innovation which accomplished this goal and went beyond it to eclipse the credibility of OMB as a source of "neutral" assessment. He added a layer of political appointees—called [political] associate directors, or PADs.

Nixon did not intend to weaken the analytic credibility of OMB. And he—as noted previously—was simply following a consensus view that the budget department had to become more attuned to political exigencies. Indeed, OMB retained much of its integrity through the Nixon administration. During the Carter administration it enjoyed—if anything—a resurgence. This owed to Carter's insatiable appetite for assessment and the relative technocratic bent of his PADs. Thus the institutional toll of the PAD system did not become fully apparent until the Reagan administration. Here David Stockman refused to engage the career officials in OMB in serious assessment of policy options—using them instead simply to fill in expenditure details on deals which he worked out with Congress. James Miller proved more benign toward career officials. However, the overarching commitment of the administration to keep career officials out of consideration of priorities meant that they still lacked a market for their analyses.

Richard Darman—the budget director under Bush—made things worse for OMB officials. He tended to use his PADs selectively, much less career bureaucrats. The state of OMB at the end of the Reagan/Bush years might prompt some to suggest that it be renamed BEB—Back-of-an-Envelope Budgeting. Early in the Clinton administration, OMB began to experience a revival. Much as during the Carter administration, both PADs and career officials began to develop a sense of working for the president. In the build-up to the 1994 budget statement, for instance, this stemmed from the president's decision to review outstanding issues in individual sessions with cabinet secretaries. However, the events surrounding the 1995–96 budget impasse between the White House and Congress left the president and key administration officials precious little time to focus on development of the 1996–97 expenditure projections. This situation once again put OMB in an institutional limbo (Gugliotta 5 February 1996).

Efforts to institute managerial reform in the United States have suffered especially from the layering of organizations with conflicting mandates. Presidents face immense obstacles if they take on efforts to reform civil service culture. The antistatist political ethos of the United States exacerbates the effects of the separation of powers on the bureaucracy (Rockman 1984, 49–52). Not only departments but offices and bureaus within them almost invariably serve three masters—the president, Congress, and client groups. The adeptness of the bureaucracy at brokerage makes it almost impervious to centrally guided efforts at administrative reform (Szanton 1981; Hansen and Levine 1988). Management reform—when it occurs—likely will emerge spontaneously within organizations. The United States is a highly managerial country and some of this rubs off on the leadership of bureaucratic organizations. This analysis holds even regarding the reformist extravaganza that Vice President Gore's National Performance Review represented. Notwithstanding the gargantuan effort, the administration made virtually no provision for an implementation gearbox. At the end of the day, it left change up to the innovative proclivities and aptitudes of individual departments and agencies.

During the 1960s and early 1970s, the view developed that management policy should receive the same type of institutional profile as did budgeting (Berman 1979, Ch. 5; Rose 1976). This served as one motivating factor behind the hiving off of the Treasury Board Secretariat from the Finance Department in Canada in 1966 (Glassco 1962). It also operated behind the creation of the Civil Service Department in the United Kingdom in 1968 (Kellner and Crowther-Hunt 1980, 78–99). Australians were slow to make their move. However, the 1976 division of the Treasury into two departments—with Finance taking responsibility for the expenditure budget—clearly sought to provide an environment in which management issues would receive greater attention.

Over the years, BOB had experimented with various approaches to giving management review greater importance. None of these efforts produced the desired results. Nixon's 1970 insertion of an "M" into the budget department's name was more than symbolic. The accompanying reforms built up a "management" side to the budget department. Under the new structure, departments' budget proposals would receive scrutiny from two desk officers—each working in separate budget and management divisions. This arrangement lasted only for a few years—although the small "special studies" divisions, which until 1994 served the budget examination divisions under each PAD, continued as vestiges of the original design. As noted previously, the fragmentation of the U. S. bureaucratic system makes central guidance of the management system difficult—even if it enjoys the full support of the president. Thus even special initiatives run out of OMB to work on particularly nettlesome management issues have found change elusive. This immobility certainly applies to the President's Reorganization Project under Carter, and Reform 88 and the Grace Commission under Reagan.

Vice President Gore's National Performance Review seems to have met the same fate. At the outset, the project relied on "volunteers" from various departments who returned to their home bases. Even the first report of the review cited many "documents" which proved, in fact, to be works-in-progress which were never finished. The report provided virtually no guidance as to where the gearbox for the reform movement would be lodged. The OMB appointee responsible for supporting the vice president in implementing the report soon went off to the White House to assume a post which only very tangentially would encompass reinventing government. Perhaps most tellingly, OMB dismantled its staff units concerned with management and shifted their personnel into budget divisions.

This section has attempted to place the two gearboxes of the modern presidency—that which links to the bureaucracy and that which connects to the administration—within the context of the art of the possible given the complexity and overlapping authority of the U. S. system.

This chapter now examines the Reagan and Bush administrations with a view to ascertaining why a difficult array of leadership and institutional issues appeared to approach insuperability. The U. S. system presents many difficulties whose severity makes the circumstances of the presidency exceptionally daunting. However, notable gaps have emerged in presidents' ability to negotiate these inhospitable waters. These performance deficits have exacerbated the governance crisis in the United States, thereby making, in turn, management of the presidency progressively more difficult for each new incumbent.

RONALD REAGAN

Through much of his presidency, Ronald Reagan maintained a high degree of public approval—even though much of the electorate indulged him in the way they would a kindly but forgetful uncle. This fact irked many students of the presidency. The scholarly community tended to view Reagan with a measure of skepticism if not contempt. He seemed to be programmed and readily manipulable by his staff. Further, much of what he did was bent on building-down the role of government in potentially damaging ways. Observers raised concerns about withdrawal of social programs from the needy, the erosion of infrastructure, and, paradoxically, huge tax breaks for the rich and carte blanche for the Pentagon. Neither Reagan nor those close to him indicated much respect for the standing bureaucracy. This could prove risky. An administration which ignores the counsel of permanent officials ultimately will become error-prone.

As if to further flout conventional wisdom among aficionados of the presidency, Reagan proceeded during his first term to do superbly with respect to our two gearbox problems. Regarding the relationship with the bureaucracy, he held very tight control over appointments (Newland 1983). Nixon had attempted this at the outset of his second term and failed (Nathan 1975). Democrats under Carter had made observers think that they had become pathologically incapable of such control.

Reagan also achieved a very high degree of centralization of decision making within the White House and the Office of Management Budget. His administration revealed a strong sense of priorities. It engaged itself efficiently and relatively effortlessly—that is without the directionless hyperkineticism of the Carter administration. To be sure, it benefited immensely from its bare-bones, stripped-down agenda—tax cuts for the rich, rolling back social expenditure, and fulfilling the wish lists of the military.

Regarding the second gearbox issue—the relationship between the president and his administration—the first term again earned full marks. The organization of the White House constitutes one of the true conundrums of the modern presidency. Certainly by the onset of the Reagan administration, observers had become chary of strong chiefs of staff. The experiences of the all-powerful Sherman Adams under Eisenhower and imperious Bob Haldeman under Nixon had given sufficient warning about the dysfunctions of hierarchical White Houses led by officials who arrogate to themselves the exertion of presidential authority.

The Carter administration served as an antidote to those who sought a White House devoid of structure. That period displayed clearly the pitfalls of a "spokes-in-the-wheel" format with several top advisers enjoying roughly equal authority and—perhaps more important—parity in access to the president.

Scholars also found under Carter that—while presidents do well to engage themselves substantially in detail—those with a compulsion in this direction need more hierarchy rather than less. That is, someone has to enforce the principle of prioritization. It seems as if presidents as often as not find it difficult to say no or immerse themselves with equal enthusiasm/diligence in everything that crosses their desks. Such incumbents need someone close by with a sense of timing and an instinct for political necessity.

What Reagan implemented holds out possibilities for future administrations. It constituted a half-way point between a strong chief of staff and the spokes-in-the-wheel format—what I have termed a "modified-spokes-in-the-wheel" system. Here three or four key aides headed up parts of the White House which represent the main components of presidential leadership. For most of the first term, the format included separate spokes for overall coordination of White House activities (James Baker—chief of staff); maintaining the president's ideological bearings (Edwin Meese—counselor); image generation and maintenance (Michael Deaver—deputy chief of staff); and foreign affairs (William Clark—assistant to the president for national security affairs).

In each case, top aides served as hubs in their own right—with the heads of key functional areas reporting to them. This meant, of course, that there was some filtering of advice to the president. However, insofar as they achieved high association with the president through access, each of the "Big Four" called upon pretty much equal credibility. As noted previously, the administration did a good job anyway at keeping its agenda simple. However, the modified-spokes-in-a-wheel format did much to further obviate the potential for overload endemic to the modern presidency.

The success of the system owed in no small part to the collegiality which the Big Four achieved among themselves—so chemistry and ability to resolve disputes played important roles in the process. As a result, the administration developed the external image of relatively concerted action. Those not in the charmed circle of four derived a sense that—even if they did not interact regularly with Reagan—at least their views were getting to the president.

As if this were not enough as a high-water point for the gearbox between presidents and their administrations, Reagan in the first term ran a cabinet that actually had group dynamics. It is very hard to sell to American audiences the need for machinery for fostering and maintaining cabinet processes. The Constitution chose to be mute on the topic. Raised in a tradition inclined toward written precepts rather than conventions, presidency scholars have tended to dismiss the applicability of collective consultation to the American scene.

The fact that Ford, Carter, and Reagan all enshrined in strong terms the principle of "cabinet government"—right down to using this exact term—did not sway skeptics. And one finds it hard to argue with performance. Carter—who incanted cabinet government more than the other two—in fact could not trust his aides to work out among themselves the schedule for the White House tennis court much less allow his cabinet secretaries to resolve their differences mutually without constant reference to him.

One can gain some ground toward attaining greater salience of cabinet government for the U. S. system. One simply has to stress that—despite the absence of written constitutional prescription or a serviceable convention—executive decision systems can improve their performance through enhancement of collective deliberations. In short, one can make the case that implementation of cabinet government might meet the standards of instrumental utility. The evidence suggests that this became the case during Reagan's first term.

Officials whom I interviewed during Reagan's first term (Campbell 1986), noted that cabinet government had not performed miracles. If we array issues on a scale of one to ten, according to their difficulty, those beyond seven would probably only be resolved even under Reagan-style cabinet government by inner groups and without broad consultation. More fundamentally, Reagan headed an ideologically homogeneous administration with a relatively macroagenda. He also eschewed detail. He, therefore, probably would have experienced relative success in keeping interdepartmental squabbles out of the Oval Office anyway. Nonetheless, any student of executive overload will still recognize how fraught these waters have become. We have witnessed in the past two decades an upsurge in the inherent complexity of governance and the byzantine nature of relations between the president and Congress. Reagan aides—in praising cabinet government—had tipped a feeling that without it a president with a strong reflex for riding above conflict would have become mired in issues at the level of six or five if not four and below!

The success of the Reagan administration in the first term had prompted some analysts to assert that the presidency had assumed a wholly new trajectory. The standing bureaucracy had suffered a pronounced deinstitutionalization of its role. Presidents would not in the future assign the same value as previously to calling upon the "neutral competence" of the public service. Instead, they would stress "responsive competence" (Moe 1985).

Such assessments urged observers to fit Reagan administration stratagems—such as centralization of political appointments and trimming of the agenda—within this context. To be sure, the new regime spelled the decline of bureaucratic power. In a democracy, however, only the ability to win elections really counts. The enshrinement of this norm was leading to a gradual institutionalization of the presidency—the condition whereby administrations would stop chasing the right decision at the end of the analytic rainbow and start placing political viability at the heart of their leadership approach.

This neo-institutional view of the presidency certainly struck a chord. It came on the heels of an administration—Carter's—which time and again overrode considerations of political responsiveness in favor of prolonging the quest for the "right" option. Yet, the neo-institutional analysis failed to capture the distinctive character of the Reagan administration. The mood of the times had made working the gearbox between an administration and the bureaucracy less complicated. A simple agenda characterized by the imperatives of making America profligately de-

fended, getting the federal government off people's backs, and eliminating or sharply curtailing do-gooder programs hardly constituted the
statecraft equivalent of rocket science.

The genius of Reagan's first term derived overwhelmingly from the
super-salesmanship of the president—the uncanny ability to wrap political expediency in drippy bromides about the inherent goodness of
America in the face of the terrible threats from "evil" forces abroad, the
marvels of unfettered markets, and the potential of individual initiative
and spontaneous charity in overcoming social ills.

The mystical force of this appeal began to dissipate by Reagan's second term. The end of the Cold War, the failure of supply-side economics and indiscriminate deregulation, and the lowering of thresholds for
social disadvantage to include vulnerable segments of the middle class
together would change radically Reagan's legacy to George Bush. Bush,
of course, would work out as a leader whose aptitudes excelled under
neither "responsive" nor "neutral" competence. He would prove the neo-
institutionalists too ready by half to decide that the modern presidency
had turned a corner of near-constitutional moment. Generally, modifications on the level of gearboxes—important as they are—do not result
in changes of a cosmic order in the political system.

This brings us to a key element of the inadequacy of neo-institutionalism for analyzing the significance of Reagan's first term. We might
grant a sea change in the relationship between administrations and the
permanent bureaucracy which would favor the former. However, this
would not necessarily establish that the control of an incumbent over
his administration would likewise function within freshly robust parameters.

For a relatively detached president, Reagan did an excellent job during his first term of guiding his administration. He did this by leaving
no doubt about his core commitments, maintaining a strong "roundtabling" norm which discouraged cabinet secretaries from making direct appeals to him, and by knowing when to roll up his sleeves and immerse himself in issues—such as the rescue of Social Security (Light
1985)—which cried out for his direct involvement.

From the beginning of the second term, it became clear that Reagan
had lost the Midas touch with regard to coordinating his administration
team. His practical noninvolvement in the process whereby James Baker
swapped jobs with Donald Regan—the first-term treasury secretary—
gave advance warning of presidential complacency. The president's de-

tachment had slipped into nonchalance and Regan brought just the level of imperiousness to the chief of staff job to occupy the vacuum.

Now all of the features which had lent such force to Reagan's direction of his administration in the first term went by the boards under Regan. Hierarchy supplanted teamwork. Conformity with the hunches of the chief of staff replaced collegiality and diversity of views. Know-it-all, executive-suite hubris overrode political sensitivity.

Cabinet stopped functioning collectively. As the administration's handling of arms sales to Iran and aid to the Contras made clear, relatively low-level White House aides counted more than cabinet secretaries. None of the resulting disarray and dysfunction would do much to lend credence to the view that the presidency had reinstitutionalized and turned the corner in its capacity for executive leadership.

The second term demonstrates an important point about the presidency under the conditions of divided government in the age of constraint. Even incumbents who have chosen to build-down government must maintain a high level of engagement and pay close attention to the design of the decision-making process. In this regard, Reagan under the first term served practically as a model. His administration did great damage not through executive incompetence but through the defects of the highly ideological policies it pursued.

In the second term, the administration proved inadequate in both regards. The result: an exacerbation of the malaise and distrust which would make gridlock core themes for those—such as Ross Perot and his followers—concerned about the intractability of divided government.

GEORGE BUSH

During the 1988 campaign, George Bush emerged as potentially an executive president—someone who would uphold the core commitments of the Republicans under Reagan yet at the same time give greater attention to detail. Things would run more smoothly. In addition, a Bush administration would engage in some fine-tuning. The argument that it would provide a "kinder, gentler" form of leadership rested on the assertion that the president and his team would know how to modulate policies according to fundamental fairness and humanity. It would not navigate so much on the automatic pilot of ideological presuppositions.

Much of the appeal of Bush as an executive president derived from his resume. We find ourselves in an age in which political outsiders have risen to power in advanced democracies in unprecedented proportions (Rockman 1991a; Peters 1991). Bush harked back to an earlier era in which chief executives had proven themselves in high office within the national government which they ultimately led. Further, unlike Carter and Reagan, Bush did not run against Washington. Much of Bush's campaign rhetoric and earlier pronouncements once elected lent support to the notion that the permanent public service performed a necessary function within the policy arena (Aberbach 1991). This seemed to restore a modicum of standing to "neutral competence" as a component of governance.

Despite these auspicious signs, George Bush flopped as an "executive" president. Instead, he functioned as a "let's deal" leader. Throughout his administration, he remained highly selective—even in foreign affairs (Berman and Jentleson 1991)—about the issues in which he would engage himself. Once he locked into a matter, he revealed little of the steady-handed direction that one expects from a pro. Too anxious for immediate results, he would launch upon hyperkinetic extravaganzas.

Some consider Bush's handling of the Persian Gulf crisis his finest hour. To the contrary, the entire episode represented the very worst dimensions of his leadership style. His administration did not adequately monitor developments in Iraq which pointed to belligerent behavior and exceedingly dangerous ventures into nuclear and chemical weapons development (Jentleson 1994). When some administration voices began to sound alarms in spring 1990, they could not attract the attention of the president and the principals in his national security team. Once the invasion occurred, the president simply shrugged until Margaret Thatcher shamed him into responding.

As if seized by a need to overcompensate, Bush then went over the top (Gordon and Trainor 1995, 153–154, 423, 431). He assembled a half-a-million-person force to remove invaders who ultimately abandoned their positions at the first sign of battle. The ensuing slaughter proved so embarrassing—the "shooting fish in a barrel" analogy employed by one British pilot still rings especially chillingly—that the allies had to call off their attack before gaining complete control of Iraq and removing Saddam Hussein from power.

It is very difficult to see how anyone could rate Bush's handling of the crisis a success. He was totally out of the game as the Iraqi threat built up. The nature and size of the allied force introduced huge distortions to the usual character of UN responses to such incidents—elements which left their signature even in small UN actions such as its intervention in Somalia. At precisely the time when Europe should have been focusing on the dangerous refragmentation of the Balkan states, Bush's leadership forced commitments which left little time or resources for attention to Yugoslavia. And at the end of the day, the approach proved less than surgical regarding the key criterion for success—removing Saddam Hussein from power. In fact, it did not even seem to have taught Hussein a lesson.

Regarding the two gearboxes under Bush, the first—that between the administration and the bureaucracy—functioned reasonably well. This owed partially to a fair amount of continuity between Reagan and Bush administrations—both in objectives and political appointees. The new administration's leadership style remained relatively control-oriented and directive.

Reagan administration appointees had proven themselves adept at devising key policies without involvement of career civil servants—apart from tapping the latter to work on details in isolation from one another. Officials developed from this situation the view that they should be seen but not heard. Indeed, many in their senior ranks migrated ideologically toward the Republicans—a truly significant development given the alleged Democratic bias of the bureaucracy (Aberbach 1991). The advancement of officials sympathetic to the Republicans had certainly quickened this process.

None of these conditions significantly eroded under Bush. On the contrary, they tended to become more firmly entrenched. What Bush had added was a supportive public rhetoric about the bureaucracy. This lent an aura of comity to what—in many respects—still involved a great deal of top-down discipline.

Unlike the first gearbox, the second—that involving the relationship between the president and his administration—operated very poorly. The use of consultative mechanisms declined notably from the outset of the Bush administration. Thus teamwork within the administration became spasmodic. Even the National Security Council—a statutorily buttressed body which normally functions fairly systematically—rarely met at the principals level. The deputies of the various council members kept in regular contact. However, they normally held their meetings through video conference calls. This served as a stricture on candor. Members of the deputies group became chary of those not in view of the cameras who might, nonetheless, be listening in on meetings. As one traces through the administration's handling of events in the build-up to Iraq's invasion of Kuwait, one can see how the irregularity of principals meetings and constraints on candor among deputies contributed to the failure of Bush to perceive and address the obvious danger.

On the domestic side, the administration developed into a dysfunctional family writ large. Certain flaws in Bush's leadership style seemed to set him up for his immense problems in this area. He saw domestic affairs as a field which could pretty much run on its own—or, at least, function under the direction of a surrogate. He enforced no roundtabling norm for resolving intra-administration disputes. And he certainly found scant occasion to meet with Cabinet secretaries over domestic issues. Even considering these factors, Bush might have performed reasonably well on the domestic side had he not chosen John Sununu as his chief of staff.

Scholars have found it hard to fathom how Bush could have selected Sununu. The former New Hampshire governor had acquired a nasty reputation for his intellectual arrogance and social bumptiousness—qualities which later served him well on CNN's *Crossfire* program. Some observers even speculated about a Machiavellian design to the appointment (Rockman 1991b, 27). Bush had cast himself as the good cop—the kinder and gentler statesman above the fray. Sununu filled the role of the bad cop—the enforcer. He would make people feel like such fools when he said no that they would not lightly make special appeals in the future. However, another reason for Sununu's elevation to chief of staff suggests itself. Bush simply sought to repay him for his pivotal role in rescuing his floundering race for the 1988 Republican nomination by providing a surprise victory in the New Hampshire primaries.

Anyone who knew Sununu as well as Bush did should have been able to anticipate difficulties. The previous unfavorable Republican experiences with strong chiefs of staff—Sherman Adams under Eisenhower, H. R. "Bob" Haldeman under Nixon, and Donald Regan under Reagan—should have given the president further pause.

It appears as if there is something about the Republican Party which leads its presidents to vest too much authority in one aide. This could relate to the relative homogeneity of the Republican administrations which gives presidents the illusion of strong mandates simply in need of disciplined implementation. It also might stem from the deep-seated sense that even cabinet secretaries soon go native—that is, become the apologists of their departments' permanent bureaucrats. Strong chiefs of staff, theoretically, can build up White House immunity to special pleading from appointees in line departments.

Whatever the points in favor of a strong chief of staff, actual experience suggests that each time a Republican incumbent has so positioned a top aide he has inadvertently damaged not just the image of his administration but the presidency as an institution. Adams kept the trains running on time and enabled his boss to keep out of minutiae. Yet he imparted to the administration such an image of automatization that even John F. Kennedy took pains to avoid the appearance of an overly institutionalized White House. Haldeman turned the White House into a nerve center for political survival and reprisal. The result was Watergate and the presidency's darkest hour in the twentieth century. Regan tried to run the affairs of state like a business. This left the image that Reagan had given up the task of political leadership.

Sununu set out to suck even the most tangential domestic issues into the vortex of the conservative agenda. He manifested much more interest in scoring ideological points than in keeping presidential trains—like efforts to reduce the deficit—running on time. On tax increases, he freely contradicted the president and infuriated even the leadership of his own party in Congress. On a host of issues, he made Bush into more of a nonconciliatory ideologue than Reagan—witness his machinations concerning the Clean Air Act and the gag-rule against abortion counseling.

Sununu, of course, left the administration in December 1991—too late to allow Bush to reverse the damage already incurred. What he had done was raise in the public mind the image of the intractable presidency. Voters quickly put this together with their already profound feelings that the Congress could not resolve the key issues facing the nation. They developed anxieties about the governability of the United States which have never before emerged to such a strong degree. This provided rich soil for the paranoid politics of Perotism—whose impact hovered over the system like an albatross. One hopes that Sununu put the last nail in the coffin of the strong chief of staff. However, the danger exists that his contribution to the failure of the Bush administration might in the long run work profounder constitutional effects.

CONCLUSION

In the middle part of this century, critical assessments of the presidential system in the United States focused on the separation of powers. Observers saw a need for greater unity between the executive and the legislative branches of government. Frustrations with the system originated largely from the left—those hoping for quicker advancement of the welfare state.

The late 1960s and early 1970s saw a cooling of interest in greater unity between presidents and Congress. The separation of powers corresponded to the fragmented nature of the American political culture. It seemed to set a viable context for pluralistic leadership in a society prone to incremental change. Further, the abuses of power under the Nixon administration raised concerns about the imperialization of the presidency.

The Carter administration functioned so ineffectively that observers fretted for a while that the presidency had become too weak. However, Reagan turned things around dramatically. He brought a strong electoral mandate to office. The Republicans controlled the Senate. The taxpayer revolt had turned many congressional Democrats into fiscal conservatives.

A theory emerged in this period that the presidency had turned a corner. Through greater internal discipline and relentless control of the permanent bureaucracy, presidents could compensate for leadership deficits associated with the separation of powers. This interpretation ultimately proved illusory. Reagan had gotten the gearbox between himself and his top advisers and that between his team and the permanent bureaucracy right at the outset of his administration. However, the delicate balance was lost by the beginning of the second term. Further, the lack of countervailance in the bureaucracy and Congress meant that the nation had overcommitted to policies which ultimately proved adverse to its long-term well-being.

The current malaise in U. S. presidential leadership relates much more to the legacy of Reaganite excesses than to the separation of powers. Indeed, adequately functioning checks and balances against the most extravagant Reagan policies would likely have mitigated the current crisis.

Two conditions greatly circumscribed presidential leadership when George Bush took office. These were the deficit—with the ceaseless pressures to reduce spending rather than raise taxes—and the sour public mood—with accompanying anxieties about the accessibility of the American dream as the United States saw its economic dominance in the world diminish. Neither of these problems went away under Bush. Indeed, his absorption with foreign policy and delegation of domestic policy to John Sununu greatly exacerbated the two conditions. By 1992, the United States had slid into the politics of distemper. Voters' support of Ross Perot as a protest vote against both the Republicans and Democrats would rob Bill Clinton of a clear electoral mandate. But the distemper persisted through Clinton's first term, leading most critically to the Democrats losing both houses of Congress in the 1994 elections.

3

Bill Clinton Encounters the Governability Gap

At the outset of his administration, at least in his more focused moments, Bill Clinton struck many observers as a "new order" president. Certainly, scenes of the newly inaugurated president climbing into his Marine helicopter holding a biography of FDR would support the view that he harbored hopes in this direction. In fact, Clinton operated from the beginning much more as a "let's deal" president. This is a viable form of leadership. Indeed, it might be the most appropriate to this particular age.

The issue of the appropriateness of "let's deal" leadership to the current age arises in part because recent presidents have found themselves so constricted by fiscal pressures. However, the rise of this style might owe more fundamentally to the types of mandates which emerge from election campaigns waged through electronic media. Electronic appeals—especially those on TV—work much more on emotions than earlier approaches that were dependent upon the print media. Television tends to highlight personal attacks rather than differentiate the policy approaches of candidates. In the process, electronic media often exacerbate divisions among the electorate. They also obscure the potential common ground for resolution of the core issues which would serve as the focus of more constructive campaigns.

Under the circumstances, deeply committed "new order" types would find it difficult to gain election. Even if they did, they would not easily rally support for dramatic policy changes. The public, on the other hand, will wink at candidates who give lip service to the importance of fundamental change—just so long as these aspirants' track records and "vibes" telegraph the fact that their fervor falls short of zeal.

Incumbents who mouth bromides about the types of bold steps required to heal what ails the country can rest assured. Most of the populace will not hold them to account for not pursuing this order of action. Still, to maintain their credibility, incumbents must rise to the occasion in those circumstances which do indeed require at least middle-range government action. In those cases, they must prove to be heat-seeking missiles. They must quickly arrive at negotiated positions and deals which will at least provide them cover from the accusation that—not only have they not acted boldly—they failed to do anything. If the "let's deal" leader fails even to rise to this occasion, he simply deepens the governability gap—that is, the seeming incapacity for the system to treat society's core difficulties.

AMBIVALENCE ALL AROUND AND A BAD START

From early in the Clinton administration, it became apparent how he likely would perform as a "let's deal" president. First, in line with the age, he received a weak and diffuse mandate. To be sure, he became beneficiary of a fair amount of good feeling immediately after his election victory. But this hardly translated into concrete support for specific actions—even if Clinton had made a host of explicit commitments. Of course, he had not—even the incantations for health care reform remained distinctly vague and tentative.

It should not have surprised many people, thus, that Clinton experienced such a truncated honeymoon—by some accounts scarcely 100 hours much less 100 days. Insofar as his difficulties related to the times, Clinton enjoyed an advantage over Bush. In an epoch in which domestic politics have assumed greater significance than foreign affairs, Clinton's strengths fit the former. Bush's had clashed with the shift in circumstances and, relatedly, popular expectations that the president should spend more time on domestic affairs.

Clinton brought another quality to the presidency which might have given him an advantage over his predecessor—an upbeat personality. This gave the public different signals from those transmitted by Bush.

Normally, they could sense when the likes of Saddam Hussein or re-
calcitrant congressional Democrats had gotten to Bush. Such incidents
would induce Bush to reveal his dark side—his tendency to personalize conflict and to couch his reasoning in harsh and vindictive terms.

Far into his first term, Clinton still managed to look very much like
the rookie coach who realizes that he will lose a few games before he
gets the hang of his job. The 1992 election campaign—involving as it
did roller coaster reversals, including intimate probes of the candidate's
draft record and marital fidelity—revealed a Bill Clinton with a hugely
resilient ego. Clinton's past behavior might in various ways have revealed character defects. However, these did not seem to touch upon his
fundamental aptitude for the rough and tumble of the modern presidency. The president does fly into temper tantrums regularly—one of
the alleged roles of Al Gore was to defuse these with humor (Berke 20
February 1994). However, only occasionally did stories appear suggesting that he had become bitter (Devroy 6 September 1993; Wines 2
August 1994).

Two problems present themselves in evaluating how suited Bill Clinton was to the "lets deal" mode of leadership. The first of these relates
to the art of the possible in the age of constricting views of what the
government should do. When asked during the 1992 campaign what his
favorite Scripture passage was, Clinton cited Galatians 6:9: "Let us not
grow weary while doing good for in due season we shall reap, but do
not lose heart" (Zapor 27 October 1992). When Bill Clinton lost his first
reelection bid in Arkansas he recognized that—in so far as "doing good"
meant pursuing the liberal agenda—discretion was the better part of
valor. Some profiles of the president's past indeed suggested that the
exigencies of Arkansas politics gave him an exceptionally high toler-
ance for compromise and even moral and ethical ambiguity while pro-
fessing to pursue noble objectives (Kelly 31 July 1994).

Yet at his core, Clinton wanted to change the circumstances of the
average American for the good. He, therefore, has found building-down
government or embracing economic policies which cater to the bond
markets extremely frustrating (Samuelson 19 May 1993). Bob Woodward even presented Clinton as railing at his staff after it became clear
that his first budget would contain no major stimulus programs and tax
breaks for the middle class: "We're Eisenhower Republicans here, and
we are fighting Reagan Republicans. We stand for lower deficits and
free trade and the bond market. Isn't that great?" (5 June 1994). If Clin-

ton actually uttered these words, we have an instance of one side of his brain berating the other.

The other difficulty that presented itself in Bill Clinton pursuing a "let's deal" style relates to the complexity of governance in our age. Even if the president chooses to base leadership on his bargaining ability, he must negotiate from the basis of well worked out principles. Paul Quirk (1991, 72) has called upon Dean Pruitt's (1982) notion of "flexible rigidity" in negotiations to underscore the need for presidents—especially under the current political circumstances—to maintain flexibility about means and rigidity about goals.

While this objective seems to be quintessential Clinton, the preponderance of analysis suggests that he never defined his goals sufficiently to enshrine his rigidities. Nor did he know when to be flexible. For the purposes of this analysis, we should distinguish between Clinton before and after the debacle of the 1994 elections. That is, the circumstances of governance changed dramatically for Clinton in the aftermath of the Democrats' loss of control of both houses of Congress. We will consider the post-1994 Clinton in a separate section.

In the pre-1994 phase, we saw at several important turning points in the administration, that observers noted that the president had failed to devise fundamental strategies (Gelb 28 January 1993), revealed a tendency to store up ideas and let them gush out without any type of thematic coherence (Broder 19 May 1993), and put his team through a seemingly endless succession of relaunches (Apple 30 October 1993). Asked to comment on yet another downturn in his approval levels, Clinton himself acknowledged his lack of a core strategy: "I think in a way it may be my fault. I keep, I go from one thing to another" (Devroy 9 November 1993).

In his analysis of George Bush, Quirk (1991) asserted that Bush displayed a tendency to get the principles of negotiation turned around—betraying a flexibility about goals and rigidity about means. Clinton seems to have rigidity about nothing. In the case of NAFTA, he embraced a Republican proposal which stood as an anathema to much of his party's core constituency—as even his pollster Stanley Greenberg recognized (Edsall 19 November 1993; Broder 19 November 1993). He then proceeded to cut deals for its passage which would impinge hugely on the utility of NAFTA to actually serve as a vehicle for free trade, often without delivering a number of votes proportionate to the cost of compromise (Wines 11 November 1993; Bradsher 17 November 1993).

Similarly, some observers have noted that Clinton's effort to co-opt insurance companies by pushing "managed competition" in health care reform rather than a single payer system created such needless complexity that the status quo in the health care sector subsequently became more acceptable than the Clinton alternative (Baker 26 July 1994). Clinton ultimately lost the support even of congressional reformers when he began, in July 1994, to suggest that he would be flexible about universal coverage and employer mandates to pay insurance premiums (Devroy and Broder 22 July 1994). In May of Clinton's first year, one aide voiced the fear that Clinton "is getting defined by his compromises, not his principles" (Devroy 7 May 1993). Even his later successes seemed to result more from expediency than from principle. One aide noted in February 1994 that the White House knew that the president was running the risk of becoming "negotiator-in-chief instead of commander-in-chief" (Priest and Marcus 20 February 1994). Clinton eventually accepted full blame for the failure of his health reform package (Johnson and Broder 1996, 125–126). However, he never really got himself off the slippery slope created by the debacle.

Clinton's problems with identifying and pursuing key goals plagued the administration in the national security field at least as much as it did on the domestic side. While it did not reflect on the resilience that he brought to office, Clinton's draft record would have made it difficult for him to gain credibility in the national security community under the best of circumstances. Scholars conventionally argue that the United States is nonstatist—that it accords no special status to the permanent custodians of the governmental apparatus (Rockman 1984). This is not at all the case with national security. Militarism—especially since the creation of the army and naval academies at West Point and Annapolis during the first half of the nineteenth century—has prospered in the United States. From that time, the armed services played a decisive socializing role for many of the nation's elite. The Civil War—which brought mankind's capacity for mass mobilization and horrific destruction of life and property to previously inconceivable heights—ran on the military aptitude amassed through the process of putting some of the most able young men in the nation through the academies.

The nation has placed three former military leaders—Ulysses Grant, Theodore Roosevelt, and Dwight Eisenhower—in the presidency since the Civil War. Indeed, Theodore Roosevelt took an interval from his political career during the Spanish-American war. He had seized the opportunity to prove his mettle. As he observed to a friend: "If I am to be of any use in politics it is because I am supposed to be a man who does not preach what I fear to practice, and who will carry out himself what he advocates others carrying out" (Cooper 1983, 38). Franklin Delano Roosevelt served as assistant secretary of the navy.

Bill Clinton—by his own admission—evaded a commitment to serve. He did this in the midst of perhaps the most trying period ever faced by the U. S. military. We might expect—under the best of circumstances— that the military establishment would resent Clinton as commander in chief. However, two factors exacerbated the potential for misunderstanding between Clinton and the Pentagon. First, candidate Clinton temporized throughout his campaign over the exact circumstances whereby he avoided military service and the motives behind his actions. This behavior simply drew public attention to his lack of credentials in this dimension of the national security field. Second, Clinton embraced the objective of equality for gays in the armed services.

The conventional wisdom has it that this second element of Clinton's problems with the military emerged unnecessarily from his desire to clinch the gay vote. That is, observers have noted that the gay vote would have gone to Clinton whatever. They further have argued that Clinton needlessly threatened the Pentagon by pressing a policy which—in its eyes—would undermine the integrity of the military culture.

In fact, this interpretation misses an essential component of Clinton's problems. During the 1992 campaign, General Colin Powell—then chairman of the Joint Chiefs of Staff—publicly criticized Clinton's plans for gays in the military. Forging a coalition with Senator Sam Nunn and other friends of the Pentagon in Congress, Powell subsequently assumed the toughest possible negotiating positions in resisting the new administration's efforts to actually implement Clinton's pledges, including threats to resign and to abandon a secret deal struck with Nunn on cutting redundant programs in the services (Gellman 28 January 1993; 30–31 January 1993; Blumenthal 8 March 1993). At one point, the president even blinked and suggested that gays might be excluded from certain types of duties—a clear instance of bending over backwards to appear conciliatory (Cohen 26 March 1993). Ultimately, a "compromise" emerged which seems to have actually made things worse for gays in the military. The Pentagon agreed to a situation whereby it would not ask either recruits or actual members of the military their sexual preference. However, it also imposed a requirement that individuals not declare their orientation. More important, it won from the administration strict sanctions against those who involve themselves in homosexual or lesbian sexual acts on or *off* military bases.

One might argue, thus, that Clinton failed to manage Colin Powell. Efforts to clarify their roles in the military responded to changes in public views about gays and fell within the compass of recent court decisions in the United States (Friedman 29 January 1993) and the more tolerant policies emerging from other NATO countries. These changes called out for attention from a Democratic presidential candidate. However, Clinton ran for cover when Powell first opposed his stance during the 1992 election.

Instead, he should have occupied the high ground by reminding the country that the commander in chief—not the chairman of the Joint Chiefs of Staff—heads the military. Without personally attacking Powell, he could then have stated that—as a potential commander in chief—he would not want his options foreclosed by the public utterances of the person whose job it is to serve the president.

Perhaps Clinton calculated that—given his draft record—he could not pull such a response off. Nonetheless, he paid mightily for not sitting on Powell immediately upon the latter's public intervention during the campaign. He essentially vacated the commander-in-chief role to the Pentagonphiles in Congress. This greatly weakened the national security side of Clinton's first gearbox—that between the administration and the state apparatus.

With the rest of the first gearbox—the Clinton administration's relation to the standing bureaucracy—we found at best mixed signals at the beginning of the administration. First, Clinton did do well in tapping the great and the good to head his key departments. With Treasury going to Lloyd Bentsen, State to Warren Christopher, the Office of Management and Budget to Leon Panetta, and Defense to Les Aspin, the new president added immensely to his cachet with the Washington establishment.

Yet a certain disjunction surfaced here between the president's youthful, sweep-with-a-clean-broom campaign and the people he called upon to head up his key departments. The president revealed an especially unimaginative approach toward staffing his national security team. Christopher, Anthony Lake—assistant to the president for national security, Samuel Berger—Lake's deputy, James Woolsey—the CIA director, and Madeleine Albright all had served in the Carter administration. They struck many observers as retreads. Indeed, Lake speculated nine months into the administration that Clinton perhaps had stressed too much building a national security team consisting of collegial, like-minded advisers: "I think there is a danger that when people work well together, you can take the edge off the options" (Friedman 31 October 1993).

When one considers that fully twelve years had passed between the end of Carter's administration and the beginning of Clinton's one cannot help but wonder if Clinton could have used a bit more initiative in making his choices. Certainly, national security constitutes one area where the administration displayed at the outset an exceptional lack of inspiration. It deferred to Bush precedents in handling pressure points such as Bosnia and Somalia. Warren Christopher—too much the cautious insider—found himself marginalized in virtually every issue he tried to tackle. Even in the case of the first clear breakthrough in the early days of the administration, the September 1993 peace accord between the Israelis and Palestinians, the administration seemed only to have bolted itself onto the process with a hastily arranged Rose Garden signing ceremony.

A few weeks into the administration, officials characterized Clinton's personal involvement in foreign policy as pedestrian (Friedman 9 February 1993). One observed, "He is there to do things when asked. But that is the extent of it."; another noted, "I think that the most interesting thing is that Mr. Clinton has not been present for a lot of the discussions. My sense of it is that he does not like this stuff because he in not a master of it."

Two messages regarding foreign policy came across during the first half of the administration. First, the core issues of global instability had truly metamorphosed—the enmity between the United States and the former communist states had almost completely dissipated. Second, several nettlesome trouble areas—most notably civil and ethnic struggles in Bosnia, Somalia, and Rwanda, the Cuban and Haitian refugee problems, and North Korea's development of nuclear arms—served up problems that called upon a delicate balance between diplomatic maneuvering and military intervention.

For the most part, the administration's handling of these intricate and sensitive problems made the United States appear peculiarly musclebound and suspect within the new framework for international relations. Clinton and his team accomplished little that assured observers that they would lead the nation into a more suitable posture for the times. And

this owed significantly to the president's limited foreign affairs attention span and constant vacillation on issues which did engage him. However, it also derived from a seeming incapacity of his cabinet and White
House advisers to organize themselves so as to compensate for the president's deficiencies in foreign policy. In this respect, Clinton was not
receiving full value from his erring on the side of experience when picking his team.

As a candidate, Clinton proclaimed time and again that he would ap-
point a cabinet which looked like America. On the foreign policy side,
this aspiration proved to be a pious hope. On the domestic side, the administration, indeed, paid a great deal of attention to diversity. However, the administration's pledges proved difficult ones to observe. The
president went through a number of agonizing decisions. Here his first
attempts at appointing a woman as attorney general proved especially
painful. Indeed, these efforts—as other abortive nominations (not all at
the cabinet level)—proved deeply damaging to the president. By stressing diversity to the degree that he did, Clinton introduced a representational imperative to cabinet making much stronger than that which has
ever prevailed normally in the United States.

Clinton's efforts exposed two pitfalls to such a representational approach to cabinet making. First, presidents who give the choice slots to
white, male members of the Washington establishment and the less crucial positions to minorities and/or women will encounter allegations of
tokenism. Second, while minorities and women fulfill representational criteria, they might encounter difficulty in actually obtaining confirmation.
Senators and the attentive groups will hold their fire rather than oppose
accepted members of the great and the good. They will show less consideration for nominees with little or no standing in Washington. However much the United States has moved from "insider" to "outsider" politics (Rockman 1991a; Peters 1991), those bent on embarrassing a new
administration will pick at unknown nominees in search of a fatal flaw.

Regarding the second gearbox—that between the president and his
own advisers, Clinton chose at the outset an eclectic approach which reflected his personality. This approach did not mean it suited the presidency at this stage. We have discussed before the difficulty of striking a
balance in the organization of the White House. Top-down, command-
oriented White Houses with strong chiefs of staff have more than failed.
They have also contributed to monocratic presidential leadership and the
abuses which seem inevitably to follow from this form of leadership.

On the other hand, a loose, bottom-up organizational approach which fits the spokes-in-a-wheel format runs into two difficulties. First, the complexity of current governmental problems and the volatility of support in the electronic era make it difficult to sustain open-ended countervailance. Prolonged examination of options in search of the best solution can make the president look ponderous and—when combined with leaks—give away hostages to the opposition. Second, especially since relative outsiders often occupy the Oval Office, not every president can call upon the ringmaster skills required of the spokes-in-a-wheel arrangement.

Almost from the day that the 1992 election was over, observers began to note that Clinton—who benefited greatly from extremely hierarchical and decisive campaign organization—returned to the inclusive and deliberative governance style which had served him well in Arkansas. As a longtime friend noted soon after the election: "Very few decisions have been made. This is Bill's style: being extremely deliberate if not slow. He always wants to do things carefully and right" (Friedman 11 November 1992). Just before the inauguration, officials were already talking about the squandered opportunity of the transition—with advisers and senior Democrats declaring, "The old Clinton is back" and "I won't even try to spin you . . . [its] awful" (Balz 18 January 1993).

Not surprisingly, Clinton pursued a spokes-in-a-wheel approach. At first, his implementation of the model seemed to have fallen short of Carter's in achieving chaos—but not by much. Clinton at least appointed a chief of staff at the outset of the administration. The first incumbent to this position was Thomas "Mack" McLarty. The chairman of a natural gas conglomerate, McLarty had no previous experience in Washington. In defining how he would function as chief of staff, he stressed his management skills and loyalty to Clinton:

> As chief of staff I will do what ever I can to help him organize, manage, facilitate and carry out the duties of President of the United States. And as his friend I will always be straight with him and he knows that. Bill Clinton has my complete loyalty and trust—always has and always will (Friedman 13 December 1992).

Some analysts wondered out loud about whether McLarty had become simply a figurehead in a White House where more assertive aides would find themselves free to pursue their own agendas. As one adviser

had noted: "They were all delighted with the McLarty appointment because it will allow them to do their thing" (Devroy 14 December 1992).

One of the key variables in determining power in the Clinton
administration was one's FOB (Friend of Bill) factor. McLarty
brought to the West Wing unrivaled credentials in this regard—having known the president since the two were three years old. McLarty
certainly did not give so much as a hint of letting power go to his head.
Thus he did not turn into a Bob Haldeman, a Donald Regan, or a John
Sununu. Indeed, he seemed to embody the "nice guy" side to Clinton's personality. Unlike the "good cop," "bad cop" act which prevailed under Bush and Sununu, the Clinton/McLarty pairing was all
good cop.

The frantic efforts of the White House to reorganize itself during May
1993—after a disastrous first three months—suggested that McLarty had
not gotten on top of the game. Clinton had not followed up on his original plan, which was to back up McLarty with a team of Washington-
savvy deputies (Devroy and Marcus 5 May 1993). To Clinton's credit,
his May 1993 reorganization proved relatively far-reaching—which is
not to say that it brought about enduring changes in the performance of
the administration.

A crucial problem with the Clinton White House was its dependence
upon those who had gained prominence during the campaign (Barr and
Kamen 11 January 1993). Here we saw a repeat of the Carter experience (Campbell 1986). Just as with Carter, Clinton could not shed aides
who—while effective campaigners—would not work well in the White
House. As well, he was so loath to differentiate between the access of
former campaign aides that he gave the run of the White House even to
those not on his staff—such as Paul Begala, Stanley Greenberg, and
James Carville—who gave him political advice (Ifill 1 April 1993; Toner
7 April 1993).

From the beginning Clinton's attachment to George Stephanopoulos
presented difficulties for the operation of the second gearbox. During
the campaign, Stephanopoulos became Clinton's most trusted and in-
fluential adviser. However, he lacked the gravitas required of a chief of
staff. President Clinton, thus, appointed Stephanopoulos White House
director of communications.

This role normally goes to the person responsible for cultivating the
president's image and developing an administration's overall media
strategy. Stephanopoulos, however, became the administration point

man by taking daily press briefings. His combative style rankled the press. In the May 1993 reorganization, Stephanopoulos retired from the public stage to the more anonymous role of "special adviser." In a moment of candor, he recognized that the campaign technique of hopping from theme to theme in order to dominate the war of sound bites did not work for a president: "On the campaign trail, you can just change the subject. But you can't just change the subject as President" (Friedman and Dowd 25 April 1993).

A defector from the Republicans and a true Washington pro, David Gergen succeeded Stephanopoulos. The results were dazzling at first for Gergen—who had earned his spurs as communications director during Ronald Reagan's first term. For instance, the administration did an excellent job of making the relatively meager results of the July 1993 Group of Seven Tokyo Summit look like true accomplishments. One problem lurked in the background, however. Stephanopoulos, as described by himself, would remain "Clinton's personal policy and political person, to make sure . . . things hang together" (Von Drehle and Devroy 29 May 1993).

The administration really seemed to be on track by late summer 1993. By focusing the fall strategy with Congress on three themes—health care reform, passage of the North American Free Trade Agreement, and "Reinventing Government"—Clinton had struck a chord for those who admired the genius of the Reagan administration at identifying a few, easy to remember themes and pushing them relentlessly. One could see the hand of David Gergen in all of this. However, many observers feared that Clinton's themes—however easy for voters to remember—touched upon goals of much greater complexity and potential divisiveness than Reagan's core commitments.

In looking through the White House and upper-level appointments elsewhere in the administration, one found an unsettling collection of Clinton mafias. He brought with him FOBs from Arkansas, Georgetown—where he received his undergraduate degree, Oxford—where he studied as a Rhodes Scholar, Yale—where he took his law degree, and the Democratic Leadership Council—in which he earned his reputation as a rising centrist in his party. His wife, Hillary, added to this list by finding places for a host of left-leaning friends. Some of these met the Clintons while they studied together at Yale. However, many—such as health and human services secretary Donna Shalala—came with connections to the Children's Defense Fund.

The political proclivities of the two Clintons clashed—to say the least. And this introduced an element of schizophrenia to the administration (Kelly 17 December 1992; DeParle 20 December 1992). Under the best of circumstances, Clinton would come off as indecisive. However, Hillary's influence at times forced him into staking out bold positions and then retreating in an unseemly manner when the political heat became too intense. And, a subplot of the administration became the competition between centrist and left-leaning prescriptions for rehabilitating the appeal of the administration. Here two figures whose prescriptions were not always compatible—Al From, the president of the Democratic Leadership Council, and Stanley Greenberg, Clinton's pollster—relentlessly pressed the need for establishment of a new Democratic governing coalition (Berke 3 December 1993; Dionne 7 December 1993; Wines 12 and 17 November 1994; Balz 18 November 1994).

The role of Hillary Clinton raised questions with constitutional and political overtones. When it became clear that she would assume responsibility for health care, some observers questioned how—as neither an elected or duly appointed official—she would be accountable (Broder 11 February 1993). As things began to go badly in areas where she had been especially involved—health care and the administration's response to the Whitewater episodes, officials began to speak out loud about the ambiguity of her role. As one Clinton friend put it: "It's hard to run a White House with nobody in charge. . . . It's especially hard to run a White House with nobody in charge and two Presidents" (Dowd 6 March 1994). Indeed, polls began to suggest that the general public had qualms as well (Broder 16 November 1993).

Even those favorably disposed toward Hillary Clinton's role conveyed the sense that she was making up for deficiencies in Bill Clinton's presidential character—by intervening to bring closure to discussions about the administration's core commitments (Woodward 6 June 1994) or providing it a moral compass (Sherrill 6 May 1993). When he seemed to be leaning overly on his wife's character as a defense against allegations concerning the Whitewater scandal, Bill Clinton provoked one of the stiffest attacks on himself yet encountered:

> Were it not because the president's own party dominates Congress and many other institutions, the assumption by Hillary Clinton of powers of an office to which she did not accede would be a constitutional crisis. It should be a constitutional crisis. But it is not. It is, instead, sublimated in scandal (Helprin 25 March 1994).

In a presidential system, the chief executive knows no peers—he belongs neither to an elected legislature nor a ministry which must maintain the support of a parliament. He gains entry to the executive-legislative arena through a constitutional mandate conveyed by a nationwide vote. No previous president has construed this mandate as shared with his wife. Clinton did. In fact, he specifically argued during the campaign that Americans would receive two leaders for the price of one—until it became clear that some voters found this formulation objectionable.

Those who place great stock in the Constitution heaved a sigh of relief when Ross Perot faded during the 1992 presidential campaign. His ascendancy—especially in the late spring—suggested that the United States had come to the brink of populism. It appeared in danger of becoming a disembodied democracy running on electronic appeals and bereft of institutional buttresses in the party system and the elected legislature.

Hillary Clinton's involvement in the administration threatened to run a close second to the presumption of a Ross Perot. This was particularly the case with her assuming responsibility for health care reform. Initially, the White House sold Hillary Clinton's role on the grounds that preparation of the health reform initiative was in disarray (Pear 22 January 1993) and, as Bill Clinton himself observed, "she's better at organizing and leading people from a complex beginning to a certain end" (Staff, *International Herald Tribune* 26 January 1993). In fact, she presided over a Rube Goldberg machine which by April had distilled the complexity into a whopping memo requiring 1,100 decisions (Priest 16 April 1993). The central motif seemed to be: "If we throw enough great minds at this issue it's got to break sometime." The task force included some 500 advisers and officials working in endless meetings. In the words of a participant reflecting upon progress by early March: "There's this sense of exhaustion and the real work hasn't begun yet" (Toner 7 March 1993).

The sense was emerging as well, that Hillary Clinton—aided by her ringmaster Ira Magaziner—was forcing Bill Clinton to embrace comprehensive and costly health care reform proposals against the counsel of cooler heads in the White House and cabinet (Pear 25 May 1993; 30 August 1993). One White House official said that notwithstanding Hillary Clinton's giving all involved license to "speak your mind," "By virtue of her position as head of the task force and by being First Lady and by virtue of her own intellect, which is really quite impressive, she commands a lot of respect and is treated with deference" (Pear 25 May 1993). By July 1994, it had become clear that Congress was not likely to pass a reform bill before the 1994 elections. One senior aide noted, "We would have been in the reality zone a long time ago" had it not been for Hillary Clinton's "health care cult" (Wines 5 July 1994).

Laurence Lynn Jr. and David Whitman published in 1981 an analysis of why Jimmy Carter's welfare reform effort had failed. Key errors included Carter's indecisiveness, the incessant meddling of outsiders with the president's ear, a penchant for secrecy and group think, and the setting of unrealistic deadlines which inflated expectations and, ultimately, made the administration look inept and torn by dissension.

The entire edifice surrounding Hillary Clinton's health reform activities gave the effort the look of Carter's welfare reform writ-large. Nobody would doubt Hillary Clinton's motives. However, she and the president took an immense risk.

Carter's failure in welfare reform scarcely registered in the public's bill of particulars against him when they went to the polls in 1980. During the early months of the administration, few advisers seemed to have seen that an abortive health care reform effort would work catastrophic effects for the Clinton administration. The issue concerned the management of 14% of GNP. It served as a focus of intense concern—especially in the business community. It had not just bolted itself to the president in the shape of a health reform czar. It had linked itself to the president's wife. Nobody seemed to have calculated that if the effort failed, the blame would go straight to a part of the administration's second gearbox which could not be hived off or marginalized. The resulting damage could ultimately compromise the future of the presidency itself.

Clinton's Problems as Symptomatic of Difficulties with
Institutionalization of the Second Gearbox

This chapter noted earlier that scholars made a great deal of the institutional strength of the presidency during the Reagan administration. However, these assessments focused on the first gearbox—that is, the connection between the administration and the permanent bureaucracy. They assumed that all was well with the second gearbox—the relationship between the president and his cabinet officers and advisers. The events of the second term, especially those surrounding the Iran-Contra scandal, suggested, indeed, that the second gearbox had broken down. Similarly, Bush encountered problems with the second gearbox. He never really connected in domestic policy. Further, closer analysis would indicate that the occasion which led to his greatest triumph—the Persian Gulf crisis—occurred because of the administration's sloppy handling of Saddam Hussein's threats to invade Kuwait.

The United States presents a special case when it comes to the second gearbox. In cabinet systems of government, such as those which prevail in Anglo-American democracies and many advanced European systems, the entire administration—as embodied in the members of cabinet—assumes joint responsibility for the policies and actions of the executive branch (Mayntz 1980, 139; Olsen 1983, 79; Weller 1985, 105–107, 131–134). Thus it becomes very important that heads of government employ formal machinery—meetings of cabinet and its committees—to arrive at decisions that will win the support of members of the entire ministry. As well, such systems almost invariably vest the head of government with an office of permanent officials who shoulder responsibility for making sure that the second gearbox runs smoothly.

We noted earlier that in the United States, the exercise of executive authority focuses very strongly upon the president. Neither the Constitution nor conventions surrounding presidential leadership sustain a collective view of the executive power. Thus only presidents who have become convinced of the instrumental utility of greater consultation with their cabinets have routinized these dynamics. Eisenhower—whose military training made him a firm believer in the need to structure decision processes—admired the British cabinet system and tried to transplant elements of it to his administration (Greenstein 1982). Following the backlash to Nixon's extremely monocratic approach, Ford, Carter, and Reagan all pursued what they termed "cabinet government" (Campbell 1986, Ch. 3). Bush, however, eschewed the concept both in the language used to describe the style of his administration and in practice.

Close analysis finds at best sporadic attention to routinized machinery for interdepartmental coordination (Porter 1980). The development and adaptation of strategic plans for administrations suffer a great deal under these circumstances. As well, administrations generally experience difficulty adhering to what commitments do emerge. The functioning of the process depends very much on personal factors and lacks institutional buttresses (George 1980). In many respects, each administration finds itself reinventing the wheel.

In the past, intellectually vigorous presidents who thrived on the cut and thrust of face-to-face exchanges with mixed groups of cabinet secretaries and advisers—typically scholars place Franklin D. Roosevelt and John F. Kennedy in this category—could keep all the policy balls in the air at once (Neustadt 1990). That is, they could keep a watching brief on all key issues and limit intensive attention to key points in the decision process. However, the system seems no longer to serve up incumbents with the agility and the self-confidence of Roosevelt and Kennedy. More profoundly, the task of governance appears no longer to provide presidents the luxury of guiding their administrations through informal and ad hoc means. Things have simply gotten too complex and interconnected.

In structuring his White House and cabinet machinery, Clinton seemed not to have gotten these two points. The evidence suggests that he in fact saw himself as another FDR or JFK. Aides reported his devouring 100-page briefings (Friedman and Sciolino 22 March 1993) and correcting advisers on points of detail (Friedman 9 February 1993). When the administration went through its first efforts to reorganize in May 1993, many aides placed much of the blame on Clinton's love affair with detail (Apple 6 May 1993) and tendency to be his own most trusted staff member in making decisions (Marcus 29 May 1993). Even if his actual abilities matched his self-assessment, Clinton would still have had to provide some evidence that he recognized that the requirements for coordination had become exponentially greater in the thirty-two years which had passed since Kennedy became president. That is, Clinton would have focused a great deal more attention than he did on the organization of his White House and cabinet systems. And he would have rejoined the iterative process—advanced the most under Eisenhower, Ford, and Reagan (first term)—whereby presidents have gradually matched tightening their hold over the standing bureaucracy (gearbox I) with institutionalization of internal administration dynamics (gearbox II).

Clinton did neither in any readily identifiable or consistent way. Indeed, his idea of organizing cabinet consisted of a weekend retreat where members shared personal accounts of their lives. This included the president's own sharing "about how he was a fat kid when he was 5 and 6 and how the other kids taunted him" (Devroy 5 February 1993).

The argument that Clinton neglected cabinet-level structures even applies to his use of the National Security Council—a part of his coordinative apparatus which—as we saw earlier—actually derives a modicum of authority by virtue of a congressional mandate given at the request of Harry Truman (Nelson 1981). The NSC—along with its supporting secretariat in the Executive Office of the President—became highly institutionalized during the Eisenhower administration. However, Kennedy virtually ignored the NSC (Destler 1982). Johnson and Nixon built up the NSC staff as a counterbureaucracy, thereby setting up the situation in which the national security advisers became major players—along with the secretaries of state and defense—in foreign affairs.

As noted before, the full blossoming of the electronic era in the executive branch meant that the Bush administration could introduce a practice which pretty much preordained the continued ineffectiveness of the NSC. He allowed much of the business of the NSC to take place on frequent video hookups between deputy agency heads, many of whom skirted around issues because the participants never knew who was looking on but remained out of view.

Bill Clinton took the downsizing of institutional buttresses of the NSC process one step further. Formal meetings of NSC principals actually chaired by the president were rare. From the beginning of the administration, the same president who immersed himself in the details of domestic affairs tended to cut meetings of his foreign policy advisers on key issues—including Bosnia (Friedman 9 February 1993). The assistant to the president for national security—Anthony Lake—did run a more systematic process than prevailed under Bush. This involved a set time for briefing the president on main developments, face-to-face meetings of deputies in the White House "Situation Room" several times a week, almost weekly meetings of cabinet-level principals, and a weekly lunch between the secretaries of state and defense and Lake (Gelb 11 March 1993; Friedman and Sciolino 22 March 1993). But with only sporadic attention from the president, this machinery did not connect well to his actual consideration and handling of the major issues facing the administration.

By October 1993, Lake had diagnosed the problem—the president had not engaged himself sufficiently in the "larger contemplative discussions" (Friedman 31 October 1993). Lake hoped out loud that Clinton would "spend more time now having more sit-back-and-think-about-this kind of meetings." This never came to pass.

On the domestic side, Clinton stuck with the division of economic and general domestic policy first instituted during the second Reagan term. As we saw earlier, standing cabinet committees with parallel secretariats have developed only very gradually. Clinton opted for a National Economic Council (NEC) and a Domestic Policy Council (DPC). Neither met with any regularity. However, during the first half of the first term, the NEC staff did an excellent job of spindoctoring its role—largely thanks to its initial head, Robert E. Rubin, who succeeded Lloyd Bentsen as treasury secretary after the midterm elections. In several newspaper stories which quoted him copiously, Rubin came across as the neutral broker par excellence (Ifill 7 March 1993; Redburn 21 June 1993). Rubin set as his model his understanding of Brent Scowcroft's role as national security adviser—acting as "an honest broker efficiently to integrate and coordinate policy across agency lines." Rubin failed to distinguish whether he meant Scowcroft under Gerald Ford or George Bush. In the latter case, Scowcroft—working as he did at the president's constant beck and call and once removed from the video conference calls conducted by deputies—had little opportunity to link up with a formal integrative process much less function as a neutral broker within it (Campbell 1991, 207–210).

The atmospherics of economic policy making in the administration seemed to belie the neutral-broker spin. From the outset, the administration proved deeply divided over key elements of economic policy (Staff, *International Herald Tribune* 15 January 1993; Ifill 21 February 1993). Clinton appeared to have been railroaded into abandoning his proposals for a stimulative package and tax breaks for the middle class in the early days of the administration (Woodward 1994). Deep rifts among cabinet officers over U. S. trade policies came to public view in April 1993 (Bradsher 23 April 1993). In the same month, the budget director—then Leon Panetta—publicly questioned the viability of the entire edifice of Clinton administration economic policy—including aid to Russia, NAFTA, and the affordability of health care reform (Staff, *International Herald Tribune* 28 April 1993). Before his becoming ensnared in the Whitewater case, Roger Altman—the deputy treasury secretary—began so to eclipse the role of Bentsen that the latter was considering leaving the administration after his first year (Greenhouse 25 August 1993). Altman's leverage rested in his cachet with Rubin and his management of the White House "war room" on the budget during summer 1993.

Even subsequent success stories related by Rubin suggested that he was more a stager than a neutral broker. He got members of cabinet strongly opposed to invocation of "Super 310" against the Japanese to hold their noses and remain silent about protectionistic measures support pressed by the U. S. Trade Representative that clearly ran against the spirit of GATT (Rowen 3 March 1994; Rosenbaum 27 May 1994). The preparation of the budget for fiscal year 1995–96 actually saw Rubin function as the president's delegate with cabinet secretaries working on an individual basis with Rubin who would then funnel issues up to Clinton (Rosenbaum 27 May 1994).

The assistant to the president for domestic policy—Carol H. Rasco—had served as Clinton's policy coordinator during the campaign. However, she brought with her little experience which would have helped her ringmaster the unwieldy domain of domestic policy—especially when we consider that the administration planned to tackle both health care and welfare reform. In any case, the Domestic Policy Council—which she was supposed to support—did not operate in a coherent fashion. And the administration's major absorption—health care reform—operated in its own separate orbit under the direction of Hillary Clinton and Ira Magaziner with the latter nominally responsible to Rasco.

David Gergen, while assistant to President Reagan for communications, once noted that cabinet-level councils—though perhaps not a philosopher's stone for resolution of coordination problems in an administration—did, when operating properly, do an excellent job of encouraging cabinet secretaries to resolve midlevel disputes before they got into the Oval Office and contributed to the excessive decision load of the president (1983 interview). The Reagan administration, of course, was aided by its stripped-down agenda, which required much less complicated management because it was not engaged in intricate efforts at positive statecraft. Still the Reagan administration's modulation of issue resolution in cabinet councils and management of the really contentious matters in the Legislative Strategy Group (discussed earlier) seemed to provide just the mix for moving its program forward expeditiously.

What the Clinton administration missed was anything like a Legislative Strategy Group (LSG). The modified-spokes-in-a-wheel organization of the White House in the Reagan administration actually provided the core for an LSG. Each of the permanent members had responsibility for an operational part of the White House and each embodied a side of the president's personality. Thus arose an exceptional team: James Baker (the chief of staff)—the pragmatist; Edwin Meese (the counselor)—the ideological conservative; William Clark (the assistant to the president for national security)—a foreign policy neophyte with strong views; and Michael Deaver (deputy chief of staff)—the communicator par excellence.

The almost organic functioning of the group helped the president in three ways. It took major issues—due to their complexity and/or divisiveness—out of the cabinet council system so that options might be narrowed before they went to the president. As well, it helped hold commitments together once the president had made a decision. Finally, it led the process of reconciling differences between the administration's commitments and what was achievable through Congress.

It might well be that an individual such as Bill Clinton would never abide a group performing such functions on his behalf. But, as I have implied before, an insistence on doing these things himself would make Clinton a president of the old school—that of FDR and JFK. That is, he would be relying upon sheer intellectual acuity and a knack for ringmastering myriad issues in direct dialogue with his advisers and cabinet secretaries. Clinton might well have displayed the first of these attributes, however, he clearly failed to demonstrate the second one.

At the outset of the administration, Clinton did not even have the individuals necessary to establish a modified-spokes-in-a-wheel format, in regard to those whom he selected for his inner circle and/or the responsibilities that he allotted to them. Mack McLarty lacked the familiarity with Washington and the decisiveness to fill the shoes of a James Baker; George Stephanopoulos lacked the maturity and control over the policy development process to function as an Ed Meese; Anthony Lake, although experienced in Washington and a competent expert in the foreign policy field, lacked the strong relationship to Clinton to serve as surrogate for a president who wanted to focus his major efforts on domestic policy. When David Gergen joined the administration in spring 1993, he soon performed a role similar to Mike Deaver's during the Reagan administration. However, he lacked operational responsibility for any specific part of the White House apparatus and the trust of those—such as Stephanopoulos—who saw running the presidency as a perpetual campaign in which possession of a very busy person's mind would provide a streetcar for advancement of pet policy ideas.

We have seen in several recent administrations the rise in the White House of a Washington insider who will serve as Mr. Fixit. During the Ford administration, in the wake of the Watergate debacle, Donald Rumsfeld—who had served three terms in the House of Representatives and as director of the Office of Economic Opportunity—and Richard Chaney—who had been a congressional aide and a deputy to Rumsfeld at OEO—both did excellent jobs as White House "staff coordinators" in a time when even the suggestion of centralization of power would have evoked the images of H. R. "Bob" Haldeman and the failed Nixon presidency. With the resignation of Donald Regan during the Iran-Contra revelations, Howard Baker—the Senate minority leader—became chief of staff. He and his successor, Kenneth Duberstein—who had twice headed up Reagan's congressional relations office—kept Ronald Reagan's White House out of trouble for the remainder of the administration. With the departure of John Sununu late in 1991, Bush first resorted to his transportation secretary, Samuel K. Skinner, but ultimately called upon James A. Baker III to leave the State Department and become his chief of staff. It was too late by then.

When Leon Panetta resigned as OMB director to become White House chief of staff in mid-1994, the question arose as to whether he could provide the steady hand necessary to get the Clinton administration on viable course. As a former chairman of the House Budget Committee, Panetta certainly brought to the White House the capacity to cope more aptly with the art of the possible inside the Beltway.

A great deal of thunder was heard around the West Wing when Panetta assumed his position in June 1994. This was based on claims of full authority from the president to make sweeping changes (Jehl 28 June 1994). Yet Panetta immediately went into reviewing-the-situation mode—with promises of a thorough "look at all White House operations," astounding words from someone who had viewed the chaos of the administration from one of the best perches available in Washington (Devroy and Marcus 1 July 1994).

As Panetta's study progressed—it took almost three months—much of the blame centered on the White House communications operation (Devroy 10 August 1994). Communications proved awkward as a major target—press secretary Dee Dee Myers had in late June been the subject of a call from the president to Panetta urging him to ease up on his criticism of Myers (Jehl 30 June 1994). In the end, it was decided that Myers would leave the White House by the end of the year. After the November election, Panetta received an in-house evaluation of his own role courtesy of disgruntled White House aides claiming that he had done nothing to reverse the campaign syndrome whereby Clinton remained "overhandled, overscheduled, overexposed" and "has suffered in stature and ability to focus" (Devroy 14 November 1994).

THE SECOND HALF OF THE FIRST TERM: A RALLY OR STRANGULATION BY TRIANGULATION?

After the Democrats faced their ignominious defeat at the hands of the Republicans in the 1994 congressional elections, Monday morning quarterbacks soon began proffering assessments of how Bill Clinton could have played the presidency better. Generally, they argued that much of the blame for the loss of both houses of Congress rested with Bill Clinton. Few saw encouraging signs that Clinton would rally the Democratic side in the second half. It looked as if the House of Representatives and the Senate would remain Republican for years to come. Little in Clinton's first-half performance would suggest that he could reconnect with Congress in such a way that the logjam of gridlock would break.

Charles O. Jones attributed Clinton's problems, and therefore the nation's, to the president's misunderstanding of the dynamics of the separation of powers (1996). Rather than working with Congress to overcome gridlock by coalitions, Clinton had chosen to play the "bank shot." He believed that he could force Congress toward his positions by "going public" (Kernell 1986). Jones advised Clinton to stop campaigning perpetually to sway the public and to engage Congress with direct bargaining, which can lead to compromise. In this regard, Barbara Sinclair's half-time analysis did not hold out great hopes for a second-half rally (1996). She believed that much of Clinton's difficulty involved poor engagement of a good congressional liaison team. He overloaded it with an excessively long and detailed gameplan. And he sent far too many conflicting signals from the sidelines. Harold W. Stanley viewed Clinton's inscrutability as of a piece with his failure to ply a "New Democrat" course (1996). He did not brim with optimism over Clinton's ability to restore this theme, which had proven so successful in his 1992 presidential campaign. But Paul J. Quirk and Joseph Hinchliffe argued that that might be precisely the point (1996). The New Democrat pitch might well restore Clinton's electoral appeal. However, he still had to contend with a secular trend whereby congressional Democrats and Republicans come increasingly from the ideological extremes of the left and the right. This drift makes translation of centrist positions into governing coalitions exponentially more difficult. Bert Rockman drew from this conundrum the logical conclusion (1996). Governing from the center does not rest well for a party, the Democrats, whose adhesive has been the desire to advance societal values through interventionist programs. Does this mean that Democratic presidents can only govern by campaigning against their own party?

Walter Dean Burnham's analysis suggests that they might at least face a long wait before their party's natural constituency reawakens (1996). To him, the Republican swing in 1994 looked like a realignment, albeit possibly a shallow one, driven by the GPWM—the Great Protestant White Middle. He speculates that substantial constituencies which seemed silent in the 1994 election might reengage when they detect clear and present dangers from the GPWM surge. We can extrapolate from this one possible strategy for a Democratic president. He can put himself forward as the defender of the public from the excesses of the GPWM. Defending rather than governing will strike many as a reversal of the division of powers in the U. S. Constitution. That is, Americans have typically looked to the Congress to protect them from presidents captured by willful majorities. However, if you are a Democratic president in an age in which minimalist views of governance prevail, a mandate to defend rather than lead might prove an enticing prospect.

Even before the midterm elections in 1994, Clinton and many of his advisers saw that they had overreached their mandate—especially with the administration's grandiose health care reform proposals. The initial defeat in August 1994 of the administration's crime bill brought this home poignantly. Fully fifty-eight House Democrats, many of whom had reversed themselves, under fire from the gun lobby, felt that they could abandon the president. Bill McInturff, a Republican pollster, chortled, "It's easier to vote against it when Clinton's name is attached . . . and he's in terrible, terrible shape" (Devroy 12 August 1994). Three days later, Clinton made several concessions to the Republicans, which brought enough of their number to his side to pass the bill (only three additional Democrats supported him). The renowned pundit David Broder characterized this as an especially "gut-wrenching" variant of governing from the middle (15 August 94).

Still, the White House divided between those wanting the president to govern as a Democrat and those urging him to become a pragmatist (Wines 11 September 1994). Indeed, part of the White House harbored the hopes of salvaging the health care reform effort. Gene Sperling, then a senior aide in the National Economic Council, asserted (rightly) that health care reform still constituted a fiscal imperative which would not go away (Wines 28 September 1994). Yet, Hillary Clinton seemed not to have gotten the message. As one White House aide noted, she was blaming Congress for playing unfairly: "She's tired. She's invested so much of herself for so long, and she's genuinely angry at Congress in particular for being so negative" (Dowd 29 September 1994). Reports even indicated that she wanted Ira Magaziner, the policy aide responsible for much of the grandiosity of the Clinton plan, to lead the effort at rejoining the battle (Pear 13 October 1994).

It was not to be. Clinton's private polls showed that he had raised the ire of 1992 Perot supporters with eight out of ten saying they would vote against Clinton in a two-way race. Clinton had not succeeded at quelling disaffection in the electorate. Those who blamed him for continued deadlock were going to express their unhappiness by voting Republican in the midterm elections.

Two motifs emerged immediately after the stark reality of the election results sunk in. The first, and most obvious, had the administration mouthing conciliatory words about issues upon which Democrats and Republicans agreed. Clinton himself highlighted welfare reform, reform of Congress, the line-item veto, and streamlining of government as areas with strong potential for bipartisan agreement (Marcus 11 November 1994). The second, however, actually articulated what the administration ultimately would find as its key to thwarting an effective challenge to Clinton's reelection prospects in 1996. To an extent perhaps beyond most observers' realization, the ball was now in the Republicans' court. As Leon Panetta put it, "There's some good news here, which is that Republicans now have to assume some responsibility to help govern this country" (Federal News Service 10 November 1994).

We will focus here on the first prong in the strategy, that is, Clinton's efforts toward occupying the center and the implications of these efforts both for his electoral prospects and those of Democrats running for Congress in 1996. Ironically, the second prong required cooperation of the Republicans as well. They would have to walk into a trap set early on by the administration. Through a very clever sleight of hand, Panetta and others would seize any opportunity which presented itself to paint the Republicans as unworthy of the trust they had received from the American people.

Here Newt Gingrich, through his hubris and erratic behavior, played right into the administration's hand. Just over a month after the election, a Gingrich outburst provoked a spot-on rebuke from Panetta: "The time has come when he has to understand that he has to stop behaving like an out-of-control radio talk show host and begin behaving like the Speaker of the House of Representatives" (Devroy 6 December 1994). Privately, an outside adviser to the White House told the *Washington Post* that the Democrats' strategy was to make the GOP look extremist without the temperament to govern: "If they provide the rope, we'll help with the hanging."

Gingrich had misinterpreted the 1994 swing to the Republicans as approbation of him. Yet polls suggested that the public had gone from chary to nearly contemptuous of him personally the longer he served as Speaker. Despite his presidential conceits (Seelye 11 April 1995), Gingrich had to end daily press briefings, because, as his spokesman argued, they "provided an opportunity for obscure journalists to come in and harangue him on their pet points" (Kurtz 3 May 1995). Late in 1995, he told his Republican colleagues that he was going to "bench himself." He had just received exceedingly negative press coverage after fulminating over a perceived slight on Air Force One and linking a grisly murder in Illinois to Democrat-backed social programs (Balz and Yang 2 December 1995).

The first prong of the administration's postelection strategy, moving toward the center, proved difficult to execute. Partially this owed to the indecisiveness of the president. To be sure, the election results sent a jolt through the administration. However, the mix of in-house and outside advisers continued to serve up a cacophony of views. Newt Gingrich's illusion was that he had become de facto president. The administration's remained that it held the corner on sheer intellect and would somehow work its way through the complexity. Late in November 1994, a White House aide had Clinton "just beginning to synthesize what happened" and trying "to do some thinking, run it through his brain" (Devroy 30 November 1994). At the same time, a briefing by Harold Ickes—the deputy chief of staff—and Panetta left chiefs of staff from departments and agencies "in a worse case of anxiety about whether they know what went on out there."

Meanwhile, Clinton's ultimate challenge seemed to have escaped both the president and his advisers. The public had lost confidence in its ability to ever get a fix on what Clinton stood for. David Gergen put it eloquently as he prepared to leave the administration: "[Americans] have lost sight of who he is. . . . People say move to the left; other people say move to the right, but what people have lost sight of is Bill Clinton's center. What they want to hear is what his core convictions are" (Devroy 15 December 1994). From the conservative Republican side, strategist William Kristol made essentially the same point—one which continued to work its effects through to the 1996 presidential election campaign. If Bill Clinton simply tried to outbid his opponents with proposals for tax cuts and shrinking programs he would come across as a "dime-store Republican."

Clinton's first prong thus required a positive thrust which convincingly connected the man, his principles, and his program. What the administration came up with appeared to be exactly what observers had warned against. In mid-December 1994, Clinton made an Oval Office speech proclaiming the "Middle Class Bill of Rights." Rather than presenting a vision, Clinton telegraphed that he was still down in the weeds trying to make sense of it all. He recited in what one observer called "drill-sergeant" fashion a wish list of tax cuts and then debated with himself out loud about whether he had become opportunistic (Devroy 16 December 1994).

Clinton elevated Al Gore's reinvention effort to the administration mainstream by implying that it could achieve the spending cuts required for a balanced budget. As much as this delighted Gore and his people (Purdum 19 December 1994), it would strike any astute critic as fanciful. How government organizes and staffs itself to fulfill programmatic mandates normally accounts for about 10% of the budget. You can shave points off this figure. But real economies come from eliminating programs—a task which any Democratic president will find difficult if not distasteful. In any case, Gore soon put the nation to sleep by continuing to promote reinvention as if his audiences consisted of six-year-olds. He even resorted to the cartoon figure Dumbo the elephant to make the point that government was simply needed to provide reassurance to communities which want to solve their own problems:

> You know the story of "Dumbo's Magic Feather"? As long as Dumbo had his magic feather, he could fly. Well, he lost his feather, but when he had an emergency situation, he found that if he tried really hard and

practiced what he had learned, he could fly without the magic feather (Raspberry 26 December 1994).

Back in the real world—with such a weak start on the "vision" side, the administration drifted with the winds of adhocery like Dumbo's lost feather. This situation continued until spring 1995, when Clinton essentially handed the task of defining his strategy over to Dick Morris— a political consultant who, since 1988, avowedly worked only for Republicans. When Clinton was governor of Arkansas, he often resorted to Morris. Morris imprinted on Clinton the concept of the "permanent campaign" (Kolbert 1 July 1995). This translates into focusing on the few commitments which will help a chief executive stay in power rather than sifting through potential policy positions and pressing those which sell on their own merits.

Morris, of course, withdrew from the Clinton team in late August 1996 after revelations of an affair with a prostitute. However, under his influence, the administration had swung irrevocably over to the resolutely pragmatic side of the ledger. Following a strategy which Morris termed "triangulation," Clinton attempted to place himself equidistant from conservative Republicans and liberal Democrats. An obvious difficulty presented itself immediately with such a strategy given the make-up of the 104th Congress. The 1994 election made each party caucus long on extremes and short on moderation. The debacle of the first half had placed a "No Exit" sign for greater accommodation toward the left. Thus Clinton would have to make his deals with the right to obtain the numbers required to govern from the middle.

The Morris ambit seemed at its height to have resulted in as much strangulation as triangulation. Clinton's new guru seemed to have triumphed in June 1995 after convincing the president that he should punt by offering the Republicans a ten-year balanced budget deal. The Clinton-Morris alliance had run roughshod over the White House aides who had served Clinton through thick or thin during the 1992 campaign and the first half of the administration (Devroy 18 June 1995). Some complained of not finding about major changes in tack until reading about them in the newspapers. Clinton's own soul seemed to be gasping for breath. When he ordered a thoroughgoing review of affirmative action to counter Republican assaults, he proclaimed, "This is what I believe" (Devroy 20 July 1995). In fact, the president's stance on affirmative action evolved from one of the few disciplined decision-making ventures undertaken by the Clinton White House (Edley 23 July 1995).

But the glimmer of hope that Clinton the man might have found how to connect principle and programs soon faded.

Frequently in this book we encounter the need for chief executives to modulate responsive competence—with an eye to continued electoral viability—and neutral competence—with an emphasis on using the resources of the executive branch decision process to get things right. Presidents who achieve a balance between responsive and neutral competence stand a good chance of attaining policy competence—that is, moving forward an agenda which works creatively within the art of the possible in order to address key issues facing the nation.

Terry Moe coined the term "responsive competence" when trying to account for the paradox of Reagan's first term success (1985). Precisely by stressing "responsive" at the cost of "neutral" competence, Reagan had retained, indeed enhanced, his electoral viability. When I first employed the Moe formulation (Campbell 1986), I took to referring to "responsive" competence and "partisan" competence interchangeably. That is, I assumed that electoral viability for the president would redound to his party and vice versa. This conclusion perhaps flew in the face of the evidence that the constellations of voters that coalesce around a party's presidential candidate frequently differ considerably from those that build around a party's congressional candidates. And Clinton's form of responsive competence—one which won him a second term—had become avowedly a-Democratic.

CONCLUSION

Occasionally, chief executives will pursue such unadulterated responsive competence that they pull entirely away from institutional fetters of any kind. In earlier work, I have termed this approach "survival politics." Bill Clinton's survival politics—which Dick Morris elegantly crafted—involved two steps. First, the president distanced himself as much as possible from congressional Democrats. Second, he placed himself as a bulwark against Republican radicals. Such triangulation silenced Bill Clinton's soul. It also meant death by a hundred or so strangulations for the liberal-Democratic agenda in Congress. Bill Clinton renewed his mandate. But he should look to the experience of Brian Mulroney in Canada to see what happens to a chief executive's place in history and the long-term viability of his party when voters twig on the vacuity of survival politics at any cost.

Frequently during the 104th Congress, the first prong of the survival strategy left congressional Democrats feeling abandoned. Early in 1995, some observers saw danger in broad accommodation of the Republicans with an eye to trying to save only the essential elements of the social safety net. The foreign affairs columnist Jim Hoagland put the risk especially clearly when he likened Clinton's strategy to what François Mitterrand had done to gain reelection in the 1988 French presidential elections (16 February 1995). In an epoch in which the trend lines favor the building-down of government, what appears to the left-center party as a tactical retreat might end up with a loss of ground which it will never regain: "Victories of the left built on centrist or right-of-center economic strategies are Pyrrhic victories, ultimately canceling out the political space the left would normally occupy in a democracy."

By mid-1995, Clinton's conciliatory moves on the budget deficit and cuts to social spending had raised the hackles of congressional Democrats. Many believed that the president's approach was pulling the carpet out from under an effective congressional strategy of scoring points against the Republicans on the social consequences of radical cuts (Rosenbaum 14 June 1995; Pianin and Harris 15 June 1995). Some Democratic analysts even began to assert that the president's desire to run on his record and leadership clashed with congressional Democrats' objective of regaining control of Capitol Hill (Mitchell 15 June 1995). By fall 1995, Clinton was busy rewriting history—claiming that liberal Democrats had pressured him into raising taxes "too much" and not pushing a more stringent welfare reform bill (Rosenbaum 21 October 1995; Devroy 3 November 1995). By early 1996, Clinton had taken to promoting the appropriateness of a disconnect between the fortunes of a party's presidential candidate and those running for congressional seats. He noted that, indeed, linking the two would be, "self-defeating. . . . The American people don't think it's the president's business to tell them what ought to happen in congressional elections" (Devroy and Harris 31 January 1996).

Through a sleight of hand, Clinton had marginalized strident voices of dissent among his fellow Democrats on the Hill. As David Broder observed, Clinton saw his future resting not in governing with a Democratic House and Senate but with presenting himself as a restraining influence on the Republican majorities in Congress (4 February 1996).

The new Clinton strategy would make the pitch that tough times require a different type of leadership from the assertive approaches which might emerge when a clear consensus has developed about what the nation should do (Williams 12 November 1995). In this regard, Clinton could even capitalize on the public perception that he at least was trying to do the right thing. Dick Morris himself styled Clinton as a synthesizer (Drew 1996, 131). Clinton would lead by following the flock as it meandered through the pasture:

> What the President is trying to do is take one from Column A and one from Column B. It's been described as centrism, as triangulation, but it's not those. It's common ground. It's a synthesis of the common wisdom of this country in the last forty-eight months.

The rise of electronically oriented populist campaigning has also greatly deinstitutionalized presidents' power bases. The facility with which Ross Perot served as spoiler in the 1992 campaign and continued—at least until his poor performance in the NAFTA debate with Al Gore—to undermine Clinton's support suggested two things. First, segments of the public have become deeply disaffected. Second, the fact that control of electronic media depends on ready cash gives carte blanche to those with populist tendencies who either have immense personal wealth or can tap unlimited resources.

We can understand why both Bush and Clinton have resorted to "let's deal" leadership approaches. However, two difficulties have emerged from adoption of this style. First, it serves up centrist, least-common-denominator solutions to problems which now seem to exceed this order of difficulty. In other words, some of the post-Reagan problems seem to call for more than incremental solutions. Second, as Bush certainly discovered and Clinton seems to be finding, it often proves difficult for presidents to successfully implement a "let's deal" style—especially if they fail to adequately rig either or both of their gearboxes.

The prognosis suggests that the nation has not turned the corner in coping with gridlock. More worrying, the specter of noninstitutional, electronically based leadership looms ever larger. It certainly reared its head with the ascendancy of Newt Gingrich in the wake of the 1994 congressional elections. A vicious circle suggests itself. Presidents and Congress will blame one another for failures in leadership. The public will increasingly blame gridlock for the resulting paralysis. Efforts will be made to short-circuit the relationships between voters and their elected representatives with direct appeals. These will undermine public perceptions of the legitimacy of presidential and congressional leadership. The respective legitimacy deficits will further exacerbate gridlock. Closing the governability gap will appear increasingly elusive.

4

Thatcher, Major, and the Problem with Leaders as Icons

Among Anglo-American leaders, the Conservatives in Britain enjoyed, until 1997, the longest run of uninterrupted power. They assumed control of the government from a discredited, demoralized, and factionalized Labour Party in 1979—at the height of the world stagflation crisis. They subsequently renewed their mandate three times—1983 and 1987 under Margaret Thatcher and 1992 under John Major.

In its final years, the luster had worn off the Conservative government. Indeed, through the latter half of their 1992 mandate, polls consistently ranked the Conservatives far behind Labour as the party for whom respondents would vote in the next election. The party had faced regular drubbings in bi-elections. It also performed disastrously in the 1994 elections for the European Parliament.

Much of the world had not caught up with the turn in Conservative fortunes. Most non-British observers with a passing interest in Britain believed that the party—especially under Thatcher—provided just what the doctor ordered. If the Conservatives had run into problems, these owed to the difficulties that any leader would encounter in following Thatcher's footsteps. Many Britons took another view. We might expect, of course, that left-leaning Labour supporters would abhor Thatcher's market-oriented policies. But many moderates—those who used to swing between the Conservatives and Labour and lodged themselves with the former after the patent failures of the latter in the late 1970s—ultimately came to the conclusion that Thatcherism left too much to markets. They also worried immensely about Conservative foot-dragging in the process of European integration. John Major's leadership certainly fell short of expectations. However, more profound doubts arose about the Thatcherite remedies for what ails Britain. Many began to see the Conservatives as fumbling witch doctors rather than brilliant physicians.

This chapter gives greater focus to this process of disillusionment. It argues that the closer one looks the more it appears that a great deal rested at the root of the Conservative's problems besides John Major's weak leadership. In part due to its initial success, Thatcherism rigidified into an ideology which struggled to capture the mind and heart of the Conservative Party. This scared off moderates. More fundamentally, Margaret Thatcher's brand of leadership fostered personalization of British politics. This exacerbated the detrimental effects of ideological rigidification.

A LIONIZED BUT EVOLVING SYSTEM

Devotees of the British executive-bureaucratic system—with its aptitude for collective decision making and permanent bureaucratic leadership renowned for "neutrality"—usually have not kept apace with developments since Thatcher took power in 1979. A close examination of the executive-bureaucratic system within this wider context might not entirely debunk the "myth." However, it raises some questions.

The British cabinet meets every week. It also divides into a complicated array of standing and ad hoc committees. Indeed, Thatcher—who always took a dim view of the committee system—performed wonders in reducing the number of standing committees to the low thirties and keeping ad hoc groups to around 120 (Hennessy 1986, 2, 101). Until summer 1992, the committee structure and membership remained closely guarded secrets—on the grounds that the manner in which cabinet divided its labor should remain a private matter to members of the government and their officials. Nonetheless, well-placed observers proved fairly resourceful in piecing together the structure. Most of it followed pretty obvious lines. These normally included committees involved with planning for legislative sessions and management of parliamentary affairs, economic strategy, overseas and defense policy, relations with the European Economic Community, home and social affairs, and security and intelligence. Under these broad headings, different clusters of subcommittees would congeal in more sharply defined fields.

For the most part, the British cabinet under Thatcher handled well the immediate issues on its plate. And it keeps in reasonably good focus how its various decisions relate to one another. Some notable lapses have occurred. For instance, the Franks Commission report concluded that the overseas and defense apparatus of cabinet had failed to monitor adequately the early signs that Argentina would invade the Falkland Islands in 1982. As well, some issues posed such wrenching conflicts that cabinet had not been able to resolve them without major rifts. This certainly pertained in the Westland affair during the latter part of 1985 and early 1986, which saw two ministers resign over whether European or American interests would receive the green light to rescue Britain's only surviving helicopter manufacturing firm. And the cabinet conflicts over British membership in the European Monetary System—which date back to the late seventies—festered even till the end of the Major administration.

The Rent-a-Bureaucracy

In comparison to presidents, British prime ministers enjoy little discretion over their main non-cabinet-level advisers. But prime ministers can work creatively to gain the maximum benefit from what ostensibly appears as a bad thing. First, they can do so by knowing how to use their Cabinet Office. Second, they can draw upon their formal status as First Lord of the Treasury to call upon the support of H. M. Treasury. Third, they can influence the tenor of the civil service by working a subtle oversight of appointments to the top mandarinate and pressing efforts toward public management reform.

The Cabinet Office has served as the core agency supporting ministers in their deliberations. Its organization has broadly reflected the structure of the cabinet committee system, with deputy secretaries responsible for the key ministerial groups, and under and assistant secretaries supporting more specialized committees. Its professional staff largely serves on the basis of temporary loan from other departments. Selection of these officials usually shows a bias toward individuals with experience in the Treasury. If individuals work in parts of the Cabinet Office concerned with macroeconomic policy or Europe then they are likely Treasury-based officials with little or no experience in line departments. If they work in "home" or overseas and defense policy, they would normally have been "starred" as potential permanent secretaries—which means that they had passed through the Treasury at some point in their career.

The Cabinet Office normally does an excellent job as a secretariat. It keeps the paper flowing, arranges meetings, gives early warning of conflicts between departments, works to give dissenters a sense that the process has taken their views into account, and circulates the results of cabinet meetings throughout Whitehall. The Cabinet Office has, nonetheless, lacked an ability to canvass alternate viewpoints. This does not mean that it has not promoted views—its officials normally share the ethos of Treasury, namely, "We know what is best because we are bright." It simply is to say that we cannot expect from Cabinet Office much of an aptitude for going beyond the received wisdom which prevails in the upper strata of Whitehall.

To varying degrees, prime ministers have sensed the extent to which the Cabinet Office might serve somewhat ambivalently and even launch its own projects. They have attempted to compensate for the resulting deficit in the policy advice on tap. Edward Heath (Conservative prime minister from 1970 to 1974) sought a think tank composed of outsiders—it did not matter whether they brought partisan credentials, he simply wanted bright people not impregnated with Whitehall folk wisdom—who would help keep his government's central goals in focus and facilitate the generation of new policy ideas as required. Negotiations between his transition people and Whitehall mandarins produced a Central Policy Review Staff—very much a horse designed by a committee. CPRS would advise cabinet generally as well as the prime minister, be located in the Cabinet Office, and include a mix of seconded officials, rising corporate executives on loan from their firms, and partisan policy professionals. The ambiguity of its function, institutional autonomy, and makeup notwithstanding, prime ministers Heath, Harold Wilson (Labour prime minister from 1974 to 1977), and James Callaghan (Labour prime minister from 1977 to 1979) and their cabinets found creative ways to employ CPRS. There did develop a secular decline in its impact the more it institutionalized its role and departed from its initial focus on the six-month strategic reviews punctuated by quick turnover of advice on issues of immediate interest to cabinet (Blackstone and Plowden 1988). The longer it operated the more difficult it found bringing cabinets to strategic issues and inserting its views on how matters before cabinet fit within this frame. Thatcher abolished it. The poor fit between Thatcher's style and efforts to keep CPRS quasi-detached had sealed the latter's fate.

Cabinet consultation can ebb and flow. The Cabinet Office can emphasize its secretariat functions or take on more interventionist stances. But H. M. Treasury tends to retain its pervasive role whatever other arrangements prevail at the time. Astute prime ministers know this. And if they recognize fully its potential, they can always invoke their formal title, "Prime Minister and First Lord of the Treasury." Recently, the Japanese have been looking at ways to reduce the concentration of levers over economic policy in their Department of Finance. The *Financial Times* of London reported on developments as if the Japanese situation stood outside the parameters of that in other advanced democracies (Dawkins 8 February 1996). The paper needed only to have looked under its own nose at H. M. Treasury to find a similar concentration of power. We certainly find in Britain a much more homogeneous structural apparatus than is found in the United States. H. M. Treasury controls all the lead central-agency units responsible for economic policy. This means that most integration of economic policies takes place in one agency—the Treasury.

Although not as severely as in the United States, the rise of new economic ideologies can usher in periods in which forecasts appear to be— somewhat more than usually the case—spins sought by political masters. By the mid-1980s, the Bank of England had in fact lost confidence in the integrity of Treasury forecasts. One senior Bank of England official lamented the degree to which Treasury forecasting had become subject to political spins:

> A problem has arisen between the head of the economics unit in the bank—John Fleming—and his opposite number at Treasury—Terry Burns who is the second permanent secretary responsible for economic advice. Fleming—a former don from Oxford—is a reconstructed Keynesian. The disagreements between the two emerge over the bank's duty to present quarterly reports on the economy . . . the tension between the two emanates from the fact that governments and administrations put forecasts in the most favorable light possible (1986 interview).

Certainly, observers generally attribute the dysfunctions of the "Lawson boom"—a surge in economic activity brought on by successive reductions of interest rates—to Treasury projections in the run-up to the 1987 election, which seriously underestimated the inflationary danger of the chancellor's, Nigel Lawson, approach to monetary policy (Keegan 1989). Analysts widely acknowledge that John Major's absorption with reducing inflation to zero after the 1992 election greatly exacerbated the conditions which led to Britain's unceremonious departure from the European Monetary System (EMS) in September 1992.

The Delicate Issue of Party-Political Advice

Prime ministers such as Lloyd George and Winston Churchill who found themselves facing a dire threat to the national security of Britain have enjoyed a great deal of latitude to insert structures which enable them to operate monocratically (Mackintosh 1977). Outside such crisis times, prime ministers who resort to such devices might prompt some to say that they have attempted to personalize the decision process. Prime ministers can—as Thatcher frequently did—narrow their consultation of cabinet to insure that they obtain legitimization from those who share their view of the government's mandate and then seek ratification from the rest of cabinet. They also can resort to setting up advisory units which serve the prime minister and no one else.

Heath's transition people wanted to do this when they began their negotiations with the cabinet secretary and the head of the civil service that ultimately led to the creation of the Central Policy Review Staff. When Wilson began his second term as prime minister, in 1974, he created a Policy Unit within No. 10 Downing Street. But until that time, prime ministers relied on the career-staffed No. 10 private office to track down policy issues. In the private office, some five civil servants on loan from other departments—as with the Cabinet Office, the Treasury normally plays mightily here—keep independent lines out to various corners of Whitehall so that No. 10 can find very quickly the origins and intensity of various departmental positions.

In serving as the prime minister's issues switchboard, the private office must maintain its credibility as an agent of neutral brokerage. Individuals within the office lose their bona fides in Whitehall if they appear to have taken a role in the development of the prime minister's priorities and pressed these as if they had become partisan operatives. The case of Charles Powell—a Foreign Office official who served in No. 10 under Thatcher long beyond the usual three-year secondment— left Whitehall for this very reason when Thatcher resigned.

Following thus upon the model that Wilson introduced in 1974, a vibrant Policy Unit can play two important roles. It can offer the prime minister a small group close by which can serve as a brain trust in the process of devising priorities and discerning the placement and timing of personal interventions in policy deliberations. Second, it can take the pressure off the private office to engage in advocacy and therefore help preserve its capacity for neutral brokerage.

Still, Policy Units have not found their way easily. Some analysts have seen their emergence as another sign of "primeministerialization"—making the central machinery too sensitive to the partisan exigencies of a government. Thatcher at first did not want to continue with the Policy Unit model—she believed that partisan advisers should largely function out of individual ministers' offices. However, she saw the potential utility of a Policy Unit around the time that she abolished the Central Policy Review Staff (1983). From that point to the end of her government, the Policy Unit figured very substantially in virtually every policy initiative—especially those associated with privatization, deinstitutionalization of professions, and educational reform. Under Major, the Policy Unit carried on this tradition. However, his first unit head—Sara Hogg, a former economics columnist with *The Independent*—chose to focus much of its work on economic policy. Thus it suffered the experience of guilt by association as the central elements of Major's economic policies unraveled.

MARGARET THATCHER

From Executive Leader to Iron Lady to Icon

After winning her third mandate, in 1987, Margaret Thatcher seemed to have established a dynasty for her party. Indeed, soon after the election, she began to make it clear that she fully intended to lead the Conservatives into the next election—thereby suggesting that her leadership would prove essential to the continuance of the mission of her party to turn Britain around.

The facts now suggest that Thatcher's perception of her situation had become delusionary if not messianic. And—just as many pundits believed that the 1987 election results seemed to enshrine the Thatcher hegemony—the executive-bureaucratic community seemed to have become resigned to the Thatcher style of governance. Ministers had learned to live with a situation in which cabinet and its standing committees simply ratified deals that the prime minister had reached in ad hoc and private negotiations. Officials lowered their sights—accepting the fact that ministers sought little by the way of policy analysis and that Thatcher thought their job was to run the public service like Marks and Spencer (the famous midprice British clothing chain). Any analyst who predicted that Thatcher would, by 1990, have pressed her luck too far and met expulsion as leader would have faced gales of laughter. In examining what went wrong, we find the short answer in the process whereby any type of executive leadership ultimately wears thin. It does so because the chief executive becomes tired and/or sloppy, and—over time—accumulates a sufficient number of resentful colleagues. The less obvious answer proves somewhat more difficult. It rests in the relatively elusive region of executive leadership associated with personality.

In the literature on the U. S. presidency, discussion of the effects of personality on behavior has centered on whether incumbents have developed and maintained positive views of their jobs and whether they pursue these in an active way. Ironically, the seminal proponent of positioning presidents in quadrants associated with the interaction of these "positive-negative" and "active-positive" axes—James David Barber—consistently drew scorn for oversimplistic application of his paradigm (Barber 1972; 1977; George 1974; Qualls 1977). The subsequent critiques of institutionalist and public choice theorists have exacerbated Barber's problems with the rest of the discipline. Yet most mainline presidency scholars pursue analyses which explicitly take into consideration the positive-negative and/or active-passive tendencies of incumbents (Hargrove 1992; George 1980, 146, 155; Neustadt 1990, 206). In fact, one derives from their work the sense that they believe that well-adjusted and productive presidents—invariably Franklin D. Roosevelt and John F. Kennedy—differ immensely from neurotic and ritualistic ones—characteristically Lyndon B. Johnson and Richard M. Nixon—in the degree to which they derived psychic income from their positive engagement in the process of governance.

To address the case of Thatcher in light of this literature, we must treat two problems—neither of which stem from the fact that we are examining the personality dimensions of executive leadership in a Westminster system while employing concepts developed in the United States. First, political scientists have revealed in their portrayals of active-positive styles a bias for the type of interventionist and expansive governance which characterized executive leadership during the apogee of the welfare state. This might have made sense in the period of interventionist governance. However, the exigences of the current epoch raise the issue of what a well-adjusted activist would look like in an era of stringency and the contraction of the state. Second, and relatedly, analysts failed to differentiate between types of activity. If activeness depends on engagement in one's job, it will take different shapes depending upon the dimensions of their position that chief executives choose to stress.

In Chapter 2, we addressed these two issues by distinguishing between four types of engagement in executive leadership—"new order," "executive," "being there," and "let's deal." Britain has not proven fertile ground for "new order" prime ministers. Winston Churchill struck a charismatic chord in his primeministership during the war. However, he proved very much a "being there" prime minister during his second administration. Clement Attlee presided over a huge amount of change. However, his style proved far from charismatic and the "new order" politics that his government followed rested substantially upon the consensus that had emerged during the war over the role of the state. It did not require a lot of pushing and shoving. Macmillan, Eden, and Hume all fit within the "lets deal" mold—with Macmillan having immense success and the latter two encountering failure. Wilson, Heath, and Callaghan operated "executive" governments—so much so that, like their American soulmate Jimmy Carter, they tended to focus upon competent engagement of the state apparatus at the cost of their electoral futures.

This assessment of Thatcher argues that she started as an "executive" prime minister. However, unlike Wilson, Heath, and Callaghan, she soon departed from this approach. Temperamentally, she lacked the patience to follow through in a concerted way with running the government. Further, she had little regard either for routinized cabinet decision making or the folkways of the permanent bureaucracy. Finally, she proved much more attentive than the others to political danger—sensing instinctively when circumstances forced her to take bold actions deviating from the counsel both of her ministers and Whitehall.

Some might mistake Thatcher's migration from "executive" leadership as a move to "new order" politics. Yet neither the objectives that she set out nor her personalization of decision making would sustain this analysis. Thatcher became increasingly a "being there" prime minister. The more she employed the regal "we" in referring to herself the more she imbibed the heady wine of symbolic politics. To be sure, Thatcherism incorporated particular policies—a special relationship with the United States, skepticism toward Europe, privatization, fiscal stringency, and running down the welfare state. But increasingly Thatcher sold herself as an icon more than a chief executive—the tough lady who had shown Britain how to regain its spine.

Nearly a year and a half after leaving the primeministership, Thatcher used language, in an April 27, 1992 article in *Newsweek,* whose form paralleled very closely that messianic language employed by Jesus in the last discourse as rendered in John's gospel. (This should not surprise us, as her former policy unit head, Brian Griffiths, an evangelical Christian, had a hand in drafting the article.) For instance, we find this caution against false prophets (i.e. John Major):

> If a man gets up and says, "Look really, I'm a very modest man," would you believe him? What about the person who says, "I care far more about people than she did"? Look at the record, and make a judgment.

Or, take these reflections on Thatcherism as against what John Major has to offer:

> There isn't such a thing as Majorism. . . . We restored the strength and reputation of Britain. We did it on fundamental principles. They bear my name, but they are far older than I am. . . . Thatcherism will live. It will live long after Thatcher has died, because we had the courage to restore the great principles and put them into practice.

These words reflect the degree to which Thatcher had turned herself into an icon. Her hubris had gone beyond extravagant claims about bringing an end to socialism. Thatcher began to see her message and the fate of the nation as organically linked. Within this context, her messianic vision of her role for the nation began to override her instinct for political survival. Eventually, her party picked up on this and jettisoned her. Yet Thatcherism still holds considerable sway in the Conservative

Party and among many Britons. Indeed, John Major's successor, the
Labour Party's Tony Blair, took pains in recrafting his party's appeal
not to attack Thatcherism frontally. Messianism does not necessarily
make a vision illusory.

Thatcher Turns Whitehall

The long duration of the Thatcher government enabled the prime minister to leave her mark on the upper echelons of the permanent civil service—perhaps more than any prime minister in this century. In this regard, a Royal Institute of Public Administration Working Group looked
into Thatcher's influence on the upper reaches of the public service and
characterized her role as "personalization" rather than "politicization",
" 'catching the eye' of the prime minister . . . may now be more important than in the past. Evidence to our group suggests that personal
contacts and impressions play a role in promotion decisions" (RIPA
Working Group 1987, 43).

In my own interviews conducted over several years, the view that
Thatcher, indeed, had strongly personalized the selection of senior personnel emerged strongly. One top Treasury official saw this as all for
the better: "The other thing the government has done is to promote a lot
of young people. And, the Treasury shows the effects of that. The management of Treasury from the chancellor to Peter Middleton [then the
permanent secretary]—and they set the tone—is young, intellectually
lively, informal" (1986 interview).

However, many officials had reservations. A Home Office official
asserted that advancement increasingly depended on individuals' willingness to cooperate with the government: "This government has a
tendency to rely on officials whom they believe are sympathetic to
their position. . . . what happens is that there are certain officials who
unquestioningly do the government's bidding and they are sometimes
rewarded by assignment to particularly sensitive jobs" (1987 interview). A Treasury official saw the process as part of a broader trend:
"There was a continuing and increasing pressure to be politically accountable. It's a fundamental change, going on for some time—even
before Thatcher. She has continued it—the politicization of officialdom. Your career wouldn't go further if you didn't take a political
posture toward your obligations, and to your advice accordingly" (1987
interview).

It appears as if the strongest symbiosis between the government and the mandarinate took place in the Treasury. A former permanent secretary associated this with a tendency of the Treasury to adapt itself to the political flavor of the day: "Treasury views the world through politically colored glasses. . . . If ministers are monetarist, then Treasury has to be monetarist" (1989 interview). However, the respondent also noted that the closeness of the relationship between Thatcher and the Treasury exceeded that of other governments. This owed both to her strong interest in economic policy and the influence of Professor Alan Walters, who worked through much of the government as a special adviser in No. 10: "No. 10's relationship with Treasury changed since the PM was more interested in economic policy and hired her own policy specialists, notably Alan Walters" (1986 interview).

The Thatcher government, indeed, institutionalized its hold on the Treasury with two key appointments. The first of these was Terry Burns, who assumed the post of chief economic adviser at the precocious age of thirty-five. In a departure from tradition, Burns—a confirmed monetarist—came directly from the London School of Business rather than from the ranks of the government economics service. The second of these saw Peter Middleton—a disillusioned academic who entered the Treasury as a press officer and became a staunch advocate of monetarism—jump a full rank to become head of the Treasury (that is, its permanent secretary) in 1983. Middleton's ascendancy in the Treasury had resulted from a bitter battle—waged before the arrival of Thatcher—between unreconstructed Keynesians and the emergent monetarists (Campbell 1983, 128).

During the 1980s, the Middleton-Burns axis in the department gained notoriety for producing economic forecasts which bent according to the preferences of the political leadership. For instance, Treasury policies during the build up to the 1987 election built on excessively rosy forecasts. These sought to evoke a favorable reception by the electorate rather than advance economic analysis. Ultimately, Treasury optimism contributed greatly to the uncontrolled "Lawson boom." Efforts to dampen this with high interest rates put excessive upward pressure on the pound for the remainder of the decade.

One former Treasury economist spoke at length about difficulties with Burns's sensitivity to political atmospherics:

> Terry Burns found it difficult to deal with people with a larger professional experience. . . . The situation was never as bad as in the U. S. where

the forecast will look like it has to be negotiated. But the risk grew with Terry Burns's involvement, because someone with a background in forecasting was nevertheless seen as a political person. . . . The Thatcher government came with clear ideas of how the economy operated, which differed from the forecasters (1987 interview).

Terry Burns succeeded Peter Middleton as permanent secretary in 1991.

The Drift toward Monocratic Leadership

BEFORE "THATCHERISM," A THATCHERESQUE VIEW OF EXECUTIVE GOVERNMENT

One of the least endearing qualities of Britain's "Iron Lady" was her determination. In the early years of her government, this trait seemed only to lead to much greater success for Margaret Thatcher than most observers would have predicted. Specifically, she shepherded her resources in an exceptionally astute way. She disciplined herself to focus only on the matters that would continue to earn the respect of the electorate for her ability to manage the affairs of the United Kingdom as well as could be expected. Most of her behavior—tough language notwithstanding—comported with the "executive" style of leadership which had prevailed during the administrations of her three immediate predecessors.

Even early in her administration, insiders noted that Thatcher took a distinctive approach to managing the decision making process. Along with a studied detachment from microeconomic issues, she already tolerated much less collective decision making through formalized cabinet committees. The prime minister eschewed the formalized cabinet committee structure in favor of ad hoc groups of ministers. She would play only with ministers who shared her view or would go along to get along. She liked to present to the entire cabinet only done deals. She loved to bat down those who voiced reservations at the eleventh hour. Soon cabinet ministers learned not to challenge her openly—no matter how egregious their exclusion from an issue deemed key to their department.

Also in the early years of the administration, insiders worried about the prime minister's criteria for the selection of the issues which would receive her attention. Some believed she did not canvass systematically enough the various matters which might require her attention. In some respects, the imperatives of monetarism and fiscal stringency provided an overarching context for the art of the possible in the government. However, the absorptions did not derive from a truly strategic approach. And, their tendency to automatize decision making meant that hosts of issues never received systematic treatment.

RULING WITH AN IRON FIST

Thatcher's style shifted over time from a selective form of "executive" government to an increasingly idiosyncratic vision that began to take on the qualities of a crusade. As my interviews progressed through the span of the government, to what degree had respondents picked up on this gradual constriction of the Iron Lady's government into the narrow parameters of Thatcherism? How did they perceive this rare phenomenon—the development of a governmental approach into an ideology—in light of the British constitutional tradition of cabinet government and the cultural integrity of the permanent civil service?

Several officials dwelt at length on the peculiar nature of the Thatcher approach. In 1989, one permanent official working in No. 10 stated approvingly that Thatcher had adopted a vertical form of organization with a "stronger sense of accountability back on finance to both Treasury and the prime minister." Whereas the three previous governments had placed considerable emphasis on consensus coordination—focusing on policy objectives across the board, Thatcher had stressed that ministers and departments state their objectives and concentrate their efforts on achieving these. Our official thus painted a stark contrast in explaining why Thatcher had disbanded the Central Policy Review Staff:

> [that was part of] the various bits which underpinned our collective discussion. I think to some extent, that was all part of the apparatus of consensus coordination, a feeling that everybody had some responsibility for things and nobody had sole responsibility for anything, which this prime minister and the general administration criticized and felt that they didn't want to continue.

However, many officials elsewhere in Whitehall saw the greatly diminished emphasis of cabinet consultation as a significant—even if not regrettable—departure from Whitehall practice. Some of these officials almost left the impression of collective government meltdown: "It is the style of this government to do less business through formal cabinet committees and meetings in No. 10. [The Cabinet Office] secretariat gets a bit less involved than it did. . . . They come in occasionally, ad hoc rather than on a continuous basis" (1986 interview).

We could not question that once Thatcher locked into an issue no manner of minutiae would escape her attention. However, one monumental lapse in her mixed-scanning approach suggested that she did not come close to achieving the selective engagement she sought. If we look at her and her government's handling of the events leading to the 1982 Argentinean invasion of the Falkland Islands, we find a succession of documented omissions and failures of judgment which together added up to near dereliction of duty (Franks Report 1983, 26–27, 33–34, 40–45, 79, 82–83).

Thatcher had given scant attention to the brewing crisis. She never even mandated her ministers to scan the matter for her. She scribbled, "we must make contingency plans" on a copy of a March 3 cable from her ambassador a month before the invasion. But her private office did not get around to conveying her comments to the Foreign and Commonwealth Office, the Ministry of Defence, and the Cabinet Office until March 8. Obviously, the matter lacked priority. Thatcher had set up a situation in which the political leadership became virtually impenetrable to those trying to give warning of the impending invasion.

Relatedly, No. 10 respondents conveyed the view that Thatcher always remained on top of the government's strategy. Yet the possibility arises that those close to Thatcher mistook ideological conviction—hers and theirs—for policy coherence. In interviews, officials in No. 10 made strong assertions of the prime minister's commanding position over policy. In the words of one official, "The PM's style is very strong, 'dominates' might be too strong. But the powerhouse of ideas and strategy come from No. 10 and her" (1986 interview). However, the approach spelled lots of problems for our respondent's previous agency—the Central Policy Review Staff—and for cabinet consultation. In the former case, Thatcher abolished the agency because it did not work within the context of monocratic governance. Yet in defending this move, the same official asserted that Thatcher's monocratic approach fell short of presidentialism, notwithstanding his awareness of the belief among many permanent civil servants that her style raised issues of constitutional propriety: "We have a very strong-willed PM who is clear where she is going. But we still have a cabinet system of government and things are still decided by groups of ministers. . . . The PM tends to have ad hoc groups meet rather than official cabinet subcommittees. Lots of civil servants will tell you this is highly improper constitutionally."

Cabinet members like Michael Heseltine, Nigel Lawson, and Geoffrey Howe eventually developed qualms of their own. Heseltine—then defense minister—left the government early in 1986 in the aftermath of his dispute with Leon Brittan—then the trade and industry minister—over the future of the Westland helicopter manufacturers. Here Thatcher employed a number of manipulative tactics in opposition to Heseltine's moves in favor of purchase by a European consortium. These included alternating between ad hoc groups and the appropriate standing committee in search of the right mix of ministers, having her press secretary convey to the media distorted accounts of ministers' preferences, and expunging from cabinet minutes any record of dissent. Heseltine subsequently claimed that, during the crisis, she read out to cabinet the results of a meeting of ministers which never took place (Bevins and Timmins 19 November 1990).

In October 1989, Nigel Lawson left cabinet over the prime minister's effort to renege on an agreement she had made in spring 1989 with other EEC leaders to ultimately enter the European Monetary System (EMS). Geoffrey Howe's November 1990 resignation from cabinet provided the final straw. In his parting shots, he noted that Lawson and he had forced Thatcher into the spring 1989 agreement on the EMS with threats of resignation. He also observed that cabinet government under Thatcher had become: "trying to pretend there was a common policy when every step forward risked being subverted by some casual comment or impulsive answer" (Goodwin 14 November 1990).

The emergence of monocratic rule made itself felt in the power of the prime minister vis-à-vis ministers in review of the expenditure budget and, by extension, the hegemony of the Treasury. In the end of the Thatcher years, budgeting by fiat had ratcheted back expenditure to the point where the government had chalked up successive surpluses. These occurred notwithstanding the degree to which the population was suffering the consequences of the decline of social provision, public services, and infrastructure.

When I first conducted interviews in Whitehall, in 1978 at the end of the Callaghan government, expenditure budgeting maintained an aura of collective deliberation. Thatcher changed dramatically the entire context of the annual expenditure review process. First, and most important, she altered the relationship between the development of macroeconomic policy and the establishment of the fiscal framework and the expenditure budget. Her actions here made the Public Expenditure Survey (PES)—that is, the interdepartmental process for reconciling spending priorities with available resources—much more subject to macroeconomic policy-making than it had been before. Second, she cut PES from four to three years. This gave departments less opportunity to enshrine their long-term spending plans. Third, she linked pay increases in the public service to "cash limits." This meant that departments which failed to hold the line in wage negotiations would have to pay in staff cuts. Fourth, she instituted limits to the assistance which would be extended to nationalized and private industries and agriculture. This greatly constricted government intervention in public and private enterprise. It resulted in turn in a building-down of the parts of Treasury and line agencies which involved themselves with state support of enterprise. Finally, Thatcher called upon the services of a "Star Chamber"—a committee of senior ministers—to arbitrate disputes between the chief secretary of the Treasury—Britain's budget minister—and departments. This committee cut drastically the involvement of the entire cabinet in deliberations over the details of the expenditure budget.

In the early Thatcher years, ministers occasionally found that they could swing the Star Chamber toward recognition of the political necessity of some expenditure. In time though, it became clear that ministers more often faced a solid line against exceptions. In the words of a key Treasury participant: "The Star Chamber has enough senior and weighty ministers on it that if they reach a view, the spending minister sees that they will prevail in cabinet as well. So, almost invariably, they don't think it is worth going to cabinet" (1986 interview). A principal finance officer for one of the big spending departments spoke of the Star Chamber as taking on almost ritualistic significance—changing little of substance: "By the end of the day, it turns on the determination of cabinet and the PM to hold public expenditure within given parameters. . . . The Star Chamber does not weaken, it becomes routine" (1987 interview).

The gradual accretion of power to No. 10 Downing St.—especially the Policy Unit—marks in another way the extent to which Thatcher's government style had become deeply monocratic. At the beginning of the Thatcher administration, there was no Policy Unit per se. John Hoskyns—a friend of Sir Keith Joseph, Thatcher's ideological mentor—worked as a special adviser without the benefit of a staff. He ran into an old problem. He found it very difficult to get papers out of the private office. He also encountered difficulties getting his views on cabinet business to the prime minister.

By summer 1983, John Hoskyns had left No. 10, Thatcher had acquired a new mandate, those in the disbanded Central Policy Review Staff with time remaining on their secondments moved to No. 10 to form the nucleus of a new policy unit, and Robin Butler—who ultimately became cabinet secretary—moved from the Treasury to become principal private secretary. Thatcher now recognized that she needed on tap a small group of advisers who would help her enshrine and implement her agenda. As one CPRS veteran who made the move noted: "The PM wanted the CPRS to help her translate her political and policy objectives into practice, and to tell her how far we could go or not, what the constraints are" (1986 interview). The same official—on loan from the private sector—observed that it took a personal agreement with the objectives of the government to make such a transition possible: "Since I was in sympathy with the government, what I was trying to do in CPRS was the same in No. 10. I think few of my colleagues could have gone to work in No. 10. They would have been horrified."

This reflex toward embracing the prime minister's goals did not confine itself to political appointees or those on loan from industry. One career official pronounced in explicit terms the degree of his commitment to the prime minister: "My loyalty was always to the PM, even when the issue involved my department. At first my department expected me to take its line. This provided unstated pressure that assumed that I would be my department's representative in No. 10" (1989 interview).

By the mid-1980s and through to the end of the Thatcher years, the Policy Unit leapt onto the radar scopes of officials throughout Whitehall—especially those working on major initiatives which would require the attention and support of the prime minister. The Policy Unit participated with the Treasury in a number of review groups taking in initiatives as diverse as the privatization of the British Airport Authority and the supplementary benefit review. In many cases, officials indicated that maintaining close ties with the Policy Unit became indispensable to serving their ministers. For instance, one respondent spoke about how keeping the Policy Unit in the loop insured that a major reform package would be guaranteed acceptance: "The minister was continuously involved and the acceptance of Treasury and the No. 10 Policy Unit was acquired all the way through" (1987 interview).

JOHN MAJOR

A Pastel Man and the Emergence of a Nonpastel Era

Just as often as it hurts, the truth comes out under the strangest circumstances. This certainly applies to two columns written by Peter Jenkins of *The Independent* the day before and the day of the 1992 election (April 8 and 9). Jenkins—who passed away shortly after the election—gave John Major a report card which did not disguise the expectation that he would not form the next government. Assuming that Jenkins had no idea that his chronic condition would take his life soon after the election, his words appear as an especially bold instance of speaking the truth to power.

Jenkins asserted that the then–Labour Party leader, Neil Kinnock, ran Major ragged in the campaign, raising serious doubts about Major's ability to continue as prime minister—"The more the country saw of Mr. Major the more it saw through him." He styled Major as an only superficially reconstructed Thatcherite—one who has equivocated on Europe, even engineering a Pyrrhic victory at Maastricht by institutionalizing Britons' footdragging in relation to Europe. Jenkins, who never disguised his pro-Europe sympathies, believed that Major had failed to wean Britain of the illusion that it only needed Europe selectively and could compete without continent-style, "government driven" industrial strategies. His first cabinet consisted of men (no women) who—like himself—rose to prominence by attaching themselves unquestioningly to Thatcher. His rewards to those who supported him in the leadership contest—for instance, Norman Lamont, who became chancellor—lavished responsibility far beyond the apparent aptitudes and proven abilities of the beneficiaries.

Jenkins confessed to having hoped for more from Major. From the outset of his primeministership, he had appeared to be "a competent and diligent technician and a thoroughly amiable man." But the election campaign had brought the harsh reality crashing down. It had:

> . . . cast doubt upon the scope of his vision, exposed once more the poverty of his language, and raised doubts about his capacity to catch the imagination of the country and move it forward.

One might find parallels between this assessment of Major in spring 1992 and assessments of George Bush that gained currency in the United States at the same time. We, of course, cannot ignore one difference:

Bush came to power while voters still suspended their disbelief about neo-liberal ideology because things were going well. As Campbell and Rockman noted in their assessment of Bush's situation when he took office: "He is a pastel political personality serving in a mostly pastel time that offers him a limited range of shades from which to choose" (Campbell and Rockman 1991a, viii—Rockman actually bears responsibility for the use of "pastel" here). Major inherited a dream unraveling as quickly as voters awoke to the illusory nature of the Thatcher vision. Peter Jenkins saw a mismatch between the political circumstances and Major's persona and style: "[his] style is of such a pastel hue at a moment when politics is entering the broad-brush phase of an election run up" (14 November 1991). Both men took over from icons. Each of them knew that he could not summon the charisma necessary to keep the spell bound. The best they could do was insure that the awakening would not be rude.

As the leader starts to send signals that he recognizes the need for change, a public previously lulled by an illusion begins to stir. Those who awake register in shrill screams the prospect that their illusion has no future. In near-prophetic terms Bert Rockman so characterized Bush's potential plight before it became a reality:

> So far, the benign context of this agendaless presidency has been its saving grace. But that context has begun to recede, and as it does so, we probably can expect precisely the kinds of conflicts that damaged the Carter administration from within. Sooner or later, Bush's bona fides as a Republican will be questioned by the "ideas" wing of the party. . . . To cover himself, he will . . . flip in one direction and then flop in the other. . . . Such a situation will make him look foolish (Rockman 1991b, 21, 23–24).

Bush walked willy-nilly into this academic prognosis. Major renewed his mandate even though he had not risen to an almost identical occasion. At the end of the day, the voters' visceral fears of a Labour government won out. Yet as events after 1992 proved, victory at the polls did not liberate Major and his party from its struggle with self-imposed paralysis.

Like George Bush, John Major inherited a "being there" regime when there was no there there. This was both because the there of his personality paled next to the conviction and compellingness of Thatcher's and the there of Thatcherism was becoming manifestly "back when."

Bush dealt with this conundrum by trying to distinguish himself as a "let's deal" president. As we have seen in Chapter 2, he failed because he could not deliver in the area of domestic policy. Major took a different tack. He tried to become an "executive" prime minister. In the early stages of his government, hopes rose that he could carry this off. Even before the challenge to her leadership that resulted ultimately in her resignation, Thatcher had lost the confidence of her cabinet. Her increasingly strident views on Europe had undermined her support. Thatcher's pique had reached the point where she began to discuss publicly the possibility of going to the people with a referendum on Britain's role in the EEC (Bevins 17 November 1990). This struck horror in the hearts even of anti-Europe MPs. As a member of the No Turning Back Group said: "It is an appalling suggestion. How can she talk about the sovereignty of Parliament and then suggest a referendum?" (Brown 20 November 1990). In the circumstances, the restoration of cabinet government became a motif of all three of the main contenders for the leadership. In so far as this criterion worked an effect on selection of the new leader, John Major's manner certainly provided reassurance.

Whatever Major's intentions, Thatcherism still worked powerful influences in cabinet and the Conservative Party. This fact become most manifest in the herculean struggles within the government over the level of integration with Europe that Britain should pursue. Major found it essential to maintenance of his power base to curry the favor of Thatcherites by appointing their darlings to cabinet and ministerial positions. He also did a very poor job of keeping them under some semblance of control.

Some officials characterized the residual Thatcherism of the Major government as stylistic rather than messianic. That is, they considered many ministers in the Major government as relative newcomers who viewed Whitehall with a high degree of skepticism. These officials did not always see this as meaning that ministers pressed radical views. The ministers simply did not have the cultural ties to the mandarinate that most British cabinets display. In the words of a senior official in the Cabinet Office:

> ... they're different in the sense that they're not long-term, long-established, traditional, knights-of-the-shire grandee types, they're more professional ... the concept of the old fashioned grandee in a department, the minister who did it through a sort of noblesse oblige, that doesn't really exist. I mean the newspapers try and talk about the more sort of

estate-agent culture, the realtor culture on the government benches, more people have come in from commerce and the city and that sort of entrepreneurial background (1993 interview).

Other officials rendered less benign interpretations of the Thatcherite style. To be sure, they noted a cohort-shift during the latter years of the Thatcher period—a young group of relatively inexperienced ministers took over almost entirely from the more conventional group that Thatcher had selected at the outset of her government. However, they also pointed up the consequences of this transformation—the emergence of a highly ideological and willful form of executive leadership. Early Thatcher ministers viewed as the prime minister's ideological soulmates at least brought their own independent experience to Whitehall. This presented the possibility for a common ground in which ministers could engage in the type of dialogue with officials which allows for creative tension.

Ostensibly, the Major government sought a consensual executive approach—both with regard to consultation within cabinet and the relations between ministers and officials. However, the prime minister's weak leadership soon led to a disintegration of cabinet coherence and trust between ministers and officials. Especially after the 1992 election, Major had imparted too much trust to inexperienced Thatcherites who then ran roughshod over their departments. Virtually every department became captured by ministers pressing idiosyncratic positions.

The combination of weak leadership on Major's part and competing signals from powerful Thatcherite ministers produced a truly schizophrenic administration. Even in the final years of the administration, Major and a handful of ministers—most prominently the chancellor of the exchequer, Kenneth Clarke, and the deputy prime minister, Michael Heseltine—tried to pursue moderate policies toward the role of government and European Union. In such cases, one caught glimmers of the possibility that the Conservatives might once again be able to speak to a nation which had gone beyond the Thatcherite paradigm. But such occurrences time and again provoked strong reactions in the Tory right. Ultimately, Major found it necessary to placate the Thatcherites by speaking to the country in their language. Such actions simply deepened the view that the prime minister vacillated. They made him appear duplicitous.

We can discern a pattern whereby Major each year put his mind to redefining a centrist message in time for the annual party conference in the fall. In the fall 1993 convention, for instance, he attempted to reenshrine "One Nation Conservatism." This view derived from Chris Patten's social market. Patten, who as party chairman had masterminded the 1992 election victory, had himself succumbed to electoral defeat and gone on to serve as governor of Hong Kong. As chairman, Patten had championed the need to produce policies that fitted within the broad frame of neo-liberalism yet provided protections for society's vulnerable.

In the Fall 1993 instance, Major's pastel approach prevented him from getting this simple message across. He chose the slogan "back to basics" to epitomize his message. In specifying what he meant by basics, Major lapsed into what appeared to be nostalgia for a more innocent United Kingdom. With regard to education, for example, he said in his 1994 New Year's address: "I don't think children go to school for 'experience'—they go to learn, and learn the basic skills they are going to need later in life—being able to read, write and do sums" (Meikle 1 January 1994). Such time warps in Major's imagery even aroused concern among moderate Conservatives that the prime minister was speaking in terms evocative of a "nanny state" (Meikle 11 January 1994).

More important, the Tory right used the back-to-basics motif as a ready hook for "highjacking"—as Kenneth Clarke put it—Major's message (White and Wintour 16 November 1993). By spring 1994, tough love supplanted back to basics. The ultra-Thatcherite then chief secretary Michael Portillo plotted to increase rents for public housing to market levels and not cover the gap with additional income support (Wintour 30 May 1994). He also threatened to crack down on benefits paid to sixteen and seventeen-year-olds who have been thrown out by their parents or left home after being abused (Brindle 2 June 1994). The Home Secretary—Michael Howard—resuscitated the already discredited proposal for military-style boot camps that would "knock the criminal spirit" out of young offenders (Travis 2 June 1994). Thatcher's experimentation with such camps in the mid-1980s had proven a failure. Major even got into the act by denouncing beggars as an eyesore and proposing that they be swept off the streets (Wintour 30 May 1994).

All of this added up to a party in deep internal division and profound denial about the associated consequences. In early spring 1994, polls indicated that Labour had taken the edge from the Conservatives even in the latter's putative forte. Respondents now believed Labour better able to deal with taxation, crime, and economic issues than the Conservatives (Linton 16 March 1994). And this was the situation before the death of John Smith found Labour selecting Tony Blair as leader. Blair, a singularly more charismatic figure than Smith, even won praise from Margaret Thatcher for his ability to instill voter confidence (Wintour 29 May 1995).

In a not-too-imaginative gambit, Major countered Blair's rising appeal with a pitch for a young persons' citizens' charter (Meikle 26 July 1994). Yet the language employed to convey what this meant struck many as hollow reincantation of rhetoric of the 1992 campaign. Major still believed he was extending the promise of "ownership, choice and opportunity" to the recipients of services through a "smaller and more efficient" government (White 28 July 1994). The public had sufficient experience with Major by this point to conclude that "smaller" and not necessarily "more efficient" would drive the bottom line. Indeed, the Conservatives' own research of eight groups of supporters suggested that not even the choir believed the preacher (Wintour 22 November 1994). As John Maples, the deputy party chairman, noted in a leaked document reporting the results of the research:

> . . . what we are saying on the economy is completely at odds with Conservative supporters' experience . . . although in the 80's the Conservatives seemed to promise a classless society of opportunity, the reality is now that the rich are getting richer on the backs of the rest, who are getting poorer. . . . [on education] talk of competition, budgets, management etc. triggers negative perceptions of treating education like a business.

The legacy of Thatcher's imperial approach to leadership had combined with Major's relative indulgence of his ministers to give the image that the Conservatives routinely took liberties with propriety. In this regard, John Major dodged a potentially lethal bullet in February 1996 through deft finessing of the Scott report. The report represented the results of a lengthy study into a complex case. This investigation centered on the deception of Parliament, the courts, and the public over ministers' and officials' complicity in sales of arms to Iraq at variance with the Conservatives' stated policy. While blaming the government for misleading Parliament, the report cleared ministers of "duplicitous intention." This let two ministers—William Waldegrave, the Treasury chief secretary, and Sir Nicholas Lyell, the attorney general—off the hook.

Knowledgeable observers could see the velvet glove of the cabinet secretary, Sir Robin Butler, in Major's handling of the report. The government negotiated an arrangement whereby Sir Richard Scott gave the government the final draft of the report eight days before its release. However, the government allowed representatives of the opposition only three hours to preview the report on the day of its publication (Peston 17/18 February 1996). Sir Robin had already headed off official dissent from the report by instituting complex procedures for whistle blowers (Burns and Kampfner 10 February 1996).

The government had stiffly lobbied Sir Richard to ease up on direct criticism of ministers after a series of leaks in summer 1995. These had proven especially critical of Waldegrave. In the end, the government successfully sanitized the report and then held it to its vest while it spin-doctored the remaining embarrassing bits. In the words of Sir Teddy Taylor, an oft rebellious Tory, it got a report which said: "You were seen throwing a brick through a window, I have a photograph to prove you threw a brick through a window, but you didn't realize it was a brick or a window" (Peston 17/18 February 1996).

The incident points up the degree to which Major had become a pre-emptive survivor. Major tended when backed into a corner to devise nifty ways of escaping. He did this late in 1994 when a rebellion of Euro-skeptics threatened him with defeat over the British contribution to the European budget. Major first made it clear to Tory rebels that he would seek a general election if he lost the vote. Then, when some re-calcitrants remained, he "lifted the party whip from them"—that is, expunged them from the party rolls. This put the members in a limbo from which they could not effectively participate in any impending leadership challenge. The most brilliant use of preemptive survivalism was Major's June 1995 temporary resignation as leader. Coming as a complete surprise, this move left the Conservatives staring at the depth of their divisions and the unlikelihood of their resolving these under any of Major's potential successors.

Bringing Chaos to Whitehall

Margaret Thatcher had palpably personalized leadership in the mandarinate. As well, her view of government had signaled to many young officials that their futures lay within the private sector. She provoked a veritable hemorrhage of the best and brightest in the mid-1980s—an occurrence which depended substantially on the confluence of her attitude toward Whitehall and the unprecedented expansion of London's financial district.

With regard to management reform in Whitehall it is important to remember that, while John Major's ministers were still in their political diapers, Sir Keith Joseph and Margaret Thatcher imbibed their neo-liberalism under the tutelage of William Niskanen (1973b). When she formed her first government in 1979, Thatcher even encouraged her newly appointed cabinet to read Niskanen. But her actual rendering of Niskanen's ideas about bureaucracy really unfolded in a highly iterative way. That is, it was essentially pragmatic. It began with Sir Derek Rayner's scrutinies. In retrospect, these amounted to relatively modest efforts to identify areas of government which might benefit from the application of private-sector management techniques.

Scrutinies ultimately led to the Financial Management Initiative (FMI). FMI relied at least as much upon public servants—especially those who had worked closely with scrutinies—who sought to generalize the benefits of a managerial approach as it did on political leadership. The initiative enjoyed the strong patronage of Thatcher and some sympathetic ministers—especially Michael Heseltine. At first blush, the initiative that followed FMI, Next Steps, might have seemed a departure from the gradualism that prevailed during the Thatcher years. However, even though Next Steps sought to reduce the number of civil servants in conventional departments by half, it fell short of radicalism. Next Steps' functions still fitted within the compass of government services. And the employees of executive agencies still belonged to the civil service.

Returning for a set of interviews in summer 1993, I found profound disillusionment over the directions that management reform had taken under the Major government. The political leadership had become almost evangelical in its belief that they could build-down government much further and make the surviving parts run like Marks and Spencer.

The period of build-down might well have spelled the end of budget-maximizing bureaucrats in line departments. But clout-maximizing offices abounded in the center. The Efficiency Unit—attached to No. 10—had gone from an elite corps of six to an increasingly bureaucratized operation of fifteen. It shouldered responsibility for the government's market-testing initiative. In 1993, it was in the process of forcing (not too strong a word) departments to come up with 1.5 billion pounds worth of business that could be given out to tender.

After the 1992 election, Major created a new agency—the Office for the Public Service and Science (OPSS), with its own cabinet member—which would shoulder responsibility for the continuation of the Next Steps process and the Citizens' Charter. The latter had evolved from the government's rhetoric about providing fewer but higher quality services to the public.

Major put William Waldegrave—who was coming off an unhappy encounter as health secretary—in charge of this organization. Anxious to recoup from an accident-prone outing in the Health Department, Waldegrave seized the opportunity to take the reins of the reinventing-government bandwagon. Within OPSS, the bureaucratization of the Next Steps and Citizens' Charter initiatives had grown apace with similar developments in the Efficiency Unit. The government replaced Peter Kemp—the very unconventional second permanent secretary who had masterminded the implementation of Next Steps—with a tried and true mandarin—Richard Mottram, from the Ministry of Defence.

Meanwhile, the Treasury energetically pressed the view that privatization need not restrict itself to state-owned corporations. It could extend to government operational units, especially those already functioning as executive agencies. This view crystallized by late 1993 into an initiative seeking to privatize most Next Steps agencies. And the Department of Trade and Industry—then under the leadership of Michael Heseltine, the president of the Board of Trade—advanced a vigorous deregulation initiative. Building-down government had become a growth industry. Ministers and officials at the center busily vied for a piece of the action.

While the proliferation of management initiatives proved great sport for central agencies, officials in line departments had to face an increasingly uncertain world. Each initiative meant huge investments in terms of institutional adjustment. And officials frequently reported being buffeted by the crosswinds of inconsistent goals. Many officials noted what struck them as logical inconsistencies between Next Steps and the new initiatives. A line department official with policy responsibilities for programs actually run by executive agencies described especially well the bind in which chief executives found themselves. According to the inspiration behind Next Steps, chief executives were given a mandate to achieve excellence in their organizations by emphasizing teamwork and flexibility. However, the official viewed the new initiatives as impinging upon these mandates by reintroducing micromanagement from the center. He cited the widespread expectation regarding market testing that it will relentlessly ratchet down chief executives' discretion:

> . . . they feel that the department is now beating them about the ears saying "You must make a contribution to the market testing program and therefore you must find something to put to tender." The agency says: "Look, I'm supposed to be managing this organization. If I thought there was anything else to market test I would market test it, believe me! I'm not interested in adding figures to programs to show to Peter Levene [the head of the No. 10 Efficiency Unit]" (1993 interview).

The same official employed such terms as "firm if not doctrinaire," "management ideology," and "little holy doctrine" to convey the belief in Whitehall that the government's perspective on reform had become driven by ideology rather than a coherent management theory.

Nobody expressed these sentiments better than one official assessing reform from the standpoint of a central agency with a key role in the process. This official observed that in New Zealand, reformers had put in place an entire theoretical apparatus—based on public choice and principal/agent theory—which then served as a point of reference for various management initiatives. In the United Kingdom, iterations in the reform process, the respondent believed, had not taken root in a logically coherent theory:

> . . . people at the top, actually, are very interested in the process of how you manage organizations and are quite keen to do something . . . the striking point between us and New Zealand . . . is if you ask people in this country to have a discussion with you about the application of principal/agent theory to their organizations they'll sort of say "What?" If you ask them, "What do you think you about Next Steps?" they'll probably say, "Well that's quite a good idea." So, it's not at all clear what's the intellectual and theoretical basis for what's being done. Moreover . . . we've actually got a whole series of things all mixed up together and being presented as though they are a single whole. . . . If you've got half-an-hour or an hour, I can do it for you. I do it all the time. But the cleverer people who I do this to often say, "That's an elegant ex post facto rationalization" (1993 interview).

The wave of initiatives washing over Whitehall after the 1992 election thus departed from the Thatcher era in two respects. First, they emerged from a context of multiple ideological entrepreneurship. As noted earlier, Major operated a seriously fragmented administration. Further, the political brokerage necessary to sustain him in power placed ideologues in positions of exceptional power. Second, the symbiosis between Whitehall managerialists and the government began to break down. Under Thatcher, the public service—despite a great deal of pain—gradually repositioned itself so it could pursue more managerial approaches. With multiple ideological entrepreneurship under Major, a sense of betrayal and confusion permeated all levels of the public service.

The effects of hyperexperimentalism concerning the public service and the boundary between it and the private sector revealed themselves as highly corrosive in several regards. Security of tenure had become a thing of the past. Increasingly, officials took the safe route. Many got out of the public service well before the normal retirement age, while they could still cash in on their connections. In 1994, for instance, four times as many public servants left Whitehall to join consultancies as did four years earlier (Hencke 13 February 1995). Late in 1993, Sir Robin Butler boasted to MPs that 500 of the top 626 civil servants in place in 1988 had left Whitehall (Hencke 24 November 1993). One in four of these had received inducements or pressure to go.

Those staying in the public service had to adjust to more than managerial experimentation. The codes which governed relations between ministers and officials almost completely eroded. Ministers commonly dodge responsibility even when things went grievously wrong in their departments. The case of arms sales to Iraqis discussed before serves as an instance of this taking place in connection with key policies of a government. Long before Sir Richard Scott finally submitted his report, the association of senior civil servants had cited the events surrounding the sale as justification for a new code of ethics in Whitehall (Norton-Taylor 16 November 1993). The association believed that ministers had become far too used to passing the buck. This pattern even provoked a now-renowned instance of a senior official balking at the wishes of his minister (Hencke 19 January 1994). Sir Tim Lankester, then the permanent secretary in charge of the Overseas Development Agency, refused in 1991 to endorse a government scheme to provide 234 million pounds for an uneconomical hydroelectric power plant in Malaysia. Sir Tim asserted that the funds constituted a bribe to the Malaysians for defense and trade orders. Major himself overruled Sir Tim. This left matters to the High Court, which ruled the use of public funds for the project illegal and economically unsound (White, Black, and Norton-Taylor 12 November 1994). However, Sir Tim's actions telegraphed an important development. Whitehall officials had become chary of situations where they might become scapegoats.

In the latter days of the Major government, accounts of questionable actions and decisions on the part of agents of the government appeared almost daily in the newspapers. In December 1995, for instance, the *Financial Times* gave a great deal of play to a case in which the regulator for the National Lottery had taken free flights from an American firm belonging to the consortium which ran the lottery on contract for the government (Kampfner 13 December 1995).

One week later, the paper covered the issues raised when the government sold the first rail franchise—South West Trains—to Stagecoach (Batchelor and Parker 20 December 1995). The company had become subject to more than twenty competition inquiries since its inception during the privatization of bus services in the mid-1980s.

Indeed, early in 1996, the government was wringing its hands over what to do about the financial liabilities of two candidates for privatization—the organization that provided atomic power to electricity companies and that which built and serviced the rails that newly privatized train lines would use. In each case, the Treasury was blocking progress toward privatization by pressing for stricter terms for financial liabilities than were believed viable for an attractive sell-off. The government had finally twigged on the fact that it had indeed sold off the family silver at a discount in previous privatizations. The *Financial Times* quoted a minister as observing: "We have heard these arguments a million times before. Every time a company approaches privatization, it complains that its viability will be jeopardized if we don't cut the debt. Then hey presto, after privatization they slash their workforces and the profits go through the roof" (Peston 14 February 1996).

Major, Cabinet, and Multiple Ideological Entrepreneurship

Early accounts of Major's handling of cabinet glowed. Ever conscious of his humble origins, the self-effacing prime minister started his first cabinet meeting by musing, "Who would have believed it" (Brown 17 December 1990). He ran notably relaxed deliberations. His consultative solicitousness extended even to backbenchers. In an early decision, he reversed himself and extended special assistance to AIDS-infected he-

mophiliacs but not without first informing Tory MPs. By all appear-
ances, his concept of the "club" extended to his noncabinet parliamentary colleagues. One member of cabinet explained the contrast with
Thatcher in exuberant terms (Hennessy 21 January 1991). He noted that
Major in cabinet sessions "sums up, but he doesn't prejudice the question, so that changes discussion." When proposals required special
preparation, Major was resorting much more to standing cabinet committees than had Thatcher.

Prime ministers might find ultimately that—no matter how sincere
their personal commitment to a consultative style—events soon press in
to the point where this style no longer is viable. Major, however, took
pains to maintain cabinet dynamics. For instance, he received very high
marks for his negotiating a compromise on the extremely unpopular local rate, called the poll tax, through cabinet—consulting earlier and more
often than Thatcher would have, allowing for genuine exchanges between ministers in cabinet meetings, and concluding agreements and
sticking to them (Bevins 7 May 1991). Indeed, Major received the im-
primatur of the most flattering source imaginable. A 1992 profile of Sir
Robin Butler—secretary of the cabinet and head of the civil service—
claimed that he derived satisfaction from Major's restoration of "the
club" and "genuine collective discussion" in cabinet (Editorial, *The Independent* 7 March 92). Major's style truly had struck a chord in some
important circles if the chief mandarin had registered pleasure with his
consensuality.

Consultativeness notwithstanding, the further Major got into his
primeministership, the more it appeared that his variant of an "executive" style saw his administration become paralyzed in the face of seemingly intractable problems. Until fall 1992, the government's inability
to ease the immense burden of interest rates loomed in many observers'
minds as an especially serious case of indecision. When Major appointed
Norman Lamont as his chancellor, some commentators asked out loud
whether Lamont would devise his own policies (Editorial, *The Independent* 4 January 1992), or would he simply follow those that had been
enshrined by the new prime minister while he was chancellor?

Interestingly, several respondents spoke of the prime minister as
someone whose Whitehall personality development had arrested when
he was chancellor of the exchequer. One official even noted that his experience in cabinet had—as well as being short—never really exposed
him to the side of Whitehall that thinks "policy":

... the prime minister instinctively is a Treasury man ... first of all, because he's cautious. Secondly, because his experience has been so strongly in the Treasury and the Department of Social Security—which is a revenue-raising and has to be very careful with money because the figures are so big. So Social Security is Treasury-minded in a way too. And his experience basically was there, not in the Home Office, Department of Environment, Foreign Office—although he was there briefly—which are departments which don't so much think numbers and cash. They think policy issues without cash. He's a banker. So, for all those reasons, I think he's instinctively a Treasury sort of man (1993 interview).

Major's bias toward the Treasury revealed itself in the way in which the expenditure review process ran during his administration. The government acted immediately after the 1992 election to revamp the Public Expenditure Survey process so as to provide a mechanism for making the tough choices that it would now have to face. The cabinet agreed to a tight public spending total for the year 1993–94. The government then used a new cabinet-level committee—EDX—to work on the details whereby individual departments would come in line with the 1993–94 targets. The chancellor—through most of the 1992 PES round, Norman Lamont—chaired EDX. This feature distinguished the committee from the former Star Chamber. The latter had worked the greatest effects when chaired by William Whitelaw—a Conservative Party eminence grise who served Thatcher as home secretary and government leader in the House of Commons.

Many officials observed that under this new format departments found themselves at the mercy of the General Expenditure Division of the Treasury—the part which deals with aggregate budget figures and reconciles these with the overarching fiscal framework—and the types of briefs that they put forward to the committee. Departments felt especially vulnerable if they lacked a minister on EDX with some experience with the matters that concerned them. Also, due to the relatively closed nature of the process, departments found it very difficult to discover what types of submissions were being made by one another. One observer—a principal financial officer—conveyed the sense of flying blind which prevailed in some departments:

> I wouldn't have described it as a Rolls Royce operation last year. I mean there was a sense of people making up the rules as they went along. . . . In a sense, on the part of some departments there was a feeling that it was all a bit mysterious, although people knew EDX existed, those de-

partments didn't really know what was going on in it always, as fully as they would have liked to have done (1993 interview).

An especially pronounced schizophrenia emerged in the Treasury as Kenneth Clarke—the chancellor after Norman Lamont's departure from cabinet in fall 1992—and Michael Portillo—chief secretary from summer 1992 to summer 1994—began to draw their battle lines. Portillo took an expansive view of his role in cabinet. He eventually strayed far beyond the usual mandate of a chief secretary. Although entitling one to membership in cabinet, the post still enjoys only secondary standing in H. M. Treasury itself. Chief secretaries, including John Major himself who filled the position from 1987 to 1989, normally have preferred to work quietly behind the scenes. Portillo, on the other hand, began to use his position as a bully pulpit for pressing his leadership of the Conservative right. On occasion, he seemed to lose a wheel here and there—sounding like a British Newt Gingrich. For instance, in a January 1994 speech to the right-wing Way Forward group he railed against the media, church, professions, and academics for promoting subversive assaults on British institutions: "The disease shows itself in a readiness to denigrate our country and praise others; to devalue our achievements and envy others; to hold our national institutions in contempt . . . to deride every one of our national figures" (Bates 15 January 1994). The chief secretary might well have included the chancellor in his critique. The latter continued to seek the high ground for his party by becoming the principal spokesman for the social market. He pressed for a mixture of "American enterprise and free market efficiency with European commitments to the welfare state" (Hutton, Kelly, and White 5 May 1994).

The "Vision" Becomes a Mirage

Major's rise to the top of politics—notwithstanding the difficulties encountered by his family during his childhood and his lack of academic achievement—played very strongly on his psyche. While selling his Citizens' Charter in 1991, Major frequently reminded voters of his humble origins. Some of his speeches shamelessly played on the voters' heart strings. For instance, in his speech to the 1991 annual party conference, Major made the connection between the Conservative's pursuit of greater choice in services and his resolve not to abandon the less advantaged:

> I know how they feel—I know what it's like for a family when a business collapses. What it's like when you're unemployed and when you have to search for the next job. I haven't forgotten—and I never will.

Indeed, Major's past and rise to the top played mightily in his adoption of the Citizens' Charter view of governance—the belief that public services have cheated average citizens of the type of choice and value-for-money that they require to advance their lives. To Major, ordinary Britons find themselves trying to climb their way up a ladder of life. Government services should encourage and facilitate this process. They should no longer sustain situations which do not promote individual enterprise and resourcefulness. In the language employed in his March 27, 1992 interview with Peter Jenkins and utilized in his first postelection speech to Parliament, Major saw no barriers for those who set their sights on the top:

> Let me tell you what I mean by the classless society and a society of opportunity. What I mean is that people from wherever they start can achieve by their own efforts whatever it is in them to achieve. That there is a ladder of opportunity they can climb and that there are incentives on that ladder, not penalties. And the artificial distinction between the value we put on the work of the blue-collar worker and that of the white-collar worker, I think they are old fashioned, old hat and socially and economically damaging. . . . I want everybody to have the same chances and opportunities.

We cannot fully understand the tremendous investment made by the Conservatives in the Citizens' Charter concept without taking into account the role of Chris Patten in developing Major's message in the build-up to the 1992 election. As noted earlier, Patten lost his bid for reelection in 1992 and became governor of Hong Kong. He had assumed the chairmanship of the Conservative Party when Major became prime minister in 1990. A practicing Roman Catholic, he maintained an almost continental notion of society, which viewed citizens' fortunes as organically interconnected. Patten saw the future of the party as balancing Thatcher's advances with the restoration of market forces in various sectors of the economy with a greater sense of social cohesiveness (Jenkins 14 February 1991). The Conservative Party would follow the lead of the Christian Democrats in Germany and maintain its appeal by promotion of the "social market"—a combination of neo-liberalism and sensitivity to the needs of the average citizen. By early 1991, Major was beginning to echo Patten (Bevins 13 March 1991). Patten had come out with this un-Thatcherite pronouncement: "People . . . express their individualism best in groups larger than themselves . . . family . . . church . . . club . . . school . . . the collective, the social is important to working out of your individuality." Major followed in the same vein: "The individual achieves his or her full identity in families, clubs, in schools, in churches, in enterprises, in public service."

We see, thus, the intellectual origins of the Citizens' Charter. We still have to account for three things. First, the pragmatism of British politics since the late 1970s does not readily accommodate organic views of society. Second, when Patten left the government, Major lacked an intellectual guiding light—no matter what his personal commitment to the social market. Third, even with Patten present in the government, Major never achieved a level of "executive" leadership that would provide an effective gearbox for implementation of an initiative of these proportions. Put simply, the Citizens' Charter amounted to a brilliantly crafted campaign slogan and little more.

One key No. 10 official gave high praise to Chris Patten for his role in developing the Conservative manifesto for the 1992 election and in giving intellectual thrust to the Citizens' Charter. She also pointed up that Patten's failure to win a seat in 1992 and his departure for the governorship of Hong Kong left a vacuum: "He was hugely important in the whole manifesto process and I think that's the best way to describe his input. He also was a strategic policy voice in cabinet, which was enormously useful . . . so there is that gap" (1993 interview).

The loss of its intellectual beacon led to a situation—as noted previously—in which some ministers pursued idiosyncratic views of Christian Democracy. Such ministers tended to canonize markets and neglect almost entirely the social costs of government disengagement from service provision. By construing the remaining government operations as "businesses" and styling citizens as "customers" they served up a brand of Christian Democracy which denied almost completely the "social" dimension to social markets.

Under the leadership of Sara Hogg through most of his primeministership, John Major's Policy Unit attempted to adapt its missions to the exigencies of the new administration and its prime minister's style. Regarding the challenges faced by the government, the unit believed that it should connect itself more vitally to immediate policy development— the preparation of the election manifesto gave focus to this activity. With respect to Major's style, the manifesto attempted to complement his own consultative approach.

In operational departments, respondents did not leave me with the impression that the prime minister's nonconfrontational style actually added up to a lower profile for the Policy Unit. This conclusion certainly applied in the two areas the unit had singled out for close attention—matters concerning Europe and the inculcation of the Citizens' Charter in Whitehall. However, like Thatcher's Policy Unit, Major's appeared to extend to review of policy initiatives or expenditure proposals which required special handling in the center.

Officials, thus, still found it essential to have the Policy Unit on-side when dealing with issues that might encounter difficulty with Treasury or other departments. Unlike the case of Thatcher's Policy Unit, I did find occasionally the suggestion that Major engaged himself less in issues than did his predecessor. As one official noted, the view had emerged that the Policy Unit was expressing views on behalf of the prime minister without his giving them deep consideration:

> . . . in the early years of Mr. Major's primeministership, and throughout last year, it was said that a lot of the letters that emerged from No. 10 said the prime minister had agreed to this and that with the matter not actually being very close to the prime minister but with it having been run through the policy unit instead. They were rather stamping things or not on his behalf (1993 interview).

Such assessments raise an interesting question. Did the seeming continued interventionism of the Policy Unit in the case of Major simply reflect an effort to compensate for the prime minister's passive leadership style? One Policy Unit official suggested as much when noting that Major had returned the United Kingdom to a nonhierarchical form of cabinet government and then observing that the prime minister tended to go with the flow:

> . . . the way departments engage with the center can be much more open and fluid than in a strictly hierarchical system of government with a heavy center and weaker departments. The more I've been here, the clearer it's come to me that cabinet government is a reality; let's say that the power of departments and departmental ministers is strong . . . this is a huge plus in the system because it creates a plurality at the center of government that is vital. I should perhaps add that this is the way this prime minister, in particular, liked to work and it very much places weight on

the views of his cabinet colleagues. He's a conciliator and therefore goes with the grain of the system of cabinet government, rather than against it (1993 interview).

Major wanted above all a nonconfrontational government. However, especially after the 1992 election, he so prized peace that he invited into his ministry views which clashed strongly. Further, he inadequately engaged himself in the process of developing policy issues. The result: a cacophony of voices and little capacity for resolution of disputes. These circumstances placed the Policy Unit in the unenviable position of attempting to fill the gap.

CONCLUSION

The U.K. system operates under substantially more favorable conditions for coherence and consistency than does the United States. No system can produce more harmony than the society upon which it is based can sustain. Thus it is questionable whether efforts to maintain the level of cohesion found in the United Kingdom would succeed in the United States. The United Kingdom is a unitary political system with relative societal homogeneity. Further, Britons share different views of governance from those which have prevailed in the United States. The separation of powers and the federal system reinforce the conscious American preference for structures which err on the side of individual and local rights. We hear much these days about the dysfunctions of "divided government" in the United States. However, it is extremely doubtful that Americans would take their governance any other way.

Even among the other Anglo-American systems that have parliamentary forms of government, the British system normally reveals itself as more capable of cohesiveness than either Canada or Australia. We can say this not only because these two systems are federal. As well, they have tended to be more experimental than the British system. This has included a willingness to adapt certain features of American governance to their systems.

This chapter has given special consideration to the experience of the Whitehall model in the United Kingdom under the leadership of Thatcher and Major. It has found that neo-liberalism can prove to be as self-deluding and replete with unintended consequences as the highly interventionist view of governance which prevailed through much of the

1960s and 1970s. Often the appearance of success which graced neo-liberalism until a few years ago rested on leaders' distortions of the circumstances which prevailed when they first rose to power. We have noted, for instance, that the seeds for more disciplined governance were first planted by Labour prime ministers. Indeed, the Winter of Discontent—for which Labour is still maligned—originated in the innate fiscal caution of James Callaghan.

Thatcher started out as a prime minister with the personal resources—especially toughness—which would have enabled her to revolutionize the way in which Whitehall did business. But three defects ultimately became drags on her performance. First, she tended to engage herself excessively with issues which had risen to a boil—with neglect of others that, though less controversial, still required some attention. Second, she tended toward monocratic governance—paying little heed to the conventions of cabinet government. Third, she let her successes go to her head—substituting leadership for solidification of her status as a national icon.

Thatcher's legacy left John Major in a perilous situation. The luster began to wear off neo-liberalism just as he took office. But his party could still invoke the ghosts of winters past to scare the public into giving Major a mandate of his own. Major would have liked the public to believe that he was defining a new form of neo-liberalism. In fact, he just wanted to appear amiable as his government pursued essentially the same agenda for building-down the state defined by Thatcherism. Indeed, his passive leadership style provided just the context in which radical proponents of Thatcherism could thrive in his own cabinet. Until the 1992 election, Chris Patten helped Major employ the continental concept of social market to provide a veneer of humanity to his appeal. When Patten left for Hong Kong, Major faced three main problems. First, how could he get himself out from under the shadow of Thatcher the icon? Second, how long could he conceal from the public the fact that Thatcherism with a smile is still Thatcherism? Third, how could he do all of this while trying to play a more positive role as a principal in European Union dynamics than that sought by Thatcher?

We have found in this chapter a great deal of erosion in Whitehall's putative reputation for policy coherence and cohesion. True collective decision making developed only very gradually in the United Kingdom. It probably reached its height in the 1950s and 1960s. Prime ministers have compensated for the weakening of collective government by adding to the coordinative apparatus at the center. Heath's creation of the Central Policy Review Staff fit within this pattern—although CPRS divided its loyalty between prime ministers and general service to cabinets. Thatcher's abolition of CPRS and enhancement of the No. 10 Policy Unit institutionalized primeministerial latitude in imposing coherence and consistency from above.

Major's Policy Unit operated less imperially than Thatcher's. However, other dimensions of the Thatcher legacy remained. Thus Whitehall functioned in a significantly less consultative manner than it did before Thatcher. Major found it difficult to resuscitate cabinet dynamics, the public service only very slowly would recover from eleven years of command leadership which stifled even constructive criticism, H. M. Treasury positioned itself as the linchpin for all that happened in Whitehall, Next Steps reenshrined the principle that true mandarins need not get their hands dirty, and various ideological entrepreneurs busied themselves picking the remains of the operational side of Whitehall.

5

Trudeau, Mulroney, Chrétien, and the Rise and Fall of Personalized Leadership

Running through the complex of relationships connecting the head of government and state functions in all Westminster governments we find the impact of electronics. Before television, prime ministers were largely gray men in gray suits. Their public personas normally did not evoke much more than an aura of overexposure to the often stuffy confines of parliamentary debate and bureaucratic machinations. The monarchs provided the bulk of glamour for the political system. For Canada, carefully staged tours allowed the monarchy to ooze as a glue for the system—the Anglophone part, at least.

The presidency of John F. Kennedy jolted Canadians from their lethargic response to the rise of electronic politics. John Diefenbaker had transformed his minority government of 1957 into an overwhelming majority in 1958. However, he failed to retain a majority in 1962 and yielded power in 1963. In a 1965 election Diefenbaker's Liberal successor, Lester B. Pearson, again faced formation of a government without a majority. Many attributed Pearson's problems to his lackluster style. Having served as leader of the Liberals since 1958, Pearson appeared in the elections of 1962 and 1963 as a poor man's John F. Kennedy. His policies struck a chord in the emerging liberal era. However, his persona fell far short of the charisma required to mobilize voters in campaigns now driven by television. As a young man, Pearson had taught at the University of Toronto. He then had pursued a diplomatic career which culminated in his receipt of the Nobel Peace Prize. No doubt a charming adornment for any dinner party, Pearson came across as wry and fumbling on television (he also spoke with a lisp). It is an excusable exaggeration to say that Pearson's style put the Liberals in the position of coping in a Kennedy-era of politics with a Warren Christopher as leader and then prime minister.

Fortunately for Canada, substance still meant more than style in executive-bureaucratic politics. Even though he toiled under minority governments, Pearson called upon his institutional bona fides with the Liberal Party and the bureaucracy to achieve an astounding degree of policy competence. Since the end of the WWII, the federal Liberals had strived to gradually advance social legislation and work toward greater national coherence. Pearson's stances and activities pushed this two-fold mission forward astoundingly considering that he held the primeministership for only five years and never attained a majority. His most important accomplishments included creating the national universal health care system administered by the provinces, successfully negotiating the very tricky waters whereby the Maple Leaf Flag replaced the British Red Ensign, and installing bicultural and bilingual policies which gave recognition to Canada's French society nationwide and not just in Quebec.

There have been six prime ministers since Lester Pearson left office in 1968. Three of these served only briefly, Joe Clark from 1979 to 1980, John Turner in 1984, and Kim Campbell in 1993. Clark and Campbell were Progressive Conservatives. Turner and Campbell proved to be transitional figures incapable of reversing the clear animosity toward their predecessor so that their party might maintain control. The three remaining prime ministers, Pierre Elliott Trudeau (1968–79, 1980–84), Brian Mulroney (1984–93), and Jean Chrétien (1993 to present), each ruled with majority governments (Trudeau headed a minority government from 1972 to 1974).

The bulk of the analysis in this chapter focuses on Trudeau (especially after returning to office in 1980), Mulroney, and Chrétien. Two of these figures, Trudeau and Mulroney, based their appeal on strongly personalized leadership. We will see, of course, that each pursued this approach in quite different ways. While focusing on Trudeau, Mulroney, and Chrétien, the chapter weaves in accounts of what occurred under Clark, Turner, or Campbell which might have had an impact on a subsequent primeministership. Before looking at individual prime ministers, however, we will examine the characteristics of the Canadian system which either advanced or hindered personalized approaches to leadership.

THE APPARATUS: NEITHER WHITEHALL NOR WASHINGTON?

As noted, in Canada executive-bureaucratic politics displayed a greater degree of immunity from personalized approaches than in the United States. However, Canada did succumb. Further, it is significant that it did so earlier and, eventually, more deeply than the United Kingdom. We might be tempted to conclude that this owed to the greater proximity of Canada to the United States and the effects of the constant drumbeat of personalized politics south of the forty-ninth parallel. A better, although not entirely different, explanation suggests itself. That is, the Canadian executive-bureaucratic system has evolved from the Whitehall format but with an unavoidable awareness of how Washington goes about its business. It has become a hybrid of the Whitehall and Washington systems. Thus some of the Canadian response to the electronic era has followed fairly deeply ingrained and predictable contours associated with its specific variant of executive-bureaucratic politics.

Personalized leadership can impinge on a government's capacity for policy competence in two ways. Most obviously, the chief executive can pursue such an unvarnished form of partisan responsiveness that he or she telegraphs a disdain for the standing apparatus, thereby prompting conditions whereby it becomes impossible to creatively engage it. This is essentially what Mulroney did. And, in this regard, he very much followed the example of his role model Ronald Reagan.

The second form of personalized leadership is more subtle. The chief executive chooses to engage the state apparatus. However, he or she embarks upon strategies designed to make the apparatus more responsive. These can involve something as simple as a high degree of selectivity in the parts of the apparatus that the chief executive engages. More profoundly, such tactics can involve efforts to reshape the bureaucracy into something which better reflects the personal preferences and agenda of the leader. Trudeau imbibed this type of personalization. He worked an exceedingly strong influence on the selection of the occupants of the highest positions in the public service. This practice reached the point where occupants of the top jobs in the permanent bureaucracy became scarcely distinguishable in their world view and priorities from the political leadership. Trudeau also reshaped the bureaucracy toward his highly rationalistic approach to complex organizations. Especially notable here was the creation of new departments and central coordinating agencies whose role it was to short-circuit the standard operating procedures of the existing bureaucratic organizations. We will see that in many respects Trudeau engaged the state apparatus but only after it had taken on the characteristics of *designer* neutral competence, that is, it had taken on his own image and likeness.

Canada as a Hybrid System

WHITEHALL A LA WASHINGTON?

Americans frequently hear their politicians say that they live in the best country in the world. Canadian politicians would rarely say such a thing. Even if they did live in the world's best country, Canadians would be too modest and cautious to draw attention to the fact.

Many Canadians thought in the immediate postwar decades that they had the best public service in the world. They believed it to have combined the best of the Whitehall tradition, with its emphasis on neutral competence, and the open, "can do" mentality of a young, energetic, and expansive society. In some respects, hybridization took on mythical proportions. However, Canadians saw it as emanating internally and, therefore, not stemming from American influences.

To be sure, one finds the elements of a British, even elitist, connection between the upper echelons of the Canadian public service and the Whitehall model. Before WWII, most recruits to the upper levels of the bureaucracy came from reasonably distinguished families (Granatstein 1982). Most had completed their undergraduate degrees at the University of Toronto, Queens University, or McGill University, which to this day draw the upper crust of Anglophone students in central Canada. A very high proportion of those who rose to the level of deputy minister had studied at Oxford as Rhodes Scholars. The entire cadre of senior professional officials was very small. Thus aspirants to positions normally had to bide their time until vacancies emerged. Ostensibly, all of this adds up to a nascent bureaucratic culture which might fool the observer into thinking that Whitehall was replicating itself on the banks of the Rideau River.

Notwithstanding obvious similarities with the upper levels of the British civil service, even the staid Canadian mandarinate of the middle part of this century differed in very substantial ways from its Whitehall counterpart. Few stopped their education after finishing at Oxford. Most topped off with MAs or PhDs at universities in the United States. For the most part, they studied economics or political science. Many who could not find a position in government immediately after completion of their education spent time teaching in a Canadian university. Here Queens University developed the strongest pipeline into the mandarinate—both for its young faculty and students—especially into the Finance Department, which emerged in the 1930s as the real power within the bureaucracy (Porter 1965, 425–428).

All of this changed radically during the 1960s and early 1970s. The rapid expansion of government made it no longer possible for the mandarinate to run on a trickle of former Rhodes Scholars with acceptable social origins. A large number of the new entrants were coming to government after working in the private sector. Several even brought with them the dreaded MBA. In a survey of nearly all senior officials in 1967, P. J. Chartrand and K. L. Pond discovered that even by that year elite Canadian universities had lost their grip on the ranks of the mandarinate (1970). To be sure, the graduates of the University of Toronto accounted for 22% of the top officials. After that, however, three Western Canadian universities—Manitoba, British Columbia, and Alberta—all produced greater proportions of the mandarins than either Queens or McGill.

In addition to becoming relatively egalitarian in its recruitment and placing a higher value on specialized training, particularly in economics and business, the Canadian mandarinate had departed from the Whitehall model in another important respect. From the time of its emergence as a significant cadre early in this century to the present day, the higher public service in Ottawa has displayed a strong symbiosis with the Liberal Party. We can certainly attribute much of the affinity upon which the relationship has taken root on the domination of Canadian politics exerted by the Liberals through this century. Until Brian Mulroney's lengthy primeministership (1984–93), Conservative governments occurred in officials' careers as mere interludes from a Liberal hegemony. Thus the boundaries between the political leadership and the permanent bureaucracy became relatively porous. Indeed, two Liberal prime ministers—William Lyon MacKenzie King (1921–1926, 1926–1930, 1935–1948) and Lester B. Pearson (1963–1968)—started their careers as public servants.

NO POLITICAL ADVISERS PLEASE WE'RE BRITISH, ER, CANADIAN.

Despite the relative symbiosis between the Liberal Party and the mandarinate, Canadian prime ministers have generally observed a taboo against extensive use of political appointees either in the Prime Minister's Office or ministers' personal staffs. In the United States, presidents have countered the tendency for fragmentation within the executive branch by creating a shadow bureaucracy in the White House. Few prime ministers have even attempted to avail themselves of this approach. And those who have failed pretty abysmally. Canadian ministers want real cabinet government and this desire places a heavy reliance on regularized consultative committees.

Although it lacks a formally prescribed role, the Canadian cabinet has enjoyed since Confederation (1867) full legitimacy based on the preamble to the Constitution Act. This states that Canada will have a "Constitution in Principle similar to that of the United Kingdom." The representational importance of Canadian cabinets, indeed, expands their salience within the system beyond that of cabinet in Westminster. The role derives from colonial precedents. Most clearly, a convention of duality operated at the heart of the Union of Canada under which Quebec and Ontario jointly had been governed since 1840. Here each department had two ministers, one from Canada East (Quebec) and the other from Canada West (Ontario) (Morton 1955, 113–125). As well, each cabinet consisted equally of individuals with French origins and those with British ancestry. The first cabinet under Confederation included five ministers from Ontario and four each from Quebec and the Maritimes. This cabinet's crafters even took care to insure representation of Catholics among the delegations from the predominantly Protestant regions, Ontario and the Maritimes.

We find that the Canadian system combines a historic symbiosis between the Liberal Party and the mandarinate, with exceptional official access to higher-level, executive-bureaucratic gamesmanship. We might ask, then, whether it would make sense for Liberal prime ministers to layer on top of this relatively auspicious foundation a private office meant to maintain the thrust of their government toward their key objectives. Such an approach might amount to killing the goose that laid the golden egg. On the other hand, Progressive Conservative prime ministers might find it tempting to create an alternate source of advice in their Prime Minister's Office.

The Liberals, in fact, only slowly developed the Prime Minister's Office (PMO). Under MacKenzie King and Louis St. Laurent (1948–1957), the head of the unit was a career civil servant. Pearson took the first steps toward a party-political PMO. However, he chose as heads of his unit individuals who fit well the overarching technocratic culture of Ottawa. As for the PC interlude between St. Laurent and Pearson, Diefenbaker kept most of the assistants in PMO whom he inherited from St. Laurent.

Canada's PMO has not even included one element which has become a permanent part of No. 10 Downing St. in the United Kingdom. Canadian prime ministers have not drawn upon a "private office" of career civil servants whose function it is to keep the prime minister informed of bureaucratic logjams and impending resistance from cabinet colleagues. For this function, Canadian prime ministers have relied upon the Privy Council Office (PCO). The office clerk of the Privy Council received formal recognition in the British North America Act of 1867. The title "secretary to the cabinet" was added in 1940. In that respect, PCO has, indeed, functioned as a cabinet secretariat along the lines of its British equivalent. Especially as the cabinet committee system formalized, PCO began to direct the formation of committees of cabinet and officials. It also frequently took the chair of many subcabinet groups. In addition, however, PCO has viewed itself much more as a resource for the prime minister than has the Cabinet Office in Britain. With the domination of the Liberals throughout PCO's development, we can see how Progressive Conservative governments might suspect the office. PCO's approach to recruitment exacerbates this difficulty. The U. K. Cabinet Office staffs itself mainly with personnel on loan from other Whitehall departments. PCO considers itself a permanent brain trust.

The peculiar folkways of the Canadian executive-bureaucratic complex pose two serious difficulties for prime ministers. First, they must work a delicate balance between inclusion of ministers in decisions—a requirement intensified by the representational imperative impinging upon cabinet's role—and maintaining some capacity for timely and coherent decision making. Second, they must take charge without violating taboos. For Liberals, tapping the normally sympathetic PCO has usually proven a sufficient resource for prime ministers to attain coherence in their approach to governance. For Conservatives, steering of this order has proven more difficult. For both parties, the absence of a strong tradition of party-political policy advice in PMO has made it difficult for prime ministers to set and adapt their policy objectives in such a way that they can sustain a viable level of partisan responsiveness.

TRUDEAU, MULRONEY, AND CHRÉTIEN (WITH THREE INTERLUDES)

Trudeau

Pierre Elliott Trudeau became prime minister in 1968 and—apart from the nine months of the Clark minority government—served until 1984. Trudeau enjoyed the fourth longest tenure of any Canadian prime minister. In this period, Trudeau—about as multiphasic a personality as one can find in a profession which seems to attract the highly multiphasic (Gwyn 1980)—went through several identifiable changes in his approach to the primeministership. However, despite the different phases of Trudeau, a central motif ran through his primeministership. Canadians developed a deep ambivalence to his approach to leadership. For once, they had a leader much more interesting and brighter than any of his contemporaries in the presidency—Trudeau's term overlapped with Johnson, Nixon, Carter, and Reagan. In the age of innocence for electronification of political appeal, Canada claimed one of the most dazzling leaders imaginable.

Trudeau had touched all the bases to rate as a member of Canada's intelligentsia. Trudeau's interests were decidedly academic. He studied under the Jesuits at the exclusive Brebeuf College—a connection which stuck in that critics often styled his behavior as "jesuitical." After graduating from the University of Montreal, he pursued advanced studies at Harvard, Ecole des Sciences Politiques in Paris, and the London School of Economics. Although he practiced law in Montreal, he developed strong ties in the scholarly community and the Francophone elite. He had become an associate professor of law at the University of Montreal. He also had been a cofounder of *Cité Libre*, a review in which many of the debates about the boundary between French national aspirations and continued participation in Canadian federalism played out.

Trudeau did not run for Parliament until 1965. In this respect, he serves as an instance of an "outsider" rising very quickly to political leadership. Lester Pearson appointed Trudeau as justice minister in 1967. He became an overnight sensation—propelled by his ability to stare down antifederalists in Quebec. Trudeau succeeded Pearson as prime minister in 1968. He quickly sought the dissolution of Parliament. The ensuing election restored the Liberals to majority government for the first time in eleven years. In an especially fractious era, Trudeau appeared to have pulled off a miracle.

PIERRE TRUDEAU "SUPERSTAR": 1968–1979

The emergence of Trudeau and his style of leadership provoked in many observers fear of "presidentialization" of the Canadian primeministership (Hockin 1971). It was one thing for Trudeau to break the mold of Canadian leadership by inciting Trudeaumania. It was another matter that he frequently displayed an arrogant contempt of his colleagues in Parliament, the media, and various segments of the public (Stewart 1972; 1973; Radwanski 1978).

Apart from his passionate engagement in the struggle over the destiny of Quebec in Canada, Trudeau betrayed little interest in specific policies. In some respects, he became in his first term a precursor to George Bush's approach to governance. Focus on the really big area, in Bush's case foreign policy and in Trudeau's Quebec, and the rest will take care of itself. Trudeau's detachment from domestic issues not intertwined with Quebec manifested itself in a "let's deal" approach. This infuriated left-of-center Liberals still harboring hopes that the welfare state might further expand.

Trudeau did not like the stuffy equivocation which emanated from former Rhodes Scholars who satisfied themselves that they had become mandarins at Whitehall on the Rideau. He was slow to make his initial moves. However, he clearly preferred the next generation of officials—technocrats with "can do" approaches. In the meantime, Trudeau did what chief executives frequently do in Latin countries when they face intransigent bureaucracy. He created counterbureaucracies. This tack took two forms. First, he presided over a proliferation of ministries, each designed to address clusters of issues which were running hot in the period between 1968 and 1972. He also greatly enhanced the capacity of the Privy Council Office for central guidance and control.

Trudeau scraped by in the election of 1972, but only with a minority government. The result was fairly predictable. The prime minister had alienated several segments of the electorate, even those who had succumbed to Trudeaumania in 1968. Left-leaning Liberals saw little indication that Trudeau would pursue further expansion of the welfare state. Although many had supported his 1970 invocation of the War Measures Act against militant Quebec separatists, they soon developed serious qualms about this action. Middle-of-the-road, English-speaking voters who had swung to the Liberals in sufficient numbers to provide them with a majority government in 1968 now had developed serious second thoughts. Trudeau seemed even less able than Pearson to resolve the constitutional impasse with Quebec. Meanwhile, his government had made a series of concessions to Quebec and Francophones throughout the country, which deeply angered many centrists. As for Quebecois, federalism was fading from fashion. The belief was gaining legitimacy that Quebec's future rested with separation.

While Trudeau did not use the Prime Minister's Office to maintain political thrust in the government, he did mend fences within the Liberal Party. His efforts toward reengaging Senator Keith Davey and Jim Coutts, both former Pearson operatives, proved to be key here. Each had become disaffected during the first Trudeau term. Each, in his own right, was a reciprocal of immense acuity in the machinations of electoral politics. More important, the two loved the challenge and fun of the political chase and worked brilliantly as a team. Trudeau turned his 1974 campaign entirely over to Davey and Coutts—with the former running a one-person war room in Ottawa and the latter managing the prime minister on the campaign trail. The excitement rubbed off. Trudeau, who previously had displayed distaste for Davey and Coutts, became a great admirer. The result was a brilliant campaign which restored the Liberals to majority government.

Once returned to power, the Liberals, although the times hardly recommended the approach, seemed to have adopted a "new order" style. A sense had developed that the party had recaptured its soul in the 1974 election. It would continue with the social democratic agenda with which it had encountered so much frustration striving for under the Pearson and Trudeau minority governments and during the personalization of leadership which prevailed while Trudeaumania held its spell.

Initially, a cabinet-level priorities and planning exercise became the mantra of the government. An elaborate machinery was set up whereby

PMO and PCO officials would then meet with ministers separately to discuss their contributions to the achievement of the government's objectives. Apart from the obvious need to right the economy, the government embraced an ambitious list of innovative social policies such as a guaranteed annual income, abolition of capital punishment, tightening gun control, liberalization of abortion laws, and decriminalization of cannabis. The worsening economy ultimately overtook the priorities exercise.

Two galvanizing exigencies would dominate the government's agenda during the rest of the mandate. The first of these, Quebec's future in Canada, took center stage in November 1976 when the Parti Quebecois won the Quebec provincial elections and formed a separatist government. From that moment until the actual referendum in 1980, with nine months off during the Clark government, a vastly disproportionate amount of Trudeau's energy went into fighting the separatist threat. In this process, Trudeau relied most heavily upon the Federal-Provincial Relations Office—a 1975 offshoot of the Privy Council Office. The second compelling matter related to Canada's burgeoning deficit and its effects on the economy. In the 1978 Group of Seven Economic Summit in Bonn, Helmut Schmidt—Germany's Social Democratic chancellor—had pushed hard the need for advanced democracies to control government spending. Trudeau and Schmidt went on a short sailing holiday after the meetings during which the latter deepened the former's acknowledgment of impending economic danger. Upon his return to Ottawa, Trudeau slashed $2 billion from 1978 allocations without even consulting the finance minister or the president of the Treasury Board. The former, Jean Chrétien, the current prime minister, received a call telling him about the cuts and almost resigned over his not being consulted.

Regarding the two gearbox issues, the third Trudeau mandate saw a relentless personalization both of relations with the bureaucracy and the internal dynamics of the government. In part this owed to the times, which would have forced any leader into bringing the wagons into a circle. However, Trudeau's determination to create a higher public service in his own image and likeness exacerbated the process. Here his 1975 replacement of Gordon Robertson with Michael Pitfield as clerk of the Privy Council and the secretary to the cabinet became the key move. Pitfield—who as a whiz kid encountered Trudeau through the Cité Libre movement—became Trudeau's Anglophone alter ego. As he rose in power, he gained unprecedented control over the government's policy agenda, machinery of government, and selection of senior mandarins.

With respect to the second gearbox, that between a prime minister and his cabinet and party-political advisers, Trudeau became increasingly monocratic as the government approached the end of its mandate. With the failure of ministers to develop and adhere to cogent and coherent strategies, Trudeau began to rely on groups of deputy ministers ringmastered by Michael Pitfield. The first of these, DM-10, planned the implementation of the 1975 Anti-Inflation Program. An even more exclusive group, DM-5, managed its termination. Ministers began to hemorrhage from the government.

An Interlude: Mr. Clark Comes to Ottawa

With the possible exception of Brian Mulroney, no prime minister in the history of the Canadian confederation has assumed office so inexperienced and ill-prepared as Joe Clark. Clark—who had become leader of the Progressive Conservatives (PCs) in 1976—turned forty slightly after becoming prime minister. He had only served in the House of Commons from 1972. Before then, he had helped build up the Alberta PCs and worked for three years as executive assistant to the leader of the opposition in Ottawa.

Clark was not going to make it to the top of his party by being a child prodigy. It would take a long, hard slog. Clark focused on building a network. He tirelessly cultivated a following. Clark's network building put him in good stead in the 1976 PC leadership convention. His positioning did not derive from his being one of the top contenders—Brian Mulroney was one of those enjoying that standing. Rather, the leadership contest had become stalemated. It became clear that the party would have to go to someone to whom deeply entrenched delegates would move in the name of party unity.

The struggle over how far right the PCs should move from the center had made consensus so difficult to achieve in the leadership convention. Try as he may, Joe Clark as leader found it hard to reconcile struggles between the left and right in his party. His fairness counseled that he should arbitrate differences. However, Clark—who never wore his political convictions on his sleeve—still could not disguise the fact that he functioned by reflex as a "pink" Tory. Thus in the prolonged build-up to the election of 1979, Clark did not present himself as a Canadian variant of Margaret Thatcher. Smart money, thus, would have to go to Joe Clark becoming an "executive" prime minister. The actual election result seemed to seal this fate. With a minority government, Clark would have to prove his mettle as chief executive, go to the public for a stronger mandate, and, then, advance to a "let's deal" approach, which might respond more directly to the urgings of the right.

Even though he would not survive as clerk of the Privy Council, Michael Pitfield read perfectly Clark's temperament and situation. Before the May 22 election, Pitfield led the higher public service's preparation of different sets of briefing books, assuming, on the one hand, that the Liberals would retain power, and on the other, that the PCs would win the election and form the next government. The PCO saw the election interval as an opportunity to crystallize some of its ideas for reorganization of cabinet business and the federal bureaucracy. The beginnings of these plans had taken shape under Trudeau in the 1978 creation of a powerful new cabinet committee—the Board of Economic Development Ministers—complete with its own central agency—and the Ministry of State for Economic Development. Each set of briefing books contained bold blueprints for restructuring the entire expenditure review process. Calling upon higher-level game theory, the documents argued that ministers will not identify spending cuts unless they can see tangible results from the economies which they have achieved. The proposed system would divide the budget into expenditure envelopes, eventually ten were created, which would follow wide sectoral lines.

Besides exploiting PCO's window of opportunity for revamping the organization of cabinet and the bureaucracy, Pitfield's sales job essentially sandbagged the government. Rather than hitting the ground running, as the new Thatcher government was doing at precisely the same time in the United Kingdom, the Clark government spent nearly five months before it even convened Parliament. During this period ministers busied themselves not only with the task of learning their portfolios but trying to make their ways through a maze of detours around reengineering sites of both cabinet and its processes. The Clark government fell on December 13 when it failed to win support from the House of Commons for its budget.

I MET THE REAL PIERRE TRUDEAU AND HE WAS A JESUIT, 1980–84

The "J" in this subtitle should perhaps be in lower case. During Trudeau's first run at being prime minister, one frequently saw in the press characterizations of him as "jesuitical." Most authors meant this as a mixed compliment in admiration of the prime minister's immense rational and persuasive abilities which doubtlessly the Jesuits had honed during his years at College Brebeuf in Montreal. When Trudeau returned to power, however, one increasingly saw reference to "jesuitical" in contexts evocative of the original use of the term in the early days of Protestant England when the population feared any member of the Jesuit order as a "... crafty schemer, cunning dissembler; casuist ..." (*Webster's*). To many, Trudeau had become a Jesuit in this sense. And those upon whom he relied for advice with increasing exclusivity—Jim Coutts and Michael Pitfield, both of whom ascended back to the throne in their previous jobs, and Mike Kirby, who took the reincarnated form of Gordon Robertson's successor as secretary to the cabinet for federal-provincial relations—began to take on palpably jesuitical traits.

It was not meant to be this way. Trudeau had announced his planned resignation as Liberal Party leader before the PC's defeat on December 13. The PC's defeat put paid to these plans. The party could not possibly select a new leader and fight a federal campaign before the February 18, 1980 election date. Pledging that he would stay in office for only two years, Trudeau agreed to resume the leadership. Again listening to Keith Davey and Jim Coutts, he devised a campaign strategy that would focus on leadership. Trudeau recognized that in the 1979 election he had dwelt too much on the constitution "rather than about things that were on people's minds" (Trudeau 1993). Clark's fumbling and misfires paved the way for Trudeau to remind the Canadian people that while he was prime minister he had at least provided coherent leadership:

> So I campaigned essentially on the issue of leadership. I said, "It's not enough to be a leader. You have to be a *good* leader. You have to know what you're doing." I attacked Clark—I think, in retrospect, rather unkindly—for acting like a headwaiter with the provinces, because he was trying to do everything that would please the provinces, and I noted that he wasn't even able to produce results by doing this (Trudeau 1993).

The energy crisis dominated much of the debate during the campaign. However, once returned to office, Trudeau focused most of his attention on defeating the Parti Quebecois in the May 1980 referendum. This referendum offered Quebec voters the opportunity of separating from Canada. However, the Parti Quebecois had committed itself to negotiating "sovereignty association" with the rest of Canada. This commitment principally involved a continuance of economic ties. The federal government trounced the Parti Quebecois in the May 1980 ballot. Trudeau misinterpreted this result as carte blanche for forcing upon Quebec a constitutional settlement. He put Mike Kirby to work fleshing out this strategy. Kirby, a systems man with a doctorate in business from Northwestern, would not have bubbled up on anyone's top-hundred list of authorities on the constitution. During the summer, Kirby crafted one of the most cynical documents ever to come under public scrutiny in Canada (it was leaked by the Quebec government just before Trudeau met with the provincial premiers in September). It essentially urged Trudeau to deliberately provoke a deadlocked first ministers meeting so that provincial premiers would appear as opponents of constitutional reform.

Kirby made two miscalculations. The first stemmed from a misunderstanding of British politics. He believed, since Margaret Thatcher retained a strong hold on the U.K. Parliament, that the U. K. government would pass a unilateral constitutional package with dispatch. The second defect was more subtle. Kirby implicitly recognized that, though he deemed unilateral patriation legal, the Canadian Supreme Court might not. Kirby, however, thought that, with rapid passage, the court would not have time to offer its views. Subsequent events would ultimately prove this assumption wrong (Russell 1993, 110–119).

Despite the leaking of the Kirby memo, Trudeau went ahead with the strategy of sabotaging his September meeting with the premiers. He then announced a unilateral patriation package on October 2. Polls indicated overwhelming majorities repudiated this approach. A committee of the British Parliament sided with the provinces in an assessment of the legality of the move. Finally, eight provinces took the matter to the Supreme Court. Meanwhile, Joe Clark managed to tie the House of Commons in knots with successive filibusters. Trudeau ultimately agreed not to press the matter further until the court handed down its opinion. On September 28, 1981, it did so: In strict legal terms the federal government could change the constitution unilaterally; however, such an action would not comport with the constitutional convention that it obtain a "substantial degree" of provincial consent.

In the face of these rebuffs, Trudeau returned to the bargaining table. He reached an accord with all of the provinces but Quebec by November 1981. The process, however, set the stage for continued tension between Quebec and the rest of Canada. The premier of Quebec, Rene Levesque, had made concessions to Trudeau which violated his commitments with the other "gang of eight" premiers who had opposed unilateral patriation most vigorously. The remaining seven premiers then felt free to obtain from the federal government terms which Quebec found offensive. This mutual betrayal defies a definitive apportionment of blame. Yet many separatist Quebecois cite it as ultimate proof that, when push comes to shove, English-speaking Canada will not respect Quebec's special claims even in situations where the latter, ostensibly, tried to work cooperatively with the former. Quebec still remains out of the settlement that the queen signed in April 1982. We will see that this issue has proved a Gordian knot for Brian Mulroney and Jean Chrétien. Trudeau's brinkmanship amounted to a technical victory in one battle. But the war has continued to grip the country in uncertainty.

In his relation with the standing bureaucracy, Trudeau essentially entrusted the management of the public service to Michael Pitfield, who, in turn, became increasingly idiosyncratic. With the departure of Gordon Robertson, Pitfield now wielded unchallenged sway over appointments that required prime ministerial approval. He continued to press his original reorganization initiatives. These resulted in fully eight central agencies, including the Prime Minister's Office, with various responsibilities for guidance of line departments. Coordination among these organizations posed a substantial challenge quite apart from that of meshing the views of various operational departments. The very nature of the cadre of deputy ministers who headed these organizations exacerbated the difficulties. They represented a generation of officials with finely honed skills in executive-bureaucratic gamesmanship. Most of them had centered their careers in central agencies.

The operation of the complex of cabinet committee, secretariats, and the Senior Coordination Committee—which now went under the acronym PEMS (Policy and Expenditure Management System, or, as some insiders began to refer to it, "Pretty Expensive Management System")—proved less than brilliant. For instance, in fiscal 1982–83, the federal government's expenditures ballooned to a whopping 150% of revenues. In 1983–84, the federal deficit amounted to 7.1% of GNP, more than twice the comparable figure for the United Kingdom in that year. The system had provided a perfect environment in which ministers could avoid making the tough decisions necessary to bring expenditures in line with declining revenues.

Another Interlude: Don't Blink, It's John Turner

Pierre Trudeau finally yielded power to John Turner on June 30, 1984. The timing put the new prime minister in a bind, as the government's mandate ran out early in 1985. Turner opted for an early September election. This put him on a campaign footing soon after taking office.

Turner had become convinced that the immense institutional dislocation resulting from PEMS more than negated any benefits from the approach. In a press conference held after he took power, Turner explicitly distanced himself from Trudeau's system of cabinet government, which he described as "too elaborate, too complex, too slow, and too expensive." He added that the highly intricate processes introduced by Trudeau had "diffused and eroded and blurred" the authority of cabinet ministers. This strong critique from a fellow Liberal perhaps drew some thrust from Turner's bitter departure from the Trudeau government in 1975. However, it struck a chord just about everywhere in Ottawa.

Turner acted decisively to abandon central elements of Trudeau's decision-making apparatus. He cut the size of cabinet from thirty-seven to twenty-nine. He reduced the number of cabinet committees from thirteen to ten. He abolished the ministries of state for Economic and Regional Development and Social Development. While not dismantling entirely the PEMS system, he took steps aimed at streamlining cabinet decision making. These included clarification of ministers' authority over their departments, control of the number of items reaching cabinet, and curtailing the role of "mirror" deputies' committees and access of officials to meetings of cabinet and its committees. However, Turner's defeat at the polls meant that he could not actually test out this streamlined system.

Mulroney

This book has stressed the degree to which chief executives struggle to attain some degree of policy competence. On the one hand, they wish to move their agenda along to respond to what the public wants. Partisan responsiveness forms an important component of this dimension of leadership, especially since chief executives want to maintain popular support so they and/or their party can continue in power. On the other hand, chief executives seeking policy competence want to utilize the state apparatus creatively. They must, of course, avoid deferring to it.

The standing bureaucracy serves as the permanent embodiment of myriad vested interests. To yield excessively to its counsel would doom any efforts toward change. Yet to underutilize the state apparatus would deny a leader an immense, although often latent, resource. Both in the devising and implementation of policy and programs the experience and expertise of the career civil service can make the difference between success and failure.

This assessment of Brian Mulroney maintains that the former prime minister neither attained a sufficient degree of partisan responsiveness—his party at the end of nine years of rule declined to two seats in the House of Commons—nor effectively engaged the state apparatus—many of his policies, indeed, placed the very survival of Canada in peril. If we can think of an immense amount of disconnected manipulation which neither achieves partisan responsiveness nor engages when crucial to the capacity of the state apparatus, we have politicized incompetence (Campbell 1986; Derlien 1993). Brian Mulroney presents us with the only case of this type of leadership among all the chief executives this book considers, although Bill Clinton at times seemed perilously close to replicating Mulroney's performance.

THE EMERGENCE OF POLITICIZED INCOMPETENCE, 1984–88

Brian Mulroney became prime minister at a time when neo-liberalism was riding a crest of popularity. In the United Kingdom, Margaret Thatcher basked in acclaim for giving her country a stiff dose of strong medicine and still pulling off a resounding electoral victory. In the United States, Ronald Reagan poised for a landslide victory in his 1984 reelection bid. With an overwhelming 211 seats in a 282-seat house, Mulroney might have appeared to outside observers as similarly placed to provide neo-liberal leadership. In fact, his electoral support fell quite a bit short of that of Thatcher and Reagan.

Mulroney came from the center of his party. Although not the "pink" Tory that Clark was, Mulroney still saw the need for the presence of the federal government in protecting social welfare. For instance, while leader of the opposition, he had supported the Liberals in their efforts to penalize provinces which allowed physicians to "overbill"—that is, charge fees beyond those covered by provincial health insurance programs. This was one side of Mulroney's personality—the papermill worker's son from the remote Quebec town of Baie Comeau. The other side was the natural pleaser who had latched himself onto the U. S.–owned Iron Ore Company of Canada as its president.

Mulroney knew that money talks. It brought out the best and worst in the boy from Baie Comeau. Deep down Mulroney knew his past and therefore could never embrace policies which seemed heartless to those in need. However, around the margins, issues which did not touch upon the personal core, Mulroney became a cavalier accommodator. Ronald Reagan had a profound belief that Americans would provide for their neighbors if the government did not. In a time in which government programs came under assault, Mulroney believed that he could protect the core social functions actually required by the less privileged. However, he liked his association with neo-liberals. He jumped on their bandwagon on matters, such as free trade, which appeared incidental. Mulroney's approach played a role in his handling of national unity issues, which revealed a tendency to bargain away matters which—on balance—the public saw as going too far in accommodating the provinces.

The PC's huge electoral victory in 1984 concealed some serious weaknesses. Those advising Mulroney as he prepared to take power recognized a very important point. Polls indicated that much of the landslide toward the Progressive Conservatives derived from a repudiation of Pierre Trudeau's legacy in so far as the public still saw this embodied in the Liberal's approach to governance. By no means did the PC's victory add up to a mandate to alter the Canadian vision of what government did.

Mulroney did bring a large majority with him to Parliament. So the public would expect more than an executive-style holding action until some salable agenda items congealed. As well, the huge PC caucus brought with it a mixed blessing. The Western populist wing of the party had dominated since Diefenbaker lost his majority in the House of Commons in 1962. Now this core group found itself awash with Ontarian and Maritime centrists and Quebecois. Mulroney would have to function as broker par excellence to keep this lot marching in step.

Those advising Mulroney faced a bit of a difficulty if the new prime minister sought even to attain a "let's deal" style. He hated meetings and preferred to spend the bulk of his working day wheeling and dealing on the telephone. The dysfunctions of this style had become clear even when Mulroney was leader of the opposition. Consistent with his view that he could yield on seemingly incidental matters in order to bolster his core, Mulroney had devolved many of his responsibilities—including chairing sessions of the shadow cabinet—to Erik Nielsen. However, Nielsen misconstrued this as a real partnership. He had opposed Mulroney's leadership challenge that had dethroned Joe Clark. Nielsen had served as interim leader during the build-up to the convention. Mulroney thought that he needed Nielsen if he was to lead caucus effectively.

In a gesture of magnanimity—to Clark as well as to Nielsen—Mulroney announced at the convention that Nielsen, the PC's savviest strategist in Parliament, would serve as his chief operating officer. This mandate soon overlapped into day-to-day management not only of parliamentary strategy but of the shadow cabinet. Mulroney—who did not even have a seat in the House of Commons when he became leader and had never served in elective office—found himself playing catch up with a deputy who knew Parliament like the back of his hand.

If they won the 1984 election because the Liberals had become discredited, the PCs could thank their relentless attacks while in opposition as much as Mulroney's campaign. The Nielsen people—that is the Western populist branch of the party—did not surprise Mulroney's people—centrists and Quebecois—when they demanded during the transition that the chairman-of-the-board/chief-operating-officer arrangement continue. They even pressed for Nielsen to chair all cabinet committees with authority over expenditure envelopes.

Those advising Mulroney did not know how to handle the Nielsen demands. On the one hand, they had seen how little interest Mulroney took in collective decision making and how poorly he ran meetings whenever he actually tried to chair shadow cabinet. On the other hand, they recognized the dangers of delegating too many of the prime minister's usual functions to Nielsen. In the end, they agreed to a situation in which Nielsen would be deputy prime minister and vice chairman of cabinet.

Nielsen himself brought little experience in executive-bureaucratic gamesmanship, although he had at least served in Clark's outer cabinet as public works minister. With Mulroney's blessing, he created a Task Force on Program Review, which would look into all government programs and ascertain which had become wasteful, redundant, or outdated. However, the process grew like Topsy. The government had not developed clear ideas about which programs should face the chopping block. Instead, it set up teams—with over 100 private sector "volunteers"—which fanned out into every corner of the bureaucracy. Over the eighteen months of the exercise, the task force suffered death by a thousand leaks. By the time it produced its twenty-one-volume final report, virtually every sacred cow had received immunization by a well-placed leak which sparked outrage in one or other special interest group. In each case, Mulroney would then intervene to assure the special pleaders that their favorite program would not be touched. The final report amounted to the largest dead letter ever produced by the government of Canada.

During the 1984 campaign, the PCs had made the usual noises about shaking up the career bureaucracy when they took office. Once it became clear that they would win the election, however, those advising Mulroney began to think more soberly. One obstacle which presented itself was a lack of experienced operatives who could effectively fill bureaucratic posts. Some in the transition team did toy with the idea that Mulroney should at least replace Gordon Osbaldeston as clerk of the Privy Council and secretary to the cabinet. Yet they abandoned this idea when some of those whom they consulted argued that if any mandarin had maintained his neutrality during the Trudeau years it was Osbaldeston. Apart from replacing a few officials elsewhere in the bureaucracy, Mulroney pretty much left the mandarinate as it was.

Once in office, indeed, the PCs found some officials more than eager to support them. Paul Tellier—whom Mulroney ultimately appointed president of Canadian National Railways—stood out in this group. He was deputy in the Department of Energy, Mines, and Resources (EMR) when Mulroney took power. Before that, he had distinguished himself as Trudeau's chief propagandist during the 1980 referendum campaign in Quebec. (Tellier had headed the Canadian Unity Information Office in the Federal-Provincial Relations Office.) In EMR, he rolled up his sleeves and dismantled Trudeau's National Energy Program—to the delight of the Alberta oil patch and the chagrin of Canadian nationalists. He so pleased Mulroney that the prime minister selected him to succeed Gordon Osbaldeston as clerk/secretary when the latter retired a year into the mandate.

During his tenure as clerk/secretary Tellier distinguished himself for blurring the line between a political operative and mandarin. He involved himself in a number of Mulroney missions which even Michael Pitfield would have concluded a clerk/secretary should stay away from. Among these were discussions with Lucien Bouchard—the separatist who eventually became premier of Quebec—in an effort to dissuade him from leaving the government; secret discussions with Manitoba first-nation leaders over details of the failed Meech Lake constitutional proposals; and forcing the condemnation of a senior official in External Affairs in a contrived attempt at apportioning blame over the granting of Canadian residency to the former Iraqi ambassador to the UN.

If part of Mulroney's challenge when taking office involved streamlining the cabinet decision-making process, John Turner—as we saw previously—did most of the tough work for his successor. Unfortunately, Mulroney reversed Turner's key initiative—reducing the size of cabinet from thirty-seven to twenty-nine. Indeed, he appointed a cabinet with forty members.

Mulroney's move took root in the inherent instability of the coalition which had brought him his lopsided majority. Here the representational imperative which impinges on all Canadian cabinet building (Campbell 1985) kicked in with a vengeance. Key, in this regard, became Mulroney's desire to develop a cadre of Quebec ministers who could assume senior cabinet posts as they gained experience. He appointed eleven ministers from Quebec even though few had ever served in Parliament before much less as ministers. The disjunction between the experience of Western ministers and those from the rest of the country manifested itself in the fact that almost half (seven of fifteen) of the members of Mulroney's Priorities and Planning Committee (P&P) came from the West. Mulroney attempted to use the ministry as a training school in executive-bureaucratic leadership and employ P&P as the inner cabinet.

Mulroney brought an old Laval University classmate and best man, Bernard Roy, with him as principal secretary in PMO. Roy had masterminded the Quebec campaign for Mulroney. A corporate lawyer from Montreal's most prestigious firm whose introduction to politics was his work for Mulroney in the election, Roy lacked the taste for behind-the-scenes gamesmanship and the knowledge of the executive-bureaucratic complex to serve effectively as principal secretary. Mulroney relied as well on Charles McMillan—a neo-liberal with an abiding enthusiasm for closer trade links with the United States from the Administrative Studies Faculty of Toronto's York University. McMillan headed a small policy unit in PMO which spearheaded the continentalist shift in trade policy and abolition of the NEP. However, McMillan's PMO unit did much less well at the usual run of issues. Indeed, its meddling was believed to have contributed to many of the government's misfires. It did little to quicken the Nielsen Task Force process when the latter seemed to have gone badly adrift.

THE CAPTAIN SAVES HIMSELF AND SINKS THE SHIP, 1988–93

To all intents and purposes, the second Mulroney mandate began to take shape by early 1988. At that point, the government had retooled itself in preparation for the next federal election. This would have to take place by fall 1989. However, Mulroney hoped to call the election as soon as possible. In Westminster systems, governments do not like to wait until the eleventh hour to go to the polls.

The prospect of an early election began to refocus Mulroney through the second half of 1987. By early 1988, the government had gotten itself in full preelectoral footing. In the process it had embraced a strategy of partisan responsiveness. That is, it focused on themes which would resonate electorally. Part of this process involved throwing caution to the wind. In enunciating its various policy objectives, the government seemed to give virtually no attention to their actual attainability and, more fundamentally, desirability.

In April 1987, the government had entered into an accord with all the provinces, including Quebec, over the constitution. The agreement called for ratification by Parliament and all ten Canadian provinces within three years. It really amounted to a pea and shell game. Essentially, it won the support of the Quebec government by so diluting the power of the federal government vis-à-vis the provinces that the latter would find it difficult to resist the temptation. Another key plank in the PC's platform became the Free Trade Agreement (FTA) with the United States. To take effect, the FTA had to receive approval from Parliament before January 1, 1989. The negotiations over the agreement had become a melee. But Mulroney's desperation for a deal had grown to monumental proportions—it had become the philosopher's stone of his economic policy. To add a final and incongruous plank, the government had announced its intention to buy a fleet of nuclear submarines to patrol the Arctic. The objective: to protect Canadian sovereignty from Russian and American intrusion. The latter consideration struck observers as a profound irony in view of the government's eagerness to set aside Canadian nationalism on the federal-politics and continental-trade fronts.

As Mulroney prepared for the 1988 election he did enjoy a few positional advantages that he lacked earlier in his mandate—a better organized cabinet and a smoother running advisory system. Regarding the former, Erik Nielsen had left the cabinet in spring 1986 in the aftermath of a conflict of interest scandal involving the regional industrial expansion minister. Don Mazankowski—a no-nonsense Albertan who had served as transport minister—succeeded Nielsen as deputy prime minister.

Mazankowski immediately took steps to bring greater discipline to the cabinet process—especially as it related to review of expenditure issues. Principal among these was creation of an Operations Committee of cabinet (Ops). In addition to Mazankowski, the committee included the president of the Treasury Board (from August 1987 to March 1988 Mazankowski filled this role himself), the heads of the three cabinet committees overseeing the three policy sectors (Economic and Regional Development, Government Operations, and Social Development), and the minister of state for federal-provincial relations.

Mulroney's key move regarding his advisory system was his 1987 appointment of Derek Burney—a career official from the Department of External Affairs—as chief of staff. Bernard Roy remained as principal secretary. However, he focused his work on Quebec affairs. Burney had attracted Mulroney's attention through his association with his department's shift in favor of free trade with the United States in the mid-1980s. He brought an unprecedented degree of discipline to PMO. More important, he provided a gearbox for Mulroney for dealing with the standing bureaucracy. Burney presented one problem as chief of staff. He so focused his efforts on the negotiations surrounding the FTA and Parliament's eventual approval of the agreement that other matters frequently fell off his and, therefore, PMO's radar scope.

The 1988 election functioned essentially as a referendum on FTA. After the vote, it became increasingly clear that the government's nuclear submarine ambit would soon fade from the political agenda. It was about as feasible for Canada, given the fiscal constraints and diplomatic complications, as Star Wars was for the United States. The action-forcing requirement for Meech Lake to receive ratification from Parliament and all of the provinces by spring 1990 began to press down on the government.

Burney left PMO to become Canada's ambassador to the United States soon after the 1988 election. However, Mulroney turned the single-issue chief of staff into an art form. He selected as Burney's immediate successor Stanley Hartt, the former deputy minister of finance, whose main job became trying to impose fiscal discipline on the government and getting the a federal Goods and Services Tax through Parliament. After the Meech Lake Accord process ended in disaster in June 1990, Mulroney went to Norman Spector with a view to his ringmastering a final effort to achieve national unity.

The Spector appointment gave a lot of observers a sense of "déjà vu all over again." A forty-one-year-old from Montreal who had worked for the British Columbia and Ontario governments, Spector had occupied the same post—secretary to the cabinet for federal-provincial relations—from which Mike Kirby had worked under Trudeau during the 1980–82 constitutional debates. Along with Paul Tellier and Mulroney, Spector had concocted a strategy whereby—three weeks before the ratification—Mulroney would stage a marathon summit with provincial premiers designed to isolate the three holdouts—New Brunswick, Manitoba, and Newfoundland—and pick them off one by one (in that order) (Editorial, *Globe and Mail* 20 June 1990). After the conference, Mulroney boasted about this plot in an interview with two Toronto *Globe and Mail* reporters (Delacourt and Seguin 13 June 1990). This scheme outraged the three premiers involved. Ultimately, the Newfoundland premier—Clyde Wells—killed the deal by obtaining adjournment of his legislature on June 22, thereby making ratification on June 23—the deadline—impossible.

Mulroney's final attempt to resolve the constitutional issue culminated in a failed national referendum in October 1992. By then, Mulroney had already brought Hugh Segal—an Ontario PC operative—to PMO as chief of staff. With approval ratings struggling to stay above the prime interest rate, Mulroney needed someone to manage the rehabilitation of his party's image. It was widely known that he did not intend to lead the PCs into the next election due in fall 1993.

The legacy of Mulroney's second mandate thus fit as well as during the first a tendency toward ad hoc arrangements which shifted according to the prime minister's whim. Emblematic of this period was the failure of one attempt to bring greater structure to the government's handling of the expenditure budget. When he won the 1988 election, Mulroney allegedly consulted with various leaders about how he could improve his performance on the deficit. As accounts go, Margaret Thatcher—who had employed the Star Chamber of senior ministers—and Bob Hawke—who had utilized the Expenditure Review Committee of ministers from the neo-liberal wing of his cabinet—each urged Mulroney to create a senior cabinet committee which would focus the government's efforts on expenditure control. Mulroney did this with great fanfare early in 1989. Patterned after the Australian format (which we examine in detail in Chapter 6), an Expenditure Review Committee (ERC) would take charge of the process of bringing expenditure in line with fiscal targets.

The prime minister was to have chaired ERC. Paul Tellier had argued that Bob Hawke—who chaired his ERC—stressed this as the sine qua non to the Labor government's success in turning a $10 billion deficit into a $10 billion surplus in two years. Mulroney, of course, never followed through on this commitment. He essentially delegated the chair of ERC to Mazankowski. During a visit to Australia in summer 1989, Tellier told his opposite number, Mike Codd, that the Canadians had come to the conclusion that having Mulroney chair ERC would comprise a huge waste of the prime minister's time. Predictably, the ERC produced few tangible results and eventually sputtered into disuse.

KIM CAMPBELL BRINGS THE PARTY TO AN END

As indicated previously, Brian Mulroney had decided early on that he did not want to lead the PCs into a third election. He had tried to engineer a situation whereby a number of cabinet ministers would emerge as contenders for the leadership. Kim Campbell had caught his eye as only one of the prospects. However, he had appointed her justice minister after her initial election to Parliament in 1988. He subsequently had provided her an opportunity to diversify her resume by moving her to the Department of Defense.

Campbell displayed a singular aptitude for setting aside her progressive beliefs, holding her nose, and coming to a workable compromise on issues as diverse as abortion, homosexual rights, gun control, and sexual assault. By the time she moved on to the Department of Defense, she had become a darling of the press. After Mulroney announced his impending resignation in February 1993, yet another mania, "Campbellmania" seized the country. The other prospective candidates for the leadership dropped off like flies. Eventually, Mulroney could only convince one minister, Jean Charest—a thirty-four-year-old minister from Quebec, to stay in the leadership race.

We find three components to the failure of Kim Campbell. First, she was succeeding Brian Mulroney. Well into the Chrétien government, voters, when asked whether they would support the PCs in an election, still cite their detestation of Mulroney as their main reason for not considering the party as an alternative. In fairness, thus, we might ask whether anyone could have rehabilitated the PCs.

Second, Campbell's faults came fully to the fore after only a few months into her primeministership. Since she had to face an election in fall 1993, she went into full campaign mode during the summer. She had come through the leadership contest as too clever by half. In other words, many of her speeches and responses to press questions appeared as stream of consciousness. She tended not to consider the consequences of much of her language—styling the opponents of the PC's economic plans as "the enemies of Canadians," the politically apathetic as "condescending SOBs," and her previous views of the Roman Catholic Church as "the evil Demons of the papacy" presenting themselves as especially egregious missteps.

After she became prime minister, her handlers put her through a barnstorming summer of visits to fairs and other community events. This, they hoped, would allow her to show her human side. The approach worked and Campbell enjoyed a bounce in popularity. Yet the old difficulties reared their heads once again when the federal election campaign began. The press contributed to the problem. By the end of the summer, they had concluded that the handlers had served up charisma without substance. But Campbell became increasingly wooly about what her program entailed. At one point, she even maintained that she could not discuss how she would cut social programs as she would fix the problem on her own once she had achieved an electoral mandate.

The third element of Campbell's failure presents a classic case of a prime minister who became paralytically mesmerized by the first gearbox issue—that is, the relationship between the government and the standing bureaucracy. We noted in our discussion of Joe Clark's experience that he succumbed to the Privy Council Office's penchant for viewing a change of prime minister or government as an opportunity for restructuring machinery of government. Unlike any other of our governments, Canada invests tremendous resources—largely centered in the Privy Council Office—to support ongoing work on possible machinery of government changes. This branch of PCO had begun work almost two years before Campbell took power on plans for a major restructuring. Its ideas all met worthiness criteria. However, their actual introduction during the Mulroney/Campbell transition presented serious problems regarding both timeliness and political sensitivity. June 1993 did provide the opportunity for a new prime minister to sweep with a

new broom. Yet Campbell had to lead her party in a federal election
some time before November. Advocates of the changes believed the
modifications would lend the new government an aura of reformism—
especially in connection with downsizing the public service and making it more efficient. Nonetheless, it has become almost axiomatic that
the public focuses on public service restructuring as only a vague objective. They pay little attention to the details of such efforts and therefore award advocates of change little credit. They will respond very neg-
atively to specific elements of the reforms if they appear to affect their
lives detrimentally or seem to alter adversely the relationship between
themselves and the state.

It was the negatives which caught public attention when the Campbell administration unveiled its machinery of government reforms. Much
of the difficulty derived from labeling. The most serious reaction centered on concerns about creation of a Department of Public Safety. This
department merged the former Department of the Solicitor General—
responsible for the Royal Canadian Mounted Police, the courts, and the
penal system—with the operational parts of immigration programs
(which had been in the Department of Employment and Immigration).
In a nation which relies upon immigrants for its growth and prides itself on its diversity and openness to outsiders, one can imagine the hue
and cry among certain segments of the public about the proposition that
immigration belonged to law enforcement. Of course, immigrant groups
became outraged. But the general public seemed immediately to twig
on the fact that "Public Security"—both the nomenclature and the structural consequences—smacked of the type of organization one encounters in repressive regimes in the developing world.

Not unrelated to her problems with the first gearbox, Campbell never
effectively engaged the second gearbox. She selected a cabinet more
with a view to representing the various factions of her party than upon
the basis of talent and experience. The reduction of cabinet to twenty-
five ministers sought to provide a workable number that would make
an inner group unnecessary. Yet Campbell rarely convened cabinet. The
situation proved chaotic. The prime minister had assumed a campaign
footing which detached her from the day-to-day operations of government even before the election was called. Meanwhile, a cabinet with a
large number of inexperienced ministers struggled in relative isolation
from one another with a reform process which a small clique of mandarins actually ran. PCO had construed the Mulroney/Campbell transi-

tion as a streetcar for its reform agenda. Campbell let it drive her government into the ground.

Chrétien: "Yesterday's Man" Soars into the Quebec Problem

In Spring 1992, Johns Hopkins University School for Applied International Studies in Washington, DC hosted a lecture with Jean Chrétien—then the leader of the opposition. At that time, few saw Chrétien as a real prospect for prime minister. Indeed, most saw him as a spent force—yesterday's man carrying the Liberal banner until someone younger and more adroit came along. Chrétien surprised his audience. He gave an excellent twenty-minute extemporaneous discussion of the main points where the Liberals departed from the PCs on such issues as national unity and NAFTA. The first question from the floor came from one of the retired academics/government officials who serve as room stuffers at such occasions in Washington. The gentleman asked the type of question which would have stumped a PhD candidate writing a dissertation on its topic. It dealt broadly with Chrétien's term as minister of Indian affairs in the late 1960s. However, it focused on a relatively arcane decision which he had made concerning Indian rights in this period. Chrétien, without skipping a beat, launched into a detailed defense of his position—outlining the advice he had received from his department, the various types of pressures exerted by Indian groups, how the cabinet had divided on this issue, and, finally, Trudeau's position on the matter. The performance so impressed an American lobbyist seated beside me that he ultimately whispered in amazement, "This guy would blow the candidates for the Democratic nomination out of the water!" Chrétien had exuded experience. Further, he had conveyed this relatively scarce commodity in contemporary politics with alacrity and humility.

Chrétien did not come readily to such grace. Indeed, he gained quite a reputation as a scrapper as he rose in the Liberal Party (Martin 1995). Like Brian Mulroney, Chrétien grew up in a mill town—Lai Bai Shawinigan—in rural Quebec. His father was a machinist. Chrétien has struggled with a facial distortion which he developed at the age of eleven as well as a relatively humble background. During the time that he served as minister of Indian affairs, he stood in the shadow of the Trudeau cabinet greats. Yet, ever the survivor, Chrétien displayed exceptional stamina and ability to learn. He ultimately served as Trudeau's finance minister, the first Francophone to occupy that position since Confederation.

Along the way he had run virtually every key department. He had also ingratiated himself to Canadians. Albertans, for instance, who love to hate the East and everything it stands for, developed in the twilight of the Trudeau years a grudging admiration for Chrétien.

Chrétien appeared to have retired from politics when the Liberals lost power in 1984. He joined a Bay Street law firm in Toronto—an action which did not exactly ingratiate him with his core Quebec constituency. He reentered politics after the Liberals' 1988 failure to present a party platform, even though their leader, John Turner, had clearly beaten Brian Mulroney in the election debates, which had mainly focused on the Free Trade Agreement.

In pursuing the Liberal leadership in 1990, Chrétien faced stiff opposition from Paul Martin—a Montreal corporate lawyer whose father had presided over installation of much of Canada's welfare state in the postwar period and ultimately had served as minister of external affairs. After assuming the leadership, Chrétien maintained a strong relationship with Martin. The latter played a pivotal role in developing the Liberal Party platform for the 1993 election. After the Liberals assumed power, Martin served as finance minister. Although Martin is bilingual and from Montreal, Quebecois viewed him as an Anglophone. Indeed, his interventions in the 1995 referendum—largely bombastic projections of the economic peril which would result from separation—became an object of separatist ridicule. Martin, thus, provided for Chrétien more a link into the board rooms of Canada than with the people of Quebec. This disfunction presented a serious problem for the government: because of Chrétien's strong federalist stances during the Trudeau governments and his defection to Toronto when he left politics, the Liberals still required a vital link to the heart of the average Quebecois voter.

The Liberals ran on a good-government platform in 1993. Their various policies, which fell well short of earth-shaking, received embodiment in a short document dubbed "The Red Book." During the campaign, it became clear that the prospective government's idea of dramatic strokes would comprise canceling two unpopular programs—the proposed purchase of $4.8 billion worth of Navy helicopters and the privatization of Pearson International Airport on economic grounds—and renegotiating some elements of NAFTA before ratification by Parliament. The government acted quickly on the former two commitments. The third it punted on, largely because the Americans refused to discuss the main outstanding points. Other than these mildly dramatic issues, the Liberals focused on the excruciatingly boring business of studying government programs with a view to possible economies. However, one such review, that of the unemployment insurance system, did hold out some expectation of relatively dramatic proposals down the road.

On the grounds that it should let sleeping dogs lie, the government remained relatively mum on the issue of Quebec. This suited most Anglophone Canadians perfectly, as many had resolved to let Quebec go rather than reopen constitutional discussions. In his initial meeting with provincial premiers, Chrétien expressly condemned the "brokerage politics" of Mulroney (Delacourt 22 December 1993). Rather than sawing off deals between warring provincial interests, he would pursue a national-interest strategy. Chrétien believed that he could win Quebec back into the fold through good, no-nonsense government in Ottawa, focusing on jobs and economic growth (Gherson 25 January 1994). Indeed, language evocative of an "executive" approach to leadership permeated the analyses of what to expect from Chrétien. The Chrétien team sent the word out from the outset that they would eschew entirely efforts to judge their first-100-days performance (Gherson 4 November 1993). In selection of his cabinet and advisers, Chrétien expressly took a "Holiday Inn"—meaning, no surprises—approach (Winsor 5 November 1993). He stressed appointees' experience and his direct knowledge of how they worked.

The Chrétien approach catapulted the Liberal government to unprecedented approval levels. By fall 1994, York University political scientist Reg Whitaker found himself exclaiming: "The polls are astonishing. We've gone from, under Mulroney, having the most illegitimate, least liked government in the world . . . to suddenly having the most approved government anywhere" (Greenspon 25 October 1994). The analysis of David Zussman—the head of Chrétien's transition team—that: "The people are fed up with lies and excuses. They want integrity and good government" resonated with voters' reasons for supporting Chrétien's relatively lackluster government. Voters seemed to have made a "value alignment" based on Chrétien's apparent fulfillment of their search for a leader who projected honesty, humility, and respect for the law (Winsor 17 November 1994).

Chrétien's relative success in striking a responsive chord with Canadians takes us a long way in explaining how his government proved too confident in its October 1995 showdown with Quebec separatists. Chrétien and the formidable team of federal strategists who had established a "war room" in Montreal decided to pursue a low-key campaign largely contingent upon the separatist leadership self-destructing. This expectation seemed to have borne itself out while Jacques Parizeau—the premier of Quebec—led the "Yes" side. However, in the last three weeks of the campaign, Lucien Bouchard—then leader of the Bloc Quebecois party in the federal parliament—supplanted Parizeau as the "Yes" side's main spokesman. The charismatic Bouchard—dubbed "St. Lucien" after losing a leg in a bout with killer bacteria—immediately transformed the entire tenor of the referendum.

Caught flat-footed, the federal side barely scraped through with a "No" vote. They obviously had not considered the possibility of a "No" victory or a result so close that it would simply reinvigorate the separatist side. This miscalculation more than anything led to Chrétien's truncated mandate in the 1997 election.

HOME COMING

It is an old saw of Canadian politics that the Liberals consider themselves the natural party of government. We have discussed earlier in this chapter the effects on the civil service that the relative domination of federal politics by the Liberals have worked. These effects have resulted in a strong symbiosis between the Liberals and the mandarinate, which took on a personalized dimension during the Trudeau years, both because of the longevity of his primeministership and his keen interest in reshaping the public service after his image and likeness. The Mulroney years saw the emergence of an a-institutional form of personalization. Mulroney tended to dip into the senior ranks of the public service and tap individuals who did his bidding.

Chrétien chose David Zussman—a University of Ottawa professor with considerable public service experience—to head up his transition team. Zussman started his work over a year before Chrétien took power. By May 1993, Chrétien had digested Zussman's recommendations and come to the conclusion that cabinet should be shrunk to around twenty-three members. Not surprisingly, since Zussman and his team tapped many of the same sources as those advising Kim Campbell, his proposed departmental labels bore some resemblance to those put forward in the PCs' May 1993 changes. The Zussman plan, however, would not have made the mistake Campbell had of creating a Department of Public Security. His plan also allowed for the first steps toward a two-tiered ministry along the lines of the United Kingdom and Australian approaches. Initially, the Chrétien government included twenty-two cabinet ministers and eight secretaries of state. The latter did not belong to cabinet. They served rather as helping ministers within specific portfolios.

Chrétien wanted his government to rely much more on permanent officials and much less on appointees. Ministers' offices—which had bloated to an average of forty staff under Mulroney—would operate with a maximum of thirteen. Chrétien himself vowed to rely heavily upon the neutral brokerage of the Privy Council Office. To this end, he took steps to rehabilitate its leadership. In February 1994, he replaced Paul Tellier's successor as clerk/secretary, Glen Shortliffe—who many believed had also aligned himself too strongly with the Tories—with Jocelyn Bourgon, whom he had promoted above the heads of many possible contenders from the position of deputy minister of transport. Chrétien selected Bourgon on the grounds that she possessed the qualities necessary to restore the independence and morale of the public service (Winsor 25 February 1994). By June, Bourgon had cleaned house on the machinery of government side of PCO and brought David Zussman in to direct the unit and staff up cabinet's reviews of government programs headed by Marcel Massé—the minister responsible for public service renewal.

One cannot understate the importance of a prime minister's relationship to PCO in setting the tone for an administration in Canada. Trudeau developed a PCO confirmed that it embodied the best and the brightest. Hence, a deus-ex-machina syndrome emerged—if we get the structure right, the rest will follow. Mulroney, if anything, underutilized the capacities of PCO in an aggregate, institutional sense. However, certain individuals and sectors of the agency became highly subject to his personal absorptions. Chrétien found a middle ground. For the most part, the agency under him did exhibit a deus-ex-machina approach. Yet it did not find itself going through contortions to respond to the whim of the prime minister.

The delicate relationship of PCO and Chrétien worked in most areas. Quebec, however, proved an exception. The actual staging of the federal "No" campaign did, in fact, follow closely the 1980 approach—with the added wrinkle of a much touted "war room" in Montreal (Winsor 8 September 1995; Ha 12 September 1995). Yet the mammoth team of seventy civil servants did not recognize until late in the game that it stood a chance to lose and, even at that point, showed little imagination in revising its strategy. Indeed, the government's moves in the immediate aftermath of the referendum—marked by recycling of twenty-five-year-old formulations—backfired badly.

BRINGING "CABINET" BACK TO GOVERNMENT

We saw previously that Jean Chrétien embraced the conventional wisdom that the size of cabinet should be reduced. Indeed, he followed the prescription more rigorously than Kim Campbell had. The notion that a smaller cabinet might actually provide a manageable group for collective and consultative government motivated Chrétien's moves. In keeping with this view, Chrétien's plan allowed for only four cabinet committees—Economic Development Policy, Social Development Policy, the Treasury Board, and the Special Committee of Council. The latter two have become permanent fixtures in the government apparatus—the Treasury Board being required by statute since 1869 and the Special Committee of Council being a time-saving mechanism for approving routine executive orders and regulations.

Chrétien's adherence to the principle that "smaller" means "more effective" cabinet government even impinged upon his administration's acknowledgment of the representational imperative. We have seen that this feature of cabinet building in Canada has helped bloat ministries. In the first term, Chrétien ignored much of the calculus associated with this imperative. He made no efforts to bolster British Columbia's representation—even though this province considers itself a separate "region," a principle which the government recognized in its 1996 enactment of a region-based formula for the amendment of the constitution. He denied Canada's smallest province, Prince Edward Island, even one minister. He resisted dipping into the appointive Senate to fill gaps. In this regard, he bluntly said of Quebec City: "They decided not to elect a [Liberal] member of Parliament so they don't have a minister" (Delacourt 2 November 1995). Chrétien's second term saw a relaxation of these strictures with cabinet reflating to twenty-seven.

A recurrent problem in the division of authority in Canadian cabinets reemerged under the Chrétien government as well. Going back at least as far as the mid-1970s, cabinet has found it difficult to make collective decisions about the expenditure budget that stick. The Canadian penchant for blurring authority over expenditure review takes root in the relative strength of the central agencies and the unwieldy elements of the cabinet process associated with the representational imperative.

Chrétien's downsizing of cabinet and streamlining of its committee system accomplished mixed results in the area of expenditure control. He seemed to plant the seeds for further confusion of authority at the outset of the government. That is, he assigned the function of cabinet-level review of programs from the standpoint of effectiveness and efficiency to a committee headed by Marcel Massé, who, as president of the Privy Council, received his most critical staff support from the PCO. He also assigned his initial president of the Treasury Board, Art Eggleton, responsibility of $2 billion which the government would parlay with the provinces for $6 billion worth of infrastructure projects. The Eggleton mission—in a reversal of the old English expression—comprised a classic instance of turning a gamekeeper into a poacher. Some of the funded projects, such as remodeling Calgary's hockey arena—The Saddledome—to accommodate executive boxes for corporate season ticket holders, struck many as more pork than barrel.

The infrastructure project dwindled to a trickle within a year of the government's taking power. Meanwhile, Massé's committee—which ultimately became styled the "Star Chamber" after a similar body in the early years of the Thatcher government—did find tangible savings. However, most observers noted that the successes the committee achieved would not have come to fruition had not the Finance Department exerted such clout in its deliberations. In other words, the Star Chamber functioned more by fiat, along the lines of its namesake under Thatcher, than collective decision making, along the lines of Australia's Expenditure Review Committee.

As noted before, Chrétien chose to rely much more heavily upon the permanent public service than did Mulroney. However, two of the appointed officials whom he retained in the Prime Minister's Office worked an especially strong influence on the government. Eddie Goldenberg—a senior policy adviser—worked for Chrétien since the latter was Indian affairs minister in the late 1960s. Goldenberg played a decisive role in the development and packaging of the Chrétien approach. He genuinely became one of those "Ask Eddie" figures—an aide who gained the reputation of knowing his boss's mind impeccably. Along with Goldenberg, Chaviva Hosek gained widespread recognition through her role as director of policy and research. Before the 1993 election, she had worked closely with Paul Martin in development of the Liberal platform. In spring 1995, Goldenberg and Hosek revived a PMO practice which had developed under Trudeau—

namely, private visits with ministers to assess the progress of the Liberal mandate.

Goldenberg often found himself at odds with some ministers. Most obviously, his cautious approach presented some problems with Lloyd Axworthy, who served as human resources development minister until he moved to Foreign Affairs in January 1996. Axworthy had headed a comprehensive review of the social security system, which sought to shift substantial funds from direct assistance to training. Goldenberg worried that Axworthy's proposals would present too many political backlashes. Because Chrétien gave little personal time to the review and the Finance Department took every opportunity to raise budgetary objections, Axworthy did not obtain cabinet approval of his legislative proposals until a month before he left the human resources development portfolio.

The results of the October 30, 1995 referendum in Quebec also worked their effects on cabinet dynamics. Right after the election, two special committees emerged—one on national unity and the other on jobs and economic growth—as responses to the crisis. However, the government became deeply divided—in the case of the former committee, between those wishing to make overtures to Quebec and those wanting to pursue a hard line, and—in the case of the latter, those wanting to relax fiscal stringency and those wanting to continue it. The January 1996 cabinet shuffle reflated cabinet to twenty-five members with special attention to the need for more Quebec representation. However, the shuffle compounded confusion over the constitution. The national unity review bifurcated before the end of 1995 into a Plan A group—which worked on accommodating Quebec and other provinces—and a Plan B group—which developed contingencies for negotiation with Quebec should it actually vote for separation in a future referendum. Massé headed the Plan A group and Allan Rock—the justice minister—chaired the Plan B group.

CONCLUSION

So far, this book has argued that effective leaders must, as Jean Chrétien seemed to have done, achieve a balance between responsive and neutral competence. Pierre Trudeau relied very heavily upon the career public service to accomplish his goals. However, he sought almost a designer neutral competence. Not content with the mandarins served up by the seniority system, he dipped down in the permanent bureaucracy to individuals in their late thirties and early forties who shared his rationalist view of the role of the state. He also created an immensely complicated apparatus for government coordination, one which collapsed under its own weight when Trudeau's immense intellectual acuity and intense focus on affairs of state began to wane.

If Trudeau's overly personalized approach erred on the side of neutral competence, Mulroney's did so on the side of responsive competence. Mulroney revealed a pathological detachment from the state apparatus. He also devolved many of his functions to two successive deputy prime ministers, placing much of what would determine the effectiveness of the administration at the mercy of the strengths and weaknesses of the incumbents to this position. A tendency toward truncated decision processes characterized the government throughout—mainly because the prime minister found it difficult to restrain himself from responding to the special pleading of ministers whose cause had not prevailed in the formal machinery. Mulroney often painted himself into corners and frequently resorted to grand gestures and brinkmanship to regain public trust. This behavior worked during the year before the 1988 election. It failed abysmally in the year before the expiration of the Progressive Conservative's 1988–93 mandate.

To be sure, Chrétien's balanced style stabilized the ship of state. Yet, Quebec reemerged as the imponderable that very substantially eroded Chrétien's support. And, as the government improved Canada's economic performance, equity also asserted itself as a concern. The two issues together cost Chrétien a strong mandate in the 1997 election.

6

Hawke, Keating, and a Balance Between Personal and Institutional Leadership

In the previous chapter we encountered the difficulties associated with overly personalized leadership. This chapter examines how two prime ministers have grappled with balancing responsive and neutral competence in Australia. That is, most of this analysis focuses on Bob Hawke (prime minister from 1983 to 1990) and Paul Keating (1990 to 1996).

The preceding chapters' treatments of executive leadership have dealt with the importance ascribed to public choice as a way of coping with the age of constraint. We noted especially the irony in the fact that the model—though first developed by American theorists—has actually been deployed much more thoroughly in the United Kingdom. We also saw that the specific character of Canada's federal system has made it very difficult to implement the model—even when it held considerable sway in the philosophic approach of the Progressive Conservative Party when it held power from 1984 to 1993.

Rational choice manifested itself in the Antipodes as a much more consciously embraced conceptual framework than pertained in any of our other systems. In New Zealand, adherence to the view even took the form of relatively elaborate theoretical amplification—with the government of the day or senior officials in the public service issuing documents and journal articles which cited extensively standard public choice work published in the United States (Scott and Gorringe 1989). In Australia, insiders coined the term "economic rationalism" as an umbrella characterization of macroeconomic policies, structural adjustments to the economy, budget constraints, and reforms of organization and management of the public sector.

Some Australian officials have accused Michael Pusey—a University of New South Wales sociologist—with popularizing economic rationalism (1988; 1991). It was obvious that the term and Pusey's use of it still rankled one very senior Australian official as recently as 1995:

> **Respondent:** . . . economic rationalism was a label that emerged out of popular debate and some very sloppy analytical work that was done by someone who should have known better. . . . It had particular point, again in the mid-1980s, when the currency was disappearing and there were arguments about what kind of a future Australia had. . . . And that became known as economic rationalism in the hands of this crazy.
>
> **Interviewer:** You're talking about Pusey, aren't you?
>
> **Respondent:** Yeah.

Yet the fact that the term had gained widespread currency among officials long before Pusey's most important work was published would suggest that he had simply become the messenger.

My own interviews in Australia conducted with John Halligan before the publication of Pusey's book clearly reflected the degree to which top officials had become conscious of a sea change in the thinking of ministers and their colleagues toward public choice. And both sides in the debate employed "economic rationalism" to encapsulate what appeared to many as a radical transformation.

It did not prove difficult to ascertain which types of individuals fit within the economic rationalist group. Many respondents believed strongly that a new breed of minister had emerged—one who actually understood economics. The strategic positioning of this group dovetailed with developments in the permanent public service that resulted in economists assuming the headships and other key roles in central agencies and line departments alike. Further, shifting perspectives in the Labor Party had led to a situation whereby market-economy rationales for policies gained increased credence. A Treasury official sympathetic to the new approach drew especially strongly the threads of economics expertise which melded the perspectives of cabinet and key officials:

There's been a great spread of PhDs in economics out running departments. Fitzgerald's running Employment, Education and Training;
Charles is running Industry, Technology and Commerce; Keating is running Finance. There is a strong breed of economists basically brought up
through the Treasury and a strong economic rationalist streak running
through this government and its policies. [As for ministers] . . . Hawke,
Dawkins, Willis and Walsh [*sic*] have economics degrees. . . . The treasurer graduated from the Treasury. We gave him his economics training.
So it's a pretty economically rational group (1988 interview).

The search for definitions of economic rationalism offered up some
slim pickings from those favorably disposed to the approach. One official defined economic rationalism as "a healthy concern for how you
get from point A to point B . . . a fair degree of pragmatism in what is
done." Another owned up to being an economic rationalist and allowed
that:

I guess I'm most interested in changing things. . . . I suppose if you wanted
to describe me or categorize me I'd be an economic rationalist. . . . I think
the emphasis these days is all on getting maximum program dollars out
for the minimum administration dollars (1988 interview).

Notwithstanding the lack of clear articulation among insiders in the
Commonwealth government of the nature of economic rationalism, its
main features reduced to three elements of the rational choice codex.
First, government had grown too large and become profligate. It had become a drag on economic performance. Second, governments had to
abandon pluralism. This element applied especially to the ethos of mutual adjustment of the various claims of economic and social groups.
Such approaches lent themselves to precisely the type of special-
interest politics that had fueled big and profligate government. Third,
rationality had to become monotonic. It required strict application of
market criteria to every decision. For instance, in an extreme form, economic rationalism would maintain that if the Australian auto industry
could not survive without tariff protection then "so be it." (Indeed, John
Hewson—the leader of the Liberal Party who many believed would become prime minister of Australia after the election of 1993—came very
close to taking precisely this view in 1992.)

One issue that arose from Pusey's analysis is the question of whether
economic rationalism amounted to a type of bureaucratic coup d'etat.
At one point, Pusey maintained "an increasingly stable and symbiotic

relationship between ministers and top bureaucrats" had emerged in the mid-1980s (1991, 8). However, the general thrust of Pusey's analysis seemed somewhat dismissive of the input of the political leadership.

The issue of economic rationalism triumphing over pluralism merits very close attention. Australia bears a close resemblance to complex and potentially fragmented political systems like the United States and Canada. Even though its population of some seventeen million would strike most readers as small, the country emerged out of six former British colonies, four of which had been established to receive convicts sent on "transportation" from the United Kingdom. The land is harsh and its agriculture is much more akin to what one finds in the American West than in the United Kingdom. The term "pastoral setting" does not leap to one's mind when viewing the Australian landscape even as close as 100 miles from the coast. There is a strong streak of rugged individualism in Australians.

The political system itself is relatively intricate. The division of powers between the Commonwealth and the state governments is more clearly defined and less a source of dispute than that between the federal government and the provinces in Canada. Generally, the Commonwealth government devolves administration of many programs that it mostly funds to the states. This system can introduce quite considerable variations in delivery which are associated with cultural differences not only in the states but in the executive-bureaucratic traditions (Halligan and Power 1990). For instance, an absorption in Canberra in the early 1990s was the uneven way in which economic rationalist principles had been adopted and adhered to in the states.

The Australian Parliament has an upper house—the Senate—which is elected on the basis of equal representation of the states. Further, the Senate has a full array of constitutional and conventional powers which make its potential sway over legislation and the budget much greater than that of the British House of Lords or the Canadian Senate. Indeed, its refusal to approve the budget contributed in 1975 to the constitutional crisis in which the governor general—peremptorily, as many have argued—dismissed Gough Whitlam as prime minister and invited Malcolm Fraser to form a government. Even as recently as the 1993 budget cycle, the Senate used delay to win several concessions from the Labor government. Keating ultimately had to accede to a new set of ground rules whereby his government would consult more fully with the Senate opposition in crafting the budget.

Locating the relationship between political executives and the career bureaucracy in developmental terms also mitigates the triumph of economic rationalism thesis. Indeed, the relationship bore some of the marks of a postcolonial administration until the 1970s. Australia, for instance, remained remarkably resistant to the concept that those starred to become its top administrators mainly come from a separate intake of young university graduates (Thompson 1994, 170–171). The first large influx of graduates to the Australian public service came in the 1960s. This period marked the height of the cadetship program whereby promising high school graduates entered the public service and pursued their degrees while working in Commonwealth departments. At the time of my initial interviews (1988), many departmental secretaries had come into the public service through cadetship—indeed, a disproportionate number of them had taken economics degrees and cut their teeth as civil servants in the Bureau of Statistics. The generational shift had laid the groundwork for the emergence of economic rationalists in the 1980s. However, by the mid-1990s the permanent heads of departments increasingly had done their university on their own steam and had not completed PhDs. Such generational shifts suggest a bureaucracy still undergoing consideration developmental transition.

A number of factors suggest that the argument that Australia under Hawke and Keating succumbed to a bureaucratic coup d'etat is counterintuitive. The size and diversity of the country, the complexity of governance—especially with the linkage between political culture and the federal system and the power of the Senate—and the tangible shift in the 1980s and 1990s toward transforming the bureaucracy from a postcolonial mind-set all would make it more difficult for public servants to pursue an overarching agenda such as economic rationalism without the instigation of the political leadership. Indeed, we might find grounds for arguing that the Hawke and Keating governments marked an instance where the political leadership achieved policy competence—namely, that they effectively meshed the requirements of their retaining public support while addressing creatively the issues faced by the state apparatus.

HOW THE TWO GEARBOXES WORK IN AUSTRALIA

The Relationship between Government and Bureaucracy

We might expect a man from Mars who was examining the relationship between the political executive and the bureaucracy in Australia to highlight factors different from the absorptions of Australian analysts. However, it is a bit disconcerting to this Canadian from Washington to find considerable disjunction between what strikes me as important about the politics/bureaucracy nexus in Australia and what many Australian observers stress. This split seems especially the case with regard to the issue of whether the Australian public service is elitist and where it is in its historical development.

AN EGALITARIAN REALITY

When observers make claims of elitism regarding one or other bureaucracy they usually stick. We cannot understand the immense power of the ministries of Finance and International Trade and Industry in Japan without beginning with the fact that these two departments skim the very brightest graduates from the University of Tokyo. When one reads the letters of recommendations for young Finance and MITI officials seeking places in American public policy schools one finds numerous references to ascriptive qualities such as how clubable the applicant is, his (inevitably) athletic prowess, and the type of family he is from. In France, both the political executives and top bureaucrats come in vast disproportion from the Ecole Nationale d'Administration (Suleiman 1974). Despite efforts at instituting alternate methods of entry, aspiring political administrators overwhelmingly come to ENA from Sciences Po in Paris an elite institute which, in turn, recruits mainly from the most prestigious lycées in the Paris area. Britain's Whitehall has demonstrated since the nineteenth century a marked preference for Oxford and Cambridge graduates who enter the public service soon after graduation (Campbell and Wilson 1995, 39–41).

The United States and Canada represent somewhat more egalitarian recruitment systems. These have founded themselves to a significant degree on specialized training. In the United States, two tracks operate— career officials and political appointees (Heclo 1977). The latter rely almost as much as the former on specialized training and have established themselves as policy professionals through a succession of positions in government punctuated by spells in think tanks or public interest organizations. There has been some variation in the prestige of the educational backgrounds of appointees in various administrations. For instance, Reagan appointees came much less frequently from Ivy League universities than did their Carter opposite numbers (Campbell 1986, 243–245). Aberbach has found a similar Ivy League bias in a preliminary examination of Clinton appointees in comparison to Reagan's and

Bush's (1996). We saw in Chapter 5 that when the Canadian public service was establishing itself as a force to reckon with, Rhodes Scholars
tended to win the bulk of prized positions (Granatstein 1982). However,
even Rhodes Scholars felt compelled to actually bring specialized skills
to their careers in Ottawa. Thus most rounded out their generalist education at Oxford with specialized training in the United States.

With the above as background, the outsider finds it difficult to access
how Australian scholars could argue so strenuously that their public service is elitist. In the 1930s, long after our other systems had established
fast tracks for university graduates, some quarters stiffly resisted the
idea of separate recruitment of graduates in Australia (Thompson 1994,
170–171). The Public Service Act of 1933 allowed a graduate intake
limited to 10% of positions in the public service. Even in the late 1950s,
the Boyer Commission still found a pronounced bias against university
graduates within the public service.

As Michael Pusey's analysis focused on the economic rationalist thesis, it pursued most vigorously the elitism of the Treasury Department
in Australia (1991). According to the popular image, the high-flying
Treasury official would have attended a prestigious private school and
graduated from the University of Sydney or the University of Melbourne
before entering the department. Readers might readily make such assumptions if their expectations for the origins of Treasury officials derive from observations about their role in Australian society. Yet anyone coming from outside Australia who has had experience with the
officials of similar departments in other systems would actually counsel that—in comparative terms—Treasury officials come across as relatively nonelite.

In the late 1980s, top Treasury officials often had received their secondary education at state-run schools in the communities in which they
grew up. Many had become cadets in government departments after
leaving school. This helped them earn their way through university. Thus
many officials had very longstanding commitments to public service.
For instance, Chris Higgins—the secretary to the Treasury who died in
1990 at the age of forty-seven—had served fully thirty years as a public servant. In the course of his career, he had completed his university
degree and a PhD at the University of Pennsylvania.

In interviews with sixty-seven official central coordinating departments in 1988–89, John Halligan and I even encountered some top officials who had left school earlier than eighteen to pursue training for

trades. Michael Keating—then secretary of the Finance Department and until 1996 secretary of the Department of Prime Minister and Cabinet—apprenticed to become a sawyer as a teenager. He completed high school while working and then entered the Commonwealth government as a cadet in the Bureau of Statistics. He ultimately completed a PhD at Australian National University. David Morgan—who was deputy secretary in the Treasury before leaving for the private sector in 1989 to become an executive vice president of Westpac Bank—began training to be an actor at the age of fifteen. He ultimately returned to school and continued all the way to the PhD degree.

The modal official in the generation ten years or more younger than Chris Higgins, Michael Keating, or David Morgan went to university under his own steam. However, members of this group also brought to their careers experiences which fly in the face of conventional wisdom. Many went to new universities like New South Wales, Macquarie, LeTrobe, or Monash rather than the more socially prestigious institutions like the University of Sydney or the University of Melbourne. The Australian central agencies have adapted fairly quickly, thus, to the expansion of the recruitment pool that resulted from the emergence of new universities.

Contrary to Pusey's conclusions, Australian central coordinating departments have not become elitist in absolute terms. Instead, they seem more to be emerging as a Canadian-style meritocracy in which expert training commands a premium. They bear virtually no resemblance to the elitism of U.K. central agencies to which individuals who did not go immediately from high school, normally a prestigious fee-paying one, to Oxford or Cambridge and then entered the public service soon after graduation would not even aspire. Australian central agencies run an exceedingly forgiving recruitment system in relative terms. This means that they bring in a highly diverse array of individuals with respect to social background. It also means that their numbers include many officials who have encountered social discrimination and economic hardship.

Under Labor, egalitarianism mixed with considerable exposure to hardship meant that—insofar as economic rationalism prevailed in the upper reaches of the Australian public service—it was tempered. Unlike the New Zealand case, the issue of social equity sustained itself as a concern of both Australian political leadership and top officials in plying a public choice approach. Paul Keating himself came from mixed social origins. His father, a tradesman, had built up a lucrative business but Paul had left school at the age of fifteen. As Treasurer his pursuit of economic rationalism did appear monotonic at times. As prime minister, he gave much greater weight to equity issues.

The Labor government in the implementation of public choice gave at least some consideration to the social consequences of its policies. This became clear when Brian Howe, a left-leaning Uniting Church minister, joined the Expenditure Review Committee (ERC) of cabinet in 1985. The ERC, as we will see later, served as the spearhead for advancement of economic rationalism. Thus any imputing of a symbiosis between the political leadership and top officials on economic rationalism during the Labor Hawke-Keating period must include the fact that each brought to the task backgrounds and agendas which inevitably mitigated any tendency toward monotonic approaches.

A PUBLIC SERVICE STILL IN A DEVELOPMENTAL PHASE

Analysts frequently enshrine what they have discovered in a snapshot as if it had become a steady state divorced from any further development. In some respects, it appears that critics of economic rationalism in Australia have made that error.

Pusey conveys his hypothesis very neatly in the subtitle of his book— *A Nation Building State Changes Its Mind.* This is too deterministic. Australia is still a state very much focused on building up the nation. The emphasis since the 1980s has been on economic viability. However, other elements of nation building still loom large. And, more profoundly, the Australian love/hate relationship with egalitarian principles (Thompson 1994) still works its subtle influences among the political executive and the higher reaches of the public service.

Pusey's analysis would make much more sense if he had placed it in a wider developmental frame. In this respect, we can identify four phases for the Commonwealth public service since WWII. During the 1950s and the 1960s, the service professionalized and graduates increasingly occupied senior posts. In this period, officials traded on their knowledge of the governmental apparatus and adherence to Whitehall-like rubrics, if not reality, of neutrality. The brief interval of the Labor government headed by Gough Whitlam (1972–75) pressed partisan responsiveness at the expense of neutral competence. Whitlam relied very heavily upon advisers from the outside—mostly lodged in the Prime Minister's Office—in a largely unsuccessful attempt to work around the standing bureaucracy (Weller 1985, 138–139). The Whitlam period, though brief, constituted a phase, because of the adjustment it required and the trauma left in its wake. The experience turned the Labor political leadership into steely realists about the task of getting a public service to do its bidding. It also worked an effect on the public service by underscoring the inevitable pressures toward responsive competence imposed by any change-oriented government.

The eight-year government of Malcolm Fraser marked a period in which the public service seemed to be lying fallow. In fact it was building a head of steam toward the emergence of economic rationalism. Previously, we noted that the 1960s saw the breaking of the dam against graduate entry. Largely entering through the cadet corps, young, university-trained officials found themselves on fast tracks to the top of the public service. Many of the very best of this group found or received time to work on PhDs. It was precisely during the Fraser years that these officials were reaching maturity. They were poised to remake the face of the upper civil service.

It becomes clear that most of the officials who held top roles during the height of the Hawke years looked back at Fraser with contempt. A cautious fuddler who saw himself as the experiential and intellectual superior of all comers in his cabinet, Fraser tried to run the Commonwealth government from the Department of Prime Minister and Cabinet (PM&C). The resulting centralization of decision making overloaded the center and antagonized the periphery. The attending operational dysfunctions led to considerable backlash to such an approach.

This takes us to the fourth phase of the Australian public service since the 1950s. Minimally, it strikes the observer as a time of symbiosis between a generation of political executives and a new cadre of senior civil servants. In short, it was a match made in heaven. Among the officials interviewed in 1988 and 1989, central agents seemed to have a difficult time restraining their enthusiasm. The positive evaluations of Hawke seemed to stem from the perception that he appointed a relatively competent ministry and learned how to resist intruding upon departmental affairs which ministers might more appropriately handle on their own. A new comity had arisen between senior permanent officials—especially those in central agencies—and the prevailing style of "executive" leadership that the Hawke administration was to adopt. This harmony set the stage for the emergence of the economic rationalist phase. Notwithstanding the residual forces of the 1960s' and 1970s' mentality, economic rationalists had dispersed themselves throughout the public service.

To begin, one could not go very far into the upper reaches of line departments without encountering former Treasury people or economists who espoused economic rationalism as if they had received their socialization in the Treasury. Many respondents in 1988 and 1989 remarked on the degree to which economics expertise attained such a premium throughout Canberra. One Treasury official dwelt on how the atmosphere had changed for Treasury officials in their relations with other departments: "We used to trot over to interdepartmental committee meetings and sit there as a very lonely Treasury voice trying to get Australia to move in a certain direction. You go to those meetings today and everybody is pushing in the same direction . . . a lot of them . . . have economics backgrounds" (1988 interview).

Several respondents explicitly associated the dispersion of economics expertise with the economic rationalism of the Hawke government. As one PM&C official noted, the 1987 machinery of government changes sharpened this trend by broadening the scope of ministerial responsibilities:

> . . . because of the change in the machinery of government structure a department like the old Department of Education may have been regarded as Sleepy Hollow—basically run by a bunch of ex-teachers and very nice people at the top. But education suddenly became the focus of Commonwealth policy and . . . became [part of] the superportfolio of Employment, Education and Training. . . . the government wanted people who were going to give effect to those policies . . . the shakers were brought in (1988 interview).

THE RELATIONSHIP BETWEEN THE PRIME MINISTER AND HIS GOVERNMENT

As we have seen in preceding chapters, the second gearbox—that between the individual chief executive and his administration—presents an entire array of separate considerations from those of the first gearbox—the relationship between an administration and the public service. We have found in the previous section that a symbiosis emerged under the Hawke government between the political executive and the bureaucracy. Although it received the tag "economic rationalism," the development did not just happen. It fit within the broader context of parallel generational changes on the political and career sides. I have asserted that we cannot assume that either cadre will remain static. Indeed, we might even expect that the symbiosis upon which economic rationalism developed might prove increasingly fragile.

When considering the second gearbox, two areas present themselves. First, we must look at how the cabinet system has functioned in Australia. Second, we must examine how the core advisory system has developed.

With regard to the cabinet system, Australia's has depended greatly upon the abilities—or the absence thereof—of individual prime ministers. However, the system does lend itself somewhat more than Canada's to coherent management. Key here is the fact that representational imperatives have not run through selection of ministers in the same way as in Canada. This has applied both in Labor and Coalition governments notwithstanding the fact that the Labor Party caucus selects from its midst those who will serve in the ministry. Few clearly discernible patterns have applied regarding how many ministers should come from each state or regions within them, whether and to what degree all of the big cities are represented, and whether the ministry covers key ethnic and religious groups. Women face a glass ceiling with few even making it into the ministry much less cabinet proper.

Unlike Canada, Australia has kept control over the size of cabinets. Until 1987, a constitutional convention prevailed whereby each minister had to head a separate department (Wettenhall 1989, 95–96; Halligan 1987). This procedure checked the growth of the ministry. Creation of new departments proved much more difficult than layering ministers within existing agencies or appointing ministers with extradepartmental functions—two practices which have been followed extensively in the United Kingdom and Canada. The practice whereby Australian prime ministers functioned with de facto inner cabinets further mitigated unwieldiness—at least in so far as this unwieldiness stemmed from size (Weller 1985, 130–131). Inner cabinets constituted roughly half of the ministry. They would deliberate separately on issues before, or even without, their going to full cabinet for formal approval.

In one bold stroke, Bob Hawke set aside the convention of one minister, one department in his major machinery of government reforms after the election of 1987. This change established a two-tier ministry. Members of cabinet would all head departments. However, radical amalgamation had reduced the number of departments from twenty-eight to sixteen. The remaining members in the ministry—fourteen in all—assumed ancillary roles toward departments. There was some reflation of the cabinet under Keating with eighteen departments and assignment of two slots to the Department of Foreign Affairs and Trade.

With regard to advisory systems, prime ministers since Whitlam have taken greater liberties than the opposite numbers in the United Kingdom and Canada. This applies both to use of private offices, theirs and other cabinet colleagues, and tapping the Department of Prime Minister and Cabinet (PM&C). Regarding private offices, Whitlam was the first to build up a significant independent source of advice in his private office (Weller 1985, 139–140). In its initial year, this unit served as the braintrust for the highly innovative Labor government. Its influence waned as the error-prone government began to lose confidence. By the end of the administration, Whitlam increasingly relied upon PM&C. It had bulked up significantly and adapted its approach to the prime minister's interest in alternative policy advice. The stage, thus, was set for the Fraser years.

This proved to be a period, as we noted earlier, in which the prime minister used PM&C as a counterbureaucracy through which to precook cabinet deliberations and micromanage the public service. Hawke broke with this pattern in two ways. First, if there was to be precooking, a preference was given to a cabinet body, namely, the Expenditure Review Committee. Second, private offices, not just for him but for all members of cabinet, came into their own. The units tapped a combination of political appointees, often styled "consultants," and career civil servants. The mix gave less of an impression of party-politicization than prevailed under Whitlam (Campbell and Halligan 1992, 203). It also created highly versatile networks which allowed cabinet ministers to coordinate their policies with a degree of independence from standing bureaucratic departments.

Just as the Australians have exerted discipline over the size of cabinet they have also limited the number of central agencies. Thus they did not go through a highly experimental phase similar to Canada's. However, in 1976, the Fraser government did hive off from the Treasury responsibility for the expenditure budget and management policy. Some insiders still consider the resulting Finance Department as the Treasury "B-Team." In fact the department plied a separate course from Treasury's and with considerable success. It clearly takes the lead in resolving budget issues with departments. The general expenditure division of the department serves effectively as the secretariat for the Expenditure Review Committee. This role greatly bolsters Finance's hegemony in budget matters as they relate to specific departments. Indeed, officials in line departments rarely dwell on the role of Treasury when asked to discuss their relations with central agencies. Finance has also put considerable thrust behind its responsibility for management reform. It has leveraged itself by linking its handling of budget questions to each department's willingness to innovate.

Two trends have appeared since the Hawke years which suggest that central-agency backgrounds count for a great deal in selection of upper-level personnel in line departments. Both have fostered the transmission of economic rationalism into line departments. First, before the rise of economic rationalism, the proportion of departmental secretaries with exposure to PM&C usually remained below 20%. In the early 1990s, this figure approached 70%—with many of these officials hailing from Treasury and moving on to PM&C. (Campbell and Halligan 1992, 172). Second, by the mid-1990s, many of the officials who became departmental secretaries brought to their work experience in Finance. This made sense. The bread and butter of Finance lends itself to the type of day-to-day interaction with line departments that could be parlayed into seeking top positions within these organizations.

TWO PRIME MINISTERS AND THE LUCK OF LABOR

The Labor governments which ruled Australia from 1983 to 1996 seemed to have been caught within the wider context of the crisis of executive leadership without actually having fallen victim of the public mood swings which made their situation so precarious. In Chapter 1, we considered the prospect that electorates in Anglo-American democracies have penalized the parties unlucky enough to be in government during the period of economic turmoil in the late 1970s and early 1980s. The Liberal Party, the main party in the Coalition government, struggled until it regained power in 1996 with precisely this type of uphill battle. It also appeared to be in a constant state of internal disarray—a condition which evoked memories of the Fraser government's final years. It was thought, too, that the Liberals would require the support of the National Party to form another government. (In fact, it gained more than enough seats to form a government of its own but chose to stick with the Coalition.) This tack made the image problems associated with disunity all that more difficult to overcome. Labor had often manifested disunity during the thirteen years of the Hawke and Keating governments. However, until 1996, it kept its act together sufficiently well to maintain public confidence.

Bob Hawke

Bob Hawke had an immense admiration for Ronald Reagan and George Bush. In fact, he would have liked Bill Clinton much more had the two leaders belonged to the same generation. Hawke, too, was a Rhodes Scholar. Although he never finished his dissertation, he had pursued a PhD in law at Australian National University (ANU). While in Canberra, Hawke mingled with some of Australia's most promising young minds—including fellow students in ANU's fledgling graduate school and recent recruits to the civil service. In today's vernacular, he even earned full standing as a policy "wonk" through his passionate interest in wage arbitration. If they were contemporaries, one could imagine Bob Hawke as just the type of individual who would appeal to Bill Clinton as a Labor secretary.

But Hawke also conveyed at ANU the aura of someone who desperately wanted to fit in. Here Clintonesque duality surfaces. On the one hand, Hawke easily won the position of scholar's representative on the university council. On the other, he sometimes carried on like a Philistine. One episode—whose recounting still makes the rounds at ANU—almost dethroned Hawke. During a night of revelry he amused his mates by swimming the length of a reflecting pool that cuts through the quadrangle of ANU's graduate residence. Hawke had to resign from the council or face dismissal from the university.

Hawke proved with age to have a serious side as well. He left ANU in 1958 to join the staff of the Australian Council of Trade Unions (ACTU). From the outset, he established himself as a tough and brilliant wage negotiator. In 1970, he became president of the ACTU. This position gave him national prominence. The ACTU serves as an all-encompassing umbrella for organized Labor in Australia. Especially in time of Labor governments, a circumstance which pertained between 1972 and 1975, the president of the ACTU performs as a prominent power broker. To capture Hawke's exposure during his period as ACTU president, it is worth noting that he served on the board of the Australian central bank from 1973 until he left the ACTU in 1980.

When Hawke won election to the House of Representatives many saw him as a potential leader of the Labor Party. He had been a professional politician in everything but name. However, he faced formidable obstacles. He had remained decidedly nonideological in his ACTU persona. This trait had led many true believers in the Labor Party to suspect his degree of commitment. Hawke also entered center stage in the middle of protracted struggle. Having lost power invidiously in 1975, the party had turned in on itself through bitter recrimination. The mounting economic storm clouds enveloped the scene in gloom. Many in Labor had drawn from the 1975 expulsion of the Whitlam government the lesson that pragmatism was in order. The world economic crisis now seemed to sound the death knell of big government. This situation gave many the sense of fighting on while selling one's soul. Hawke's pragmatism evoked in many neurotic anxiety.

As soon as Hawke arrived in Parliament, he began stalking the Labor leader, Bill Hayden. Indeed, Hawke pressed a full-dress challenge in 1982. This gambit failed. However, Hayden freely relinquished the leadership early in 1983. Polls showed he stood little chance against the Liberal prime minister Malcolm Fraser in the impending election. Hawke found the road clear for the leadership of Labor. The public found in Hawke a regular bloke whose pragmatism gave Labor renewed credibility as a party of government. Labor did not have time to alter its platform before the election. Hawke ran on generalities, stressing consensus leadership toward addressing Australia's economic ills. Playing the "things are much worse than even we thought" card, Hawke moved quickly when taking the reins of office to put his government on a no-nonsense, economic rationalist course. As we have seen, he found aid and comfort both among the right-wing members of his cabinet and the forty-something generation at the higher levels of the public service.

Hawke, thus, was no "new order" prime minister. In fact, his rise to power based itself on a repudiation of that reflex within the Labor tradition—the one which had contributed to Gough Whitlam's early demise. The times and part of Hawke favored an "executive" approach. And this tack would have prevailed if, as Michael Pusey has suggested, the bureaucracy had been able to channel entirely the thrust of the government in the direction of economic rationalism. However, Hawke's humanity entered into the equation at various important intervals. Hawke-the-pragmatist warred constantly with Hawke-the-conciliator.

Hawke did not embrace bold new ideas about helping the dispossessed. However, he often proved ready prey to arguments focused on the equitable distribution of the societal costs of economic rationalism. He also wanted his cabinet—which contained representatives of the left as well as the right—to function as a team. All of this pulled Hawke toward a "let's deal" approach based on reconciling various claimants:

> ... the recognition and negotiation of claims is the centrepoint of government and the leader is required above all to establish communication between claimants. This is Hawke's chief claim for himself in politics, and underlies his maneuvering in regard to the party and the party platform which aims at preserving some broker's flexibility outside his partisan responsibility. In Hawke's political style human relations—consensus, reconciliation, accord—to some degree take the place of abstract fidelities (Little 1983, 434).

Thus the style of Hawke's government became multiphasic. Swings from an "executive" to a "let's deal" approach and back again to the "executive" occurred at various stages of a mandate. Hawke tended to relax adherence to economic rationalism when electoral considerations loomed less large. However, he tended to give in to pressures from the right in his cabinet as elections approached. Since members of the House of Representatives receive only three-year terms, governments must go to the polls three years after each general election.

This lent a roller-coaster effect to Hawke's shifts of style. (Hawke had gone back to the electorate in 1984 largely because half of the Senate members' six-year terms had expired.) He drifted away from economic rationalism in late 1985 and early 1986. But Paul Keating, the Treasurer, lunged the government back on course with his famous May 1986 speech given while Hawke was visiting the People's Republic of China. Keating alleged that Hawke's deviations from economic rationalism had further taken Australia down the road to becoming a "banana republic."

The point that Keating was chafing at the bit to assume the Labor leadership and swung—in his utterance—the full weight of his prestigious department and the bond markets was not lost on Hawke. He became more Catholic than the pope. He ran the 1987 election on an unadulterated economic rationalist platform. Once he had received a new mandate, he introduced an ambitious structural adjustment program and put the civil service through a wrenching downsizing. Hawke again strayed from economic rationalism in the middle part of his third term. He became sufficiently concerned with equity issues surrounding budget cuts that he created a Social Justice Committee of cabinet. This body reviewed expenditure policies from the standpoint of the burdens assumed by various social groups. Still, as the third term approached its end, Keating again asserted himself, and the government swung back to fiscal conservatism. Indeed, Keating himself has admitted that his stringent 1990 budget proved too much good medicine by half. Australia plunged in the early 1990s into a recession much deeper in its consequences than that of most other Organization for Economic Cooperation and Development (OECD) countries.

Few—even in the Labor cabinet—expected Hawke to pull the government out of the fire in the 1990 election. In the immediate aftermath of the victory, Hawke stumbled badly. Part of this owed to burnout after seven years as prime minister—which even involved medical problems that slowed Hawke down. However, the core difficulty was that people were looking over Hawke's shoulder to Keating—wondering when the Treasurer would claim what he doubtlessly saw as his rightful inheritance. Thus Hawke's final year and a half in government sputtered along with greatly diminished coherence. Hawke no longer had the energy to lift his game from "executive" to "let's deal" politics. Keating challenged him in June 1991 and left the cabinet when he failed. He relaunched his effort in December 1991 and brought the Hawke primeministership to an abrupt, some might say "merciful," end.

GOOD AT GEARBOXES

Despite Hawke's foibles and tendency to shift from an "executive" to a "let's deal" style according to the winds of the time, he did an excellent job of working the two gearboxes that have proven so crucial to executive leadership in the age of volatile politics. To be sure, Keating buffeted him to the point where the question often arose "Who's prime minister here?" But the Labor government under Hawke proved uncanny in its ability to modulate partisan and neutral competence. It achieved the former sufficiently to renew its mandate three times—in the case of 1990 against very heavy odds; it attained the latter by coping with the new politics of constraint as well as any OECD country. At the end of the day, Hawke, not Keating, was prime minister.

REDEFINING THE RELATION BETWEEN THE POLITICAL
LEADERSHIP AND THE BUREAUCRACY

Like other Anglo-American administrations, the Hawke government sought to change dramatically the nature of the public service. This involved a two-prong strategy—the first concerning the responsiveness of the bureaucracy; the second, the efficiency and effectiveness with which the bureaucracy accomplished what it had been mandated to do.

The Hawke government adopted freshly coined American nomenclature to capture its approach to improving the responsiveness of senior bureaucrats. In 1979, the United States had created a Senior Executive Service (SES) which brigaded the top 6,000 or so career officials in a common corps with the 1,500 or so political appointees holding key jobs which did not require Senate confirmation. The original crafters of the Australian SES envisioned a greater number of political appointments within departments. Ultimately, Hawke chose instead to limit political slots to ministers' personal staffs. Thus the Australian variant of SES was a bit of a misnomer, as it never accomplished an expansion of the appointive cadre and a pooling of this with the career civil service.

While the Australian SES did not lead ultimately to a pooled service consisting of political appointees and career civil servants, many of its features laid the groundwork for a stronger linkage between the political leadership and permanent officials. For instance, the reforms made it clear that departmental secretaries were responsible to their ministers and could be removed from office. This procedure eventually formalized itself in an arrangement by which secretaries have five-year contracts. SES members encompassed five levels down in the corporate structures of departments.

The full potential of the Australian SES toward alteration of the civil service culture came to the fore in the massive machinery of government changes of 1987. Many "permanent" heads found that the abolition of their departments spelled the end of their careers. When all the sorting had run its course—twelve secretaries found their departments cut out from under them—the new top mandarinate bore all the marks of economic rationalism. The SES shed 179 individuals, 43% of whom left the public service entirely (Public Service Commissioner 1988, 7).

A thrust toward making the bureaucracy more effective and efficient took many forms during the Hawke government. Furthermore, the administration—and the Finance Department brain trust which took the lead in the various stages of the reforms—kept adding iterations to the process. These have served as central elements of the management reform effort.

Labor took pains to explain the structure and goals of its reforms—both inside and outside of government (Commonwealth 1983, 1984; Department of Finance 1988). The wealth of information on the reforms had even engendered remarkably open and lively debates between practitioners and observers who took a special interest in public service management (Keating 1988; Keating and Holmes 1990; Yeatman 1987; Considine 1988; Hood 1990).

The first reform—the Financial Management Improvement Program (FMIP)—emerged in 1984. Even before the Hawke government came to power, in 1983, Finance had formulated means whereby managers would become more conscious of the link between their resources and specific results. And, Labor—though in opposition—had placed a strong emphasis on management reform in the public service (Parliamentary Labor Party, 1983). John Dawkins—the first Finance minister under Hawke—picked up enthusiastically on the reform effort and pushed FMIP vigorously. The administration eventually moved to install the next phase of reforms—Programme Management and Budgeting (PMB) in time for the 1986–87 fiscal year.

Your author and John Halligan have examined the effect of these reforms in much greater detail elsewhere (Campbell and Halligan 1992, 144–162). Their implementation was not perfect in every respect. However, the experience stands in sharp contrast to the much more heralded case—that of New Zealand. A positive image of the administrative state permeated the Australian reforms. Thus the effort operated with a higher degree of autonomy from quasi-experimental impulses among economic rationalists bent on putting the operational departments in their place. The movement benefited greatly from the patronage of two powerful and effective ministers—Dawkins and his successor, Peter Walsh. Here the fact that Australia separates responsibility for budgeting and management policies from that for other economic functions played an important role. The Finance Department, especially under the leadership of Mike Keating—secretary from 1986 to 1992—dedicated considerable resources to conceptualization and implementation of reforms.

HAWKE'S CONSULTATIVE STYLE AND THE KEATING FACTOR

To many observers, the Hawke years present ambiguous signals if we ask what he contributed to the legacy of his government. His oscillation between "let's deal" and "executive" approaches makes it difficult to assess which worked the greatest effects. As well, Hawke continually faced situations in which Paul Keating would steal the limelight.

Generally, officials applauded Hawke's consultative style—especially in contrast to the monocratic approach of Malcolm Fraser. However, a disjunction developed in the government between Hawke's stylistic preferences and the tremendous force of Keating's approach. In Westminster systems, the constitutional position of the treasurer does differ somewhat from that of his other cabinet colleagues. In such systems, the treasurer—or his counterpart—shoulders responsibility for advising the government of the day on macroeconomic policy. He also takes the lead in devising the fiscal framework of the budget. In these systems, cabinets ascribe such value to the norms of secrecy that often only the prime minister and the treasurer establish key budgetary policy, without reference to cabinet or even an inner group of ministers.

The fact that Australian treasurers—or their opposite numbers in other Westminster systems—often can establish key economic and fiscal policies without vetting these before cabinet colleagues other than the prime minister makes them somewhat more than equal ministers. Further, research on central agencies in other Westminster systems suggests that officials in the Treasury or the equivalent ministry might begin to see themselves as guardians of special departmental constitutional prerogatives (Campbell and Szablowski 1979, 85–88; Campbell 1983, 57, 127–130; Campbell and Wilson 1995, 205–206). We can add to this perception the immense weight of any powerhouse of economic analysis during a time in which financial issues greatly constrict the art of the possible in all advanced democracies.

In the case of Paul Keating as treasurer, we find that sheer personality added a great deal of thrust to an already powerful office. Treasury officials heaped lavish praise on Keating's effectiveness in cabinet—even going so far as to assert that his role had eclipsed that of Hawke. As one respondent enthused: "We have a very strong treasurer who's the de facto prime minister. . . . I don't think anyone here would want to be under anyone else because you want to be with strength. So everyone in the Treasury likes the treasurer, you will discover" (1988 interview).

Many officials made the obvious connection between Keating's power and the fact that economic issues had the predominant sway over the government's agenda. Others, however, stressed the fact that Keating's acuity at swaying his cabinet colleagues and selling his positions to the rest of the Labor Party made the critical difference. As one respondent said:

> ... [the treasurer] gets his way over nearly everything. That puts us in a very powerful position ... [he] is so powerful because he can carry cabinet and he can shut down everybody else in Parliament. ... He's persuaded his colleagues to do things that none of them would ever have contemplated doing five years ago. When he's away overseas and Parliament is sitting, the government looks decidedly seedy if they come under sustained attack from the opposition (1988 interview).

The relative, in comparison to Fraser, detachment of Hawke from the day-to-day affairs of departments coupled with Keating's role as ringmaster of economic rationalism should not lead readers to conclude that Hawke let the administration run on automatic pilot. In fact he worked intensely at the teamwork side of cabinet government. In this respect, the Expenditure Review Committee became the center ring for the government.

Initially, ERC served as the core group for the economic rationalists. It emerged early in the government as a body designed to impose budgetary control. As was seen in Chapter 4, the Star Chamber in the United Kingdom—a secret committee of "nonspending" ministers which emerged at the outset of the Thatcher administration—served as a partial model for ERC. However, ERC differed in very substantial ways from the Star Chamber. First, it functioned year-round and not just during the height of the budget season. Second, unlike Mrs. Thatcher, Hawke assumed the chair of ERC and attended the bulk of its meetings. Third, the ERC involved itself in virtually all contentious issues between the minister of finance and departmental ministers. The Star Chamber, on the other hand, usually engaged in the eleventh hour of the budget process and focused only on matters in which lengthy negotiations between the chief secretary (the U.K.'s Treasury's minister responsible for expenditure) and spending ministers had broken down.

Through an iterative process of top-down discipline, the Star Chamber eventually fell into disuse. Ministers got the point that they had better settle out of court with the chief secretary. In the case of ERC, the discipline—although far from totally collective vis-à-vis cabinet— achieved a much higher degree of encompassment of key players in the ministry. An Australian respondent familiar with the operation both of ERC and the Star Chamber put it this way:

ERC meets on a regular basis—at least once every month. In theory it's
similar to the Star Chamber type of thing in the UK where it was basically an expenditure cutting thing. But, because it's a grouping of economic ministers coming together to discuss an aspect of macro policy,
its discussion gets to be much broader than just expenditure cutting (1988
interview).

The activity of ERC ebbed and flowed depending upon the preoccupations of the government and where it found itself in the annual budget cycle. However, during the most intense period building up to the
annual May economic statement, ERC went through a stretch of two or
three weeks in which it met virtually every day. Sometimes its sessions
would run for hours.

Similarly, Hawke's involvement in ERC shifted according to electoral or budget cycles. Immediately before the 1987 election, Hawke
was not attending ERC on a regular basis. After the election, he chaired
most meetings—even marathon sessions that went long into the night.
In this same period, the treasurer and the minister of finance also regularly involved themselves.

A treasury official articulated especially well the degree to which the
government strategy for bringing along the rest of cabinet worked. The
cohesion and effectiveness of the core group had preempted the possibility of "collusion" among spending ministers. This would have played
the prime minister, the treasurer, and the finance minister off the middle in an effort to forestall cuts:

> . . . at the end of the day . . . [the prime minister] is the adjudicator when
> very difficult conflicts arise in the expenditure review process between
> the treasurer and the minister of finance on the one hand and the spend-
> ing minister on the other. . . . But, it is within the context of the govern-
> ment's overall strategy already determined, with . . . [the] prime minis-
> ter's involvement, so the direction is not at risk by a high degree of
> collusion. On the contrary, the "collusion" has produced the direction. . . .
> It has definitely been led, rather than coming from the grass roots. But,
> it has been effective. A good illustration of this is [the inclusion] of Brian
> Howe [then minister for social security] (1988 interview).

ERC made a key contribution to the strong symbiosis which appeared
during the Hawke government and key segments of the public service.
We have noted previously that ministers, officials in central agencies,
and the secretaries of many departments shared a common economic ra-

tionalist perspective. As we observed, some respondents maintained that a synergy of views and interests made short shrift of sectoral interests and microeconomics. Group dynamics helped sustain this synergy. Officials accompanied their ministers to ERC and felt free to participate in the give and take of its deliberations. The prime minister, treasurer, and finance minister brought supporting officials with them to ERC. Nonmember ministers attended ERC when issues touching directly on their portfolios arose. Most brought along officials to provide support at critical points in discussions.

Paul Keating

A few years ago, Bill Gates, the computer software multibillionaire, visited several world political leaders to discuss the information superhighway. One of his first stops was Canberra and a session with Paul Keating, in February 1994. As he walked away from this encounter, Gates apparently allowed that "Keating was one of the smartest leaders he had met" (Gordon 22 October 1994). Since he was acquainting himself with world leaders, Gates might well have noted an obvious irony. He could easily have asked himself whether Australia—with its relative societal homogeneity and remoteness from the epicenters of global economics and politics—presented a sufficient challenge to a Paul Keating to engage fully his interest and energy. If economics and politics were globalizing as quickly and readily as information technology, the media, and telecommunications, Keating would certainly have emerged as a Bill Gates, or a media mogul like Conrad Black, Rupert Murdoch, or Ted Turner.

Scripture says that a prophet is never accepted in his own land. For an Australian prime minister, this means that he has the worst of both worlds. He cannot project himself very authoritatively on the world stage. However, he inevitably will wear out his welcome at home. This proves especially the case in Australia because "tall poppies"—those who aspire to leadership in the world as well as domestic stage—as often as not evoke resentment and derision among fellow countrymen.

Keating is a self-educated and self-made man. He left school at fifteen and worked his way up through the labor movement in New South Wales into politics. This history should not tempt readers to draw parallels between Keating and John Major. The Keating story does not strum at heart strings with accounts of a dysfunctional family and trouble at school. John Major should probably have been told when lured into politics, "Don't give up your day job." Politics was—from the age of fifteen till his party lost the March 1996 election—Keating's day job. And he was quite good at it, thank you very much. Accounts of Keating invariably pointed up his arrogance. However, the qualities which most sharply distinguished him from John Major and many other contemporary leaders were drive, raw intelligence, a sense of political architectonics, and, above all, hot and cold running ruthlessness. The following sketch by Paul Kelly, one of Australia's leading political commentators, will perhaps make the reader consider Keating as a John F. Kennedy who came up through the school of hard knocks:

> Possessed of a sharp brain and an artist's eye, Keating was a born political salesman. He was an enthusiast, a talker, a schemer, a manipulator, with an architect's mind in its penchant for clear lines and pure constructs. In the topsy-turvy world of politics Keating operated at one speed—fast, fast, fast. He began as boy politician in the Labor Youth Council and became a premature political veteran. He liked making friends and was never afraid to make enemies. Keating left school at fifteen, completed his Leaving Certificate at night and had no tertiary qualifications (Kelly 1994, 26).

As a self-educated man, Keating revealed a tendency to use his various jobs to expand his knowledge and ability. When he became treasurer, he put himself through a veritable course in economics. At first, this placed him somewhat at the mercy of his Treasury department tutors. In time, however, he became very much the master of his department and its subject matter.

Keating faced another problem when he became prime minister. He had to learn which issues to focus on and which to delegate either to ministers, collectively or individually, or his officials in the Prime Minister's Office or the Department of Prime Minister and Cabinet. Two difficulties constrained his development in this regard. He knew that a Malcolm Fraser—a person who attempted to run everything—would encounter the risk of becoming a jack of all and master of nothing. However, a collective approach—modeled after the operation of the Expenditure Review Committee under Hawke—also presented problems for Keating. ERC had become associated in most observers' minds with economic rationalism, an asset in Keating's previous persona as treasurer but a liability when he sought to expand his appeal beyond his role as promoter of markets par excellence.

Keating chose a modulated approach. Rather than chairing ERC he delegated this to the treasurer and focused his attention on deliberations with the treasurer and the finance minister in a "troika." This group afforded the principal ministers of the government the opportunity to set the broad outlines of its core strategy and make adjustments when ERC ran into major snags. Keating had reservations about whether chairing ERC as Hawke had would be a good use of prime ministerial time. More important, as some officials argued, his reconstruction in the eyes of the public required a certain distancing of himself from the tough decisions made over specific programs in ERC. As one respondent suggested, Keating had to paint on a larger canvas when he became prime minister:

> If I can make one observation that is somewhat of a political nature, I think the prime minister early on had to move a fairly definite way to establish his wider political credentials and his concern for social policy at large, not just economic management, so that had to be taken into consideration in deciding how much time he would give to the day-to-day decision-making process in the ERC (1994 interview).

We saw earlier that Hawke's style oscillated between an "executive" approach—largely associated with his involvement in ERC and need to keep his government's economic rationalist bona fides with the markets—and a "let's deal" approach—which he adopted when he had some breathing space between elections and became concerned about the social consequences of his administration's policies. Not totally surprisingly, Keating's eschewing of too strong an attachment with ERC meant that he veered strongly in the direction of a "let's deal" approach. This presented some problems. The chief executive who tries to operate as a "let's deal" leader must bring to his work an acute ability to scan the entire menu of issues and focus on those which truly require his involvement.

Many observers questioned whether Keating commanded this type of adroitness. Such doubts frequently emerged in the media. Jack Waterford of the *Canberra Times* put the issues especially cogently:

> Paul Keating, a poor cabinet chairman at the best of times, and a man who public servants and other ministers complain cannot and will not

read briefs, pays attention only if there is trouble, and concentrates on the "higher issues." . . . [he] waits for trouble to come to him, and often does not even know about problem areas (25 March 1994).

Most observers note that Keating generally got it right in the management of foundational issues. The work behind his two major statements, "One Nation" at the outset of his government and "Investing in the Nation" just before the 1993 election, enshrined the principle that the government would pursue a socially sensitive variant of economic rationalism. Along with concern about not leaving any groups behind along the road to economic prosperity, the government had proven effective at focusing attention on the need for longer-range views of investment—including, of course, infrastructure.

Similarly, most commentators gave Keating high marks for his handling of the aftermath of the Australian High Court's 1992 Mabo decision (Brennan 1995, 38–80). The decision recognized for the first time that aboriginal peoples in Australia may lodge claims for lands which were historically theirs and never formally transmitted to the sovereign (the government) or other parties. Initially, the decision did not cause a great stir. However, mining and agricultural interests soon twigged on the possible consequences of Mabo for development of their industries. Keating set his mind to providing a legal framework which would accommodate aboriginal aspirations regarding land claims while stanching impending panic in Australia's vital primary industry sector. He accomplished his objective in December 1993 with the passage of the Native Title Act.

Keating's emphasis of the big picture did not always lead to such good results. For one thing, he frequently engrossed himself in issues more on the basis of interest than foundational importance. Keating fancied himself as an authority on aviation. On occasion he had needlessly become ensnared in issues surrounding reorganization and privatization of Australia's national carriers. He likewise was sucked excessively into disputes surrounding expansion of the Sydney airport—an especially intractable issue for Labor because every conceivable solution affected constituencies at the core of its voter base in New South Wales.

In the telecommunications area, where huge debates waged over such essential issues as cable television, Keating became exceptionally subject to interventions from moguls whose favor he felt he had to curry to obtain necessary media support. One official familiar with the area portrayed a chaotic process in 1995:

> We can't do things in committees because we fear leaks. If word gets to the likes of Rupert Murdoch about some of our ideas, we can expect unfavorable news coverage and a blast from Keating the next morning. We try to work things out with just us and PM&C. But, we frequently find that our work is rendered still-born by a leak and an irate intervention from the prime minister (1995 interview).

A PLATEAUED STATE APPARATUS

The period of the Hawke government saw an unprecedented time of innovation in the Australian public service. The process included devolution of spending authority to lower levels of the bureaucracy and rationalization of the departmental structure. The Keating government did not successfully take the public service beyond these initiatives. One detects then a sense that the reform movement reached a plateau in the mid-1990s.

With regard to management innovation, respondents stressed two things. First, serious concerns about accountability had emerged, owing to some abuses associated with devolution. Second, the forked-tongue problem—whereby the Finance Department talked devolution but continued to involve itself in microsurveillance of departments' expenditures (Campbell and Halligan 1992, 144–62)—continued to undercut the perceived legitimacy of the reforms.

The accountability problems arose largely because the management reforms focused excessively on techniques and inadequately on the human element to implementation of the changes. Even one respondent who had played a critical role in pressing the reforms during the 1980s acknowledged this: ". . . we basically thought we had the management framework right, but there's a long way to go in terms of making it work. I mean just changing the culture, it always will inevitably take time" (1995 interview).

Under the circumstances, a bit of a stand-off emerged between central agencies and departments. This stalled further iterations in the process. A widespread view developed concerning evaluation—the centerpiece of the reform effort in the late 1980s—that it constituted hoopjumping for the Finance Department. As one top official in a line department put it:

> Evaluations do not address the threshold questions, like should there or should there not be such a program. Very rarely do you see an evaluation that says "this program is worthless, you should get rid of it"—per-

haps because there aren't many such programs. . . . evaluation has become a whole industry in itself, there are complex reporting requirements
to the Department of Finance. . . . it's a process with good intentions
which have been imposed and people have to go through the hoop when
professional line managers would have done the necessary parts of it anyway. But, instead you have to go beyond that and write elaborate stories
about what your plan is for the following year and what you did last year
(1995 interview).

Prime ministers do not usually spend a great deal of time worrying
about the fine points of management reform. Keating fitted within this
mold. The great thrust in the 1980s essentially came from the Finance
Department and two exceptionally able ministers, John Dawkins and Peter Walsh, aided by an extraordinarily strong team of officials. As Treasurer, Paul Keating took little interest in management reform. He had
little experience to carry over into his primeministership.

The rationalization of the departmental structure which took place under Hawke's machinery of government changes conceivably might have
earned a higher place in Keating's scheme of things. To be sure, the reforms emanated almost exclusively from PM&C with virtually no direct participation of cabinet. However, their key elements comported entirely with the economic rationalist view espoused by Keating. One
would expect, thus, that Keating as prime minister would want to hold
the line against any dilution of the reforms' impact—especially the core
concept that portfolios and cabinet slots should be based on managerial
rather than political rationales.

Keating, in fact, presided over a considerable softening of the economic rationalist concept of machinery of government. During his time
as prime minister, he created a separate portfolio for Tourism and he
split Transportation and Communication into two separate departments
each with its own minister. Further, he violated the 1987 concept of only
one cabinet minister per department by giving two cabinet posts to the
Department of Foreign Affairs and Trade. One PM&C official, while
acknowledging that these changes departed from the original thrust of
the machinery of government changes, viewed Keating's actions as inevitable in a period when the circumstances perhaps allowed for a less
monotonic commitment to efficiency over politics:

The 1987 reforms were driven very much by concern for the purity of
the decision making process with little consideration of personal political pressures. We are now getting something which reflects the pressures

of politics. . . . in order to devise changes of the magnitude of the 1987 reforms, you have to have a sense that things are a lot worse out there than they currently are. . . . you have to have an enormous premium on efficiency which doesn't happen all the time (1994 interview).

THE ECONOMIC RATIONALISTS' LOSS OF HEGEMONY

The "let's deal" style of Paul Keating visited upon his government a true irony. The imperatives of diversifying his image and power base led Keating as prime minister to soften economic rationalism as a core policy stance. In turn, life became substantially more complicated for the remaining cabinet ministers bent on maintaining some semblance of the discipline of the 1980s.

Keating, of course, had to reconcile his commitments to maintaining Australia's economic solvency while adhering to his oft-evoked pledge to build a society which will not leave the less advantaged behind. In the course of his government, Keating also took special interest in building a better infrastructure for Australian society and business. Within this framework, a view entrenched itself in the government that further cuts of programs and efforts to push structural adjustment on industry might do more damage than good. Apart from chiding the states to cut their bloated bureaucracies and rationalize their utilities, the government did not distinguish itself as an articulator of the economic rationalist view.

This reality provoked in the media a nostalgia for the old Paul Keating. In 1994, writers drew the parallels between Australia's current account deficit coming out of a recession (around 4% of GNP) and the circumstances in 1984 when economic rationalism first began to take hold (Wood 5 March 1994). Even Keating's intervention to provide relief to farmers during the drought of 1994 prompted at least as much contempt as understanding. One journalist chided the kinder, gentler Keating for going soft on the deficit:

> Just as Paul Keating, as the Grim Reaper of the 1980s, combined with Peter Walsh [the finance minister then] to turn the Budget from heavy deficit to substantial surplus in just four years, so Keating the statesman must now recover the ruthlessness, sense of mission and genius for statesmanship that enabled him to raise taxes, cut spending and have Australians accept it (Colebatch 6 October 1994).

For his part, Keating took every opportunity to adhere to his redefined persona. In spring 1994, he chided Australian business for exces-

sive profit taking and insufficient investment, warning it that unions
might come in with claims that reflect more labor's contribution to the
economic upswing (Robinson 20 March 1994). In October 1994, he even
appeared to revoke his 1986 banana republic speech when he minimized
foreign debt as largely business transactions "between consenting adults,
consenting borrowers and consenting leaders" rather than "sovereign
debt of the South American variety" (Dwyer 11 October 1994).

Keating's obvious retreat from economic rationalism exacerbated
problems associated with the functioning of cabinet—especially the crucial Expenditure Review Committee (ERC). As we saw before, Keating did not follow Hawke's practice of chairing ERC. He preferred to
delegate this function to the treasurer. Two difficulties arose here—one
associated with ERC's dynamics and the other with the personalities of
the two treasurers under Keating.

With respect to the first issue, as a general rule committees exert an
impact in direct relation to their status. In a system in which the prime
minister is first among equals, it follows that ERC received a demotion
in the minds of many through Keating's decision not to chair it. If ERC
decisions claimed less authority than they did previously then ministers
would take advantage of this modification to press their cases privately
with the prime minister. Excessive use of this recourse would further undermine ERC's authority and it soon would find itself in a vicious circle.

One strategically placed PM&C official reflecting upon the rather disastrous budget process of 1993—which led to the resignation of the then
treasurer John Dawkins—believed that end-runs around ERC had not
reached the point where they had undermined the committee's authority. Indeed, the officials almost invited more such activity as a way of
inserting the political component to budget decisions which had proven
somewhat lacking in the 1993 round: "I guess the overriding feeling
coming out of the last budget is that there would have been benefit in
a bit more of that. That the last budget was not politically sensitive
enough" (1994 interview).

With regard to the second difficulty, neither John Dawkins—treasurer
until January 1994—nor Ralph Willis—Dawkins's successor—had
proven especially effective as surrogate chairs of ERC. Dawkins badly
misread the government's vulnerabilities associated with its lack of control of the Senate. He failed to identify in advance items in the 1993
budget which would face stiff resistance from two minor parties—the
Greens and the Democrats. In an eleventh-hour deal, he got the budget

passed by the Senate by promising in the future to give members advance knowledge of especially contentious budget proposals. This truly constituted the government kicking the ball in its own goal. No other Westminster government (if we accept that New Zealand, because it has changed its electoral system might no longer belong to this category) has had to commit itself in advance to private negotiations with the opposition to smooth passage of its budgets. However, in this instance, the opposition did demonstrate restraint in its use of this access.

Willis's problems related more to a misfit between his personality and the difficulty of achieving discipline in a Labor government at best ambivalent about economic rationalism. Willis did not even come close to the forcefulness of a Paul Keating. Yet his ERC encompassed a much wider swath of the Labor cabinet than it ever did under Bob Hawke, which resulted in a lack of unanimity in the committee. Willis did not shrink from setting tough targets. However, he encountered a bit of a credibility gap. Many questioned his ability to actually deliver. One Finance official put it succinctly at the outset of Willis's term. Reviewing the factions in ERC itself: "In essence, if you were to look down—speaking very plainly—and looking down that list, you would have to say that Mr. Willis is going to have a hard time" (1994 interview).

Labor under Keating, thus, eased off on economic rationalism. And the main vehicle through which Labor pursued it—ERC—became badly carboned up. Keating's determination to remain once-removed from its day-to-day activities perhaps added to ERC's problems. However, a deeper point emerges from this analysis. It became clear that, unlike their opposite numbers in New Zealand, the political leadership and top bureaucrats under Labor only cautiously embraced economic rationalism. They consistently modulated their approach both when faced with electoral exigencies and when motivated by concern for the relatively disadvantaged in society. The bottom line for governance is not always markets. In fact, governance without humanity would seem to be a betrayal. Even the Conservatives in Britain pressed under Major the importance of social markets.

One finds in Canberra a ready-made cadre of tough officials who played mightily in the most stringent iterations of 1980s-style economic rationalism. However, at their core, they still believe that cutting back the state too much could make it impossible to build the type of country that they believed Australia was capable of being. This attitude came through strongly in interviews conducted in 1994 and 1995. For instance, one key PM&C official lamented the emphasis in the 1993 budget-round on tax issues. He believed that the country would better spend its time focusing on the type of society it was trying to become through its tax **and** expenditure structure: "I would have preferred the debate not to have gone onto the tax increases. Rather, we should have focused on what sort of society we want and how you can spend the money in the context of the society you want" (1994 interview). A top Finance official echoed these thoughts and amplified their consequences in an assessment of the 1994 budget round: "We are moving into the harder issues and a lot bigger issues of gray. The need to address these issues is still weighed very strongly on both sides of the political divide. It's just a manifestation of Australia and our place in the world and the things that we've got to do to make sure that all our kids have a good future."

Michael Pusey has suggested that the rise of economic rationalism under Hawke spelled the end of interest in nation building among the political leadership and bureaucratic elite in the Commonwealth government. The epitaph of the Keating years should perhaps say: "Here lie the nation builders whose demise was greatly exaggerated."

JOHN HOWARD, A BRIEF PRELUDE

In 1996, Australia went through a transition to a new prime minister, a transition which proved wrenching for the public service. The Coalition government—consisting of the Liberal and National parties and under the leadership of John Howard—took office in March 1996. It essentially maintained the departmental structures set out by Labor in 1987. In fact, it retrenched the number of cabinet-level departments to fourteen. This essentially rolled back the accretion of new portfolio ministries which had occurred under Keating.

The Howard government took an aggressive stance toward the public service. This posture became manifest in the government's plans to find $8 billion in expenditure savings over its first two years. Here it took the classic "we didn't know the cupboard was so bare" stance to partially justify cuts of such magnitude. However, it also pressed the view that the public service remained bloated. The order of envisioned cuts seemed to take such an argument beyond reason. It appeared at best questionable that a public service which had experienced relentless rationalization since the mid-1980s could still render cuts in running costs (staff and other management costs) in the order of 25%. The Coalition's draconian rhetoric probably set objectives which were not attainable without greatly impairing the core capacities of the Commonwealth government. It also cast a pall over Canberra.

Labor set up the top echelon of the mandarinate for the biggest Coalition encroachment on the permanent public service. Fully six department secretaries left the public service altogether because the new government wanted them out of their departments. Each was given an offer of an unpalatable position elsewhere. Keating had put departmental secretaries on five-year contracts. This had meant that they no longer could construe their positions as "permanent" until retirement. The Coalition seemed to follow no particular rhyme or reason in its choices. Although some of the officials had worked for Hawke or Keating in the Prime Minister's Office, they all had remerged with the general mandarinate years ago. One could only speculate that these individuals had had brushes—either because of their personalities or the difficulty of their portfolios—with the Coalition while it was in opposition.

Howard further placed the public service under threat by accelerating the retirement of Mike Keating, the secretary of the Department of Prime Minister and Cabinet, which was to have taken place at the end of 1996 in any case. In the 1990s, Liberal governments in the Australian states relied increasingly on hired guns in any shake-up (which is different from shaping up) of their civil services. One of these, Max Moore-Wilton, earned the handle "Max-the-Axe" when he advised two successive Liberal premiers in New South Wales. Howard elevated him to Mike Keating's former position even though Moore-Wilton never previously served as a departmental head, much less a secretary of a key central agency, in Canberra. He had, after leaving the NSW government, gone to the private sector. Doubtlessly on the grounds that private-sector blokes know a great deal more than public-sector ones about management, Howard embraced Moore-Wilton even though the latter came from a relatively minor position—national director of the Australian Stock Exchange's policy and priorities review.

When your author was visiting Canberra shortly before the March 1996 election, the Finance Department had almost completed a major review of its role. Finance finally had faced reality and recognized that it had to overcome the forked-tongue problem discussed previously. That is, it had to devise ways of getting expenditure reviewers in the supply divisions to become management consultants as much as budget examiners. The Howard government essentially aborted this process. It made it clear that it wanted Finance to go back to focusing simply on inputs. This perspective meant, of course, that even if the Coalition met its draconian budget cuts, it probably would not advance materially the managerial competence of the public service. In fact, it more likely would create such a demoralized cadre that the issue of competence would become moot in the extreme.

It seemed, thus, that Howard's actions in the realm of gearbox-I almost amount to a list of "don'ts" for anyone inheriting a public service. His moves on the gearbox-II front seemed less worrying. He kept control of the cabinet system by limiting the number of portfolio departments and committees. The Expenditure Review Committee (ERC) remained the most important cabinet body. However, Howard had to insure that it did not become a Star Chamber. Observers began soon to speculate about the return of a "Razor Gang" mentality in ERC. The emergence of a cut and slash approach would doubtlessly wear thin on the cabinet if it became clear that a clique of hardliners had taken control of expenditure decisions. Howard did initially take an active role in ERC. Direct prime ministerial participation can provide ballast against Razor Gang reflexes.

Howard took Australia for the first time on the road toward a Central-Policy-Review-Staff (CPRS)-like body in the Department of Prime Minister and Cabinet. He refashioned the Cabinet Office, which used to serve solely as the secretariat for the flow of cabinet business, as a source of independent advice on issues and the government's strategic policy directions. This refashioned unit drew staff both from within and outside of the public service. A long-time Liberal adviser with experience in the Department of Prime Minister and Cabinet, Peter L'Estrange, headed the unit. Previously, he had run the Menzies Research Center, a Liberal Party think tank. Such a unit, especially under the leadership of a person with L'Estrange's combination of skills, might achieve the difficult task of balancing a prime minister's need for party-political advice with intelligent engagement of his advisory resources in the permanent bureaucracy.

CONCLUSION

The pursuit of neo-liberalism by Hawke and Keating was relatively slow and cautious but steady. Labor under Hawke built on a firm foundation of supporting legislation and programs. If the explicit directions were not always apparent, they received plausible vindication in respective elections. For the same leader to obtain for his party four separate mandates constitutes a major accomplishment in Australia—especially since Hawke and Labor swam against the tide of public antipathy toward left-of-center parties which prevailed throughout the 1980s.

In several respects, Hawke fit the mold of electronically oriented chief executives. He pursued a highly personalized style. He engaged in re-crafting the roles of cabinet and bureaucracy in ways which did not shy from impinging upon perceived institutional prerogatives. Especially in the build up to elections, he stressed responsive over policy competence. This became especially the case in mid-1986 when the government clearly panicked and entered a prolonged period of survival politics.

Normally, analysts give low marks to political executives who adopt survival politics. They fear that leaders' desire to keep in power at any cost will lead them to indulge in "crisis inflation" (Campbell 1986, 10–13). That is, leaders who adopt survival politics will seize upon elements of national malaise which make circumstances appear to approach emergency proportions. If convinced of the urgency of matters, the public might suspend its disbelief and allow the government to take actions which abuse the government's prerogatives regarding the state apparatus and abandon long-term goals in favor of empty rhetoric and quick fixes.

Many critics of Hawke accused him of precisely these tendencies. However, we find less "crisis inflation" in Hawke's approach than in other leaders. Further, Hawke returned to his more characteristic style— a broker politics—once he had secured a third mandate and reversed the more adverse economic indicators. More important, Hawke's variant of survival politics—unlike most others—paid a great deal of attention to the gearbox between the political executive and the public service and within the cabinet. Rather than overriding—or even co-opting—the bureaucracy and cabinet, his approach identified the points of symbiosis and creatively engaged in a two-way dialogue.

Those who still saw a need for state provision of infrastructure, intervention in and regulation of the marketplace, and responsive social programs justifiably found grounds for bemoaning some of the consequences of the coalition between Labor and the upper ranks of the public service under Hawke. However, analysis does not suggest a new-right conspiracy in the economic rationalism which directed the

government through the period of survival politics. Rather, the symbiosis came from a prime minister who knew what kind of message
would restore confidence in his government and recognized that, if his
rhetoric was to stand the test of time, he would have to deliver upon it.

Auspiciously—both for Hawke's electoral success and place in history, a large and strategically located cadre of reform-minded officials
was waiting in the wings. So, he used them. If anything, Hawke and the
economic rationalists worked so well together because they recognized
a shared stake in an exceedingly difficult enterprise. This involved an
infinitely more ambitious task than that of the new-right administrations
in the United States and Britain. Hawke and the economic rationalists
did not set out to dismantle the socially responsive state. Instead, they
struggled with the task of making it viable in an environment in which
the public increasingly resented the role of government and economic
conditions began severely to constrict the art of the possible in responding to human needs. Readers who want to see what happens when
a government fails to adequately devise, enshrine, and implement a strategy for defending the social functions of the state need only look to the
case of Canada's Brian Mulroney. His administration remained in a near-
paralytic condition for eight years. It neither downsized nor reformed
the public service. Nor did it deal with the policy dilemmas which
emerged from the fiscal crunch.

Hawke's leadership style and the overarching strategy which guided
his administration relied very heavily upon the collaboration of the so-
called economic rationalist ministers, especially Paul Keating. In many
respects, Hawke owed much of his success to Keating. Through the
sheer force of his intellect and the power of his personality, Keating became the hub of the administration's most crucial coalitions. Not even
Hawke rivaled Keating in his adeptness at mesmerizing cabinet colleagues, forging bonds with the top mandarins, bludgeoning parliamentary opposition, wooing the business community, and cajoling unions.

No small irony confronts us when we look at Keating's record as
prime minister. To be sure, he kept Labor in power through yet another
mandate. However, the Nixon-goes-to-China magic of a Labor government resolutely pressing a neo-liberal agenda began to wear thin. And
Keating—the genius at executive-bureaucratic machination—could not
rise to the challenge in the task of projecting a kind and gentle image—
even though, in many respects, he relented on neo-liberalism more readily as prime minister than he had as treasurer. The softening of eco-

nomic rationalism left the way open to John Howard. In the 1996 election, Howard essentially ran on a platform of more of the same only more kindly and gently. However, the Liberals executed a classic bait-and-switch. Their post-election rhetoric made it seem that Australia had yet to encounter real neo-liberalism. Some observers began to grip themselves for politicized incompetence if the Coalition government persisted in administering neo-liberalism as if the Coalition had introduced it for the first time to the Commonwealth government.

7

Toward a Rehabilitation of U. S. Executive Leadership

This book has focused on the U. S. presidency within the wider context of crises of executive leadership in Anglo-American democracies. Its emphasis takes root in the commonality of the crises encountered by the United States and the other democracies. Until the past twenty years, all had proven immensely adaptive democracies with shared histories and constitutional traditions. They seem now to have plateaued. Their electoral systems only erratically produce the types of leaders that the times seem to require. The consensus about governance which prevailed in these systems in the 1950s and 1960s appears to have dissipated.

To be sure, the United States and other Anglo-American systems function under vastly greater physical dispersion than, say, the nations of Scandinavia. Yet they keep close tabs on one another. Language and shared antecedents seem to run deeper than location in Europe, the Americas, or the Pacific Rim. Perhaps it should not surprise us that neo-liberalism has spread as the flavor of the generation throughout the Anglo-American community. Structural and cultural vagaries have affected the passage of these countries into market-centered views of governance. However, few would question that, among advanced democracies, these nations belong to a separate club in the degree to which they have adopted the prevailing approach.

We might argue that Anglo-American systems have found their true selves in neo-liberalism. Three of them maintained sufficient suspicion of government intervention in citizens' lives that they devised federal structures. These serve to various extents as breaks on the power of national government. The United States stands alone in its adherence to separation of powers between the executive, the legislature, and the judiciary. However, Canada's 1982 constitution's embrace of a charter of rights established a new-found independence for the judiciary. As well, the European Council of Human Rights now very substantially impinges on British courts. This influence, in turn, has allowed the courts to deviate from decisions which adhere to relatively narrow interpretations of the will of Parliament.

None of our nations would fit neatly into "statism" as we know it in continental Europe and parts of Asia. We find in none of the systems a strong cultural tradition whereby citizens look to the state to provide national cohesion. The public in none of our countries thinks by reflex that only state intervention can resolve the crucial problems facing the populace. Each of our nations experienced an immense expansion of the welfare state in the middle part of this century. Yet a strong cultural undercurrent maintained ambivalence about the state assuming an interventionist role. This uncertainty made the programs highly vulnerable when the economies of the four nations began to feel the pinch of globalization.

Our publics—especially the economic middle groups within these—have since the early 1980s increasingly assumed boutique views of governance, supporting state provision of goods and services so long as benefit accrues to them personally. Otherwise, they lose interest. We have seen this especially strongly in the United States. For instance, baby boomers' parents became ambivalent about supporting public education once they got their children through school. Boomers themselves had fewer children and, thus, less interest than their parents in supporting schools. However, political leaders who dare even to moot changes in pension programs court strong backlashes from both boomers and their parents.

All of this has amounted to middle-class flight from the view of governance which prevailed in the 1950s and 1960s. The process has begun to tear the fabric of even the minimalist state which neo-liberals envision. This presents serious problems for executive leaders. Neo-liberalism brings its own cluster of unintended consequences. But the prevalence of the boutique view of governance leaves leaders little latitude for addressing these outcomes. This makes the middle even more estranged.

THE STYLISTIC DEFICIT

This book has examined in detail ten presidents and prime ministers: three American presidents—Ronald Reagan, George Bush, and Bill Clinton, and seven prime ministers—Margaret Thatcher and John Major (the United Kingdom), Pierre Trudeau, Brian Mulroney, and Jean Chrétien (Canada), and Bob Hawke and Paul Keating (Australia). In examining these leaders the conclusion that our systems have encountered considerable slippage in the capacity of leaders to deliver appears inescapable. And much of the responsibility seems to rest with the leaders themselves. Generally, it appears that style has supplanted substance. This development increasingly colors how chief executives modulate their approaches to leadership. It clearly works an effect on voters. However, one important caveat suggests itself here. Voters make their decisions increasingly on style. Indeed, they might develop messianic expectations for leaders in response to clever manipulation of symbols. However, they frequently have turned into a lynch mob when disillusionment sets in.

This book has attempted to eschew a bias toward any leadership style over another. In fact, it has pressed the principle that reduced public expectations for the state's involvement in their lives should prompt chief executives to adjust their sights accordingly. Profound difficulties have arisen, however, when leaders overcorrect. Many have come to the conclusion that reduced public expectations mean that they can pay less attention to the substance of governance. The 1980s presented chief executives with acute managerial challenges in living up to their promises to provide more with less. Few rose to the occasion. In the 1990s, their successors struggled with the less for less paradigm, a shrinking art of the possible for governance as the public clung increasingly to boutique views of what the state does and the types of resources it requires.

In our analysis, we discussed four styles of executive leadership. The age of boutique governance appears to have spelled the end of one of these styles. Studies of chief executives in the 1960s betrayed a pronounced preference for "new order" leaders. The times seemed to call for presidents and prime ministers who would present to the public bold plans for treating what ailed society with more government intervention. For many, John F. Kennedy became the darling of the era. His mastery at persuasion with electronic leadership became a model for leaders in our other systems, even though none of the prime ministers of the time brought Kennedyesque charisma to the political arena.

What some of the others did share with Kennedy during this era was a certain nobility of bearing in the face of opposition. This demeanor largely took the form of resilience under fire, the ability to promote one's agenda without showing rancor toward those bent on confounding you. Canada's Lester B. Pearson proved the master at this dimension of "new order" leadership. Indeed, he quietly advanced the frontiers of the interventionist state more than any president or prime minister of the time. Along the way, he never enjoyed a majority government. As well, he embodied the embarrassment many Canadians reveal about the notion of "glamour."

A decline in esteem of the "new order" paradigm for chief executives coincided with emergence of the age of constraint. Part of the process owed to changes in the public view of leadership. For instance, the Americans experienced a double disillusionment. Lyndon B. Johnson revealed what happens when a leader lacks the resilience to remain buoyant under fire. Richard M. Nixon struck horror in most of the public when it became clear what happens when a leader lacks a rudder, apart from an insatiable desire to gratify his ego. As Americans became inoculated against the imperial presidency, Britons, Canadians, and Australians began to worry about the "presidentialization" of the primeministership. None of our Westminster Anglo-American systems had produced anyone as mean as Johnson or as venal as Nixon. However, prime ministers' use of electronic appeals to enhance the leverage of their office did scare many observers.

None of the presidents or prime ministers we looked at in detail successfully adopted the "new order" approach. Clinton, of course, toyed with it at the beginning of his administration but ultimately saw that he could not pursue it and retain the presidency. Our leaders therefore are left with three approaches, namely "executive"—bringing one's resume to bear in an attempt at doing better at running government; "being there"—manipulating the symbolic resources of office with a view to making the public feel better about their nation, and "let's deal"—seeking paths toward building-down the state that will preserve the most vital functions.

Whatever the style chosen by our leaders, they all have encountered difficulty. Ronald Reagan and Margaret Thatcher opted for the "being there" format—although the latter in her early years attempted the "executive" approach. Reagan clearly confused style for substance. Especially during his second term, he seemed to have lost the plot. Thatcher became so enamored of her ability to deal on the symbolic level that she turned herself into an icon. Her legacy proved a considerable impediment to the Conservatives in seeking a realistic paradigm for governance in the 1990s.

Although several of our leaders have aspired in some way to "executive" politics (Thatcher, George Bush, John Major), only two have sustained the style. Ironically, Pierre Trudeau—who went through every one of our four styles during his lengthy tenure as prime minister—did very well at using "executive" politics between 1972 and 1974 as a means toward rehabilitating the image that the Liberals had enjoyed for providing efficient government. His flamboyant character otherwise found him alternating between "new order" pretensions and "being there" conceits. If we only looked at Jean Chrétien's mastery of doing less with less, we would find a genius at "executive" leadership. Unfortunately, governance as good management proved less compelling in coping with the challenge of Quebec separatism.

Our leaders who ended up taking the "let's deal" route seemed to have encountered a similar type of difficulty. The style appears to call upon special skills at modulating approaches. On the one hand, it requires an ability to sense when one should short-circuit standing operating procedures and seize the opportunity to work a deal. On the other hand, it must include a firm mastery of detail and core commitments. I find myself going back once again to Paul Quirk's distinction to the effect that "let's deal" leaders can show flexibility about means but not about ends. A chief executive who becomes too facile will lose sight of this crucial element to the approach.

George Bush—given the experience he brought to government—surprised many observers by not rooting his "let's deal" approach in a sound balancing of means and ends. Bill Clinton did worse. His unfamiliarity with the Washington arena meant that he often did not even know when he was compromising ends in order to enshrine means. John Major brought to the table an exceedingly weak personal core and a gaggle of cabinet colleagues, many of whom represented caricatures of Margaret Thatcher's worst qualities. The resulting cacophony put Major in a ceaseless spin over means, ends, and everything in between. Brian Mulroney knew so little about the distinction between means and ends that he impaled his own party. Bob Hawke, on the other hand, enjoyed a cabinet with a high degree of ideological consensus and, with the obvious exception of Paul Keating, an aptitude for suppressing the impulse to gratify one's ego by winning over means. The Hawke government did the best of any we have examined closely at responding to the age of constraint without ripping the fabric of the state. Keating tried to continue this accomplishment. He largely succeeded. But he lacked two Hawke qualities—the ability to communicate to the people what he was attempting and a talent for getting the best out of his cabinet. His demeanor did not help with an Australian public that had become susceptible to the argument that "Enough is enough." Only Pierre Trudeau could have rivaled Keating in behavior that critics could label "arrogance."

In more auspicious times deficits in leadership approaches would amount to failures in rising to immense possibilities and not making the best of these. Certainly, the sense that Eisenhower had underachieved in this way constituted the central motif of the American public's embracing Kennedy. After eight years of a president who proved chary of seizing new opportunities, the electorate eagerly followed Kennedy into the "New Frontier." In fact, George Bush at the height of euphoria over victory in the Persian Gulf attained the only approval ratings ever to exceed those of Kennedy just before his assassination.

Deficits in the current age of protracted public skepticism and fiscal constraint have amounted to a different complex of issues. The experience of the United Airlines pilot who successfully crash-landed (if that is not an oxymoron) a DC-10 that had lost its hydraulic system comes to mind. Rather than soaring into the wide blue yonder as leaders did in the 1950s and the 1960s, many of their counterparts these days find themselves trying just to land safely under seemingly insuperable odds. To use another airplane analogy, leaders today at least find themselves in the situation of the Air Canada cabin crew of a Boeing 767 who discovered over the wilds of Manitoba they had no fuel and were miles from Winnipeg—the closest airport. Voila! The pilot was a weekend glider-enthusiast and the copilot had been stationed in a closed Canadian Air Force base within gliding distance of the fuelless 767. The two coaxed their aircraft down to a safe landing on the abandoned runway.

The ascendancy of style over substance does not help in an age in which the circumstances call for more, not less, adroit chief executives. In buying into the view that government must shrink, the public seems also to think that governance has become easier. The growing penchant for "outsiders" as against "insiders" reflects this difficulty. No one would ever ask a weekend Cessna pilot to take over the controls of a Boeing 747. But publics in Anglo-American systems, especially during the 1980s, have flirted with the view that amateurs work better than professionals as presidents and prime ministers.

Error-prone governance emerges from the current complex of forces on executive leadership. Both the "executive" and "let's deal" chief-executive approaches require immense patience and resilience, the latter more so than the former. However, incumbents—selected as they are more on the basis of style than substance—have not revealed great quantities of these attributes. As a result, many have tended to make a hash of a fairly straightforward though difficult proposition like gliding a 767 to a safe landing. Some have choked up completely when their hydraulic systems have gone.

Everyone of the leaders we have examined closely has encountered sizable difficulties in managing the building-down of governance. Ronald Reagan became so ensconced in his own mythsphere that he could not see the mounting deficit for all the tax cuts, failures to cut domestic spending, and profligate indulgence of the Pentagon. In the second term, the American public's inattention to the internal contradictions of his administration lulled Reagan into thinking that he could take still longer afternoon naps. One result was the Iran-Contra debacle. The president saved himself from ignominy in this instance because his argument that he did not know what was going on appeared to many as eminently plausible.

By ignoring mounting signs that Saddam Hussein had gone a bit off, George Bush had made U. S. policy in the Persian Gulf into a DC-10 without a hydraulic system. He recouped, but at the cost of inattention to other global hotspots and domestic politics. Bill Clinton's resilient personality made him act as if he was soaring into the wide blue yonder. Actually, he was having a devil of a time deciding whether he should land his fuelless aircraft at National Airport, Dulles, or Baltimore Washington International. Meanwhile, the passengers' knuckles became whiter and whiter.

Margaret Thatcher's inattention to cabinet government led to the Argentine invasion of the Falkland Islands. At the outset, the British effort to retake the Falklands appeared to be a matter of bringing down a 767 with no fuel. However, events turned into a more drastic DC-10–sans-hydraulics situation. The Argentines learned that the aluminum superstructures of Royal Navy frigates burned to a crisp when hit by French Exocet missiles. Yet Thatcher derived exactly the wrong lesson from the Falklands victory. She began to pump up the job of transitioning to the age of constraint to another feat of flying without hydrolics crisis. When the alarmism began to wear thin, she struck out at European integration as a dire threat. John Major had to live with the dysfunctions of Thatcher's approach to leadership. When several little Mrs. Thatchers tried to run a country a cacophony resulted which hardly instilled public confidence. The inability of the Conservatives to fashion viable British responses to continued European integration persisted as an intractable problem for the United Kingdom. Major essentially destroyed his credibility as a leader just a few months into the Conservatives' final term. Being too clever by half, he proclaimed that he would talk inflation down to zero. The perverse effect of this policy amounted to an explosion in the government's baggage compartment. The hydraulic system blew in the shape of a run on the pound.

Pierre Trudeau piloted the Canadian state over a span of sixteen years. In his early years, Trudeau might have handled the forbidding array of problems arising with the crisis of Quebec and the emergence of stagflation with the aplomb of the real-life 767 pilot. In fact, he had become quite ham-handed by the late 1970s. From then until he left office formally, he deeply embittered Quebecois and Westerners through mean-spirited and divisive initiatives in response to both the constitutional and energy crises. Meanwhile, he let the deficit balloon far beyond economists' wildest fears. When the Progressive Conservatives took over from the Liberals, the state had become a hydraulicless DC-10. The notion that bonhomie could substitute for hydraulics constituted the central folly of the Mulroney years. Governance, from handling the national unity crisis to reducing the deficit to supplying the military with new toys, became a tissue of delusions spinning uncontrollably from whole cloth. Between November 1993, when the Liberals again resumed power, and October 1995, when the separatists almost won the referendum in Quebec, Jean Chrétien began to make Canada look like a 767 with fuel. His personal approval ratings exceeded those of any other chief executive among advanced democracies. A number of tough decisions rationalizing and reducing what government does even helped restore confidence in the financial community. The Quebec referendum placed much of the increased confidence in question. Liberals found themselves in wind shear. The 767 might well have been fueled. But the conditions were pulling it wildly both horizontally and vertically.

The experience of Bob Hawke as prime minister and Paul Keating as treasurer in Australia from 1983 until the latter resigned from the cabinet in 1991 certainly evokes thoughts of a pilot/first officer relationship that worked. Australia's 767 clearly was running out of fuel by 1986. Hawke had sustained Labor through two elections with bonhomie. Temperamentally, he would have cast the 1986 crisis as one simply requiring more of the same. Keating, on the other hand, had gotten religion. He knew that Labor definitively had to chart a course for neoliberalism. He, thus, challenged Hawke publicly in his famous banana republic speech. When Keating left the government, Hawke had become so shopworn that he could not even summon bonhomie. Yet, as Hawke's successor, Keating found that he lacked this precious emollient. When voters embraced the Coalition's "Enough is enough" slogan in the election of 1996 they clearly had directed their anger at Paul Keating and not at neo-liberalism.

Problems with gearboxes have frequently revealed themselves in our analysis. These gearbox problems have played substantially in our leaders' difficulties. Two fallacies have prompted chief executives to pay insufficient attention to mechanics. The first, associated with gearbox-I, has them concluding that they can get along without the neutral competence proffered by the permanent bureaucracy. The second, related to gearbox-II, finds them assuming that—by having made the standing civil service more pliant—coordination of their cabinet and/or political appointees will follow much more readily.

Several of our leaders encountered serious difficulties with gearbox-I. The Reagan administration proved highly error-prone because it chose to build walls between political appointees and career officials. Bush attempted to bring these barriers down but only partially succeeded. Clinton's poor sense of boundaries—as represented most egregiously in the health care reform effort—meant that the standing bureaucracy found itself with too many masters and a sea of confusing signals.

Thatcher revealed a love/hate relationship which had her cleverly engaging some officials and parts of the apparatus and summarily dismissing others. The cumulative effect of the Thatcher approach made Whitehall very substantially more responsive to party-political stimuli than before. This became a huge problem under Major. A cacophony of voices in the political leadership supplanted the monocratic force of Thatcher's style.

Trudeau also brought about cultural change in his permanent bureaucracy. The problems which emerged under him related, however, much more to the complexity of design—largely stemming from his rationalistic approach—rather imperiling the public service's aptitude for neutral competence. Mulroney could not have contrasted more sharply with Trudeau in that he abhorred structure. He might have adopted a Thatcherite-style selective engagement, but his attention span could not sustain that. Chrétien inherited a public service which had become deeply demoralized due to Mulroney's inability to manage gearbox I. Chrétien proved adept at modulating advice emanating from the bureaucracy with the preferences of his cabinet and party caucus except in a few instances. Unfortunately, his handling of the 1995 Quebec referendum fit within the "poor modulation" bin.

Hawke receives high marks from this analysis for getting the most out of his public service. Critics believe that they have spotted a conspiracy in which the Hawke government identified like-minded officials, termed "economic rationalists," and forged an unholy alliance. This interpretation falls very wide of the mark. Two generational shifts, one among the political leadership and the other in the top levels of the bureaucracy, produced the symbiosis which became known as economic rationalism. By the time Keating came along, the economic rationalists had pretty much done their dash. The fact that Keating wanted to make policy on his own made development of a new symbiosis virtually a nonstarter.

Our chief executives also encountered considerable difficulty with gearbox-II. Reagan's disciplined administration became a shambles during the second term, as indicated by the Iran-Contra fiasco. The events leading to Saddam Hussein's invasion of Kuwait strongly suggest that coherence had proved an elusive commodity in the Bush administration's handling of foreign affairs. On the domestic side, striving for coherence took the form of augury about John Sununu's state of mind. Clinton would have to achieve viable coordination of his mind and his heart and the right and left sides of his brain before even thinking of achieving greater coherence in his administration.

Thatcher achieved coherence through intimidation. This provided a united front, especially in times of crisis. However, it also meant that a great deal was not brought to cabinet and properly discussed for fear of primeministerial ridicule. This made the government error-prone in some instances, most notably the lead-up to the Argentine invasion of the Falklands. Any prospects of Major achieving coherence went out the window when he squandered the political capital gained from achieving his own mandate on the foolish objective of zero inflation.

Trudeau's experience with cabinet government ebbed and flowed. At its best, it brought some of the finest political minds ever assembled in the cabinet room to bear on the issues of the day. At its worst, it turned into a rudderless graduate seminar led by a professor whose great mind was elsewhere. Thus coherence became somewhat hit or miss—more the latter in Trudeau's final years. Mulroney's cabinets were certainly not into great minds. And whatever their efforts at collective decision making, Mulroney's tendency to short-circuit cabinet processes undermined participants' belief that their recommendations would actually stick. Chrétien brought to the cabinet table immense experience. This included a healthy respect for the need of achieving coherence through collective deliberation.

Through his investment in cabinet and its committees, principally Expenditure Review, Hawke gave vastly more time to collegial processes than any of our other leaders. This involvement provided a focal point for the symbiosis which developed around economic rationalism. Hawke kept himself close to the pulse beat of the difficult process whereby a left-of-center government attempted to reconcile neo-liberalism and concern for society's vulnerable. Keating tried to do all of the balancing in his head. Under him, a palpable disjunction emerged between the level of political machination (a domain ruled by Keating) and that of getting the most out the public service (the domain of the Expenditure Review Committee).

FROM PASTEL BACK TO BROAD-BRUSH?

Writing separately in 1991, two sage observers of executive leadership— Bert Rockman (Campbell and Rockman 1991, vii) and the late Peter Jenkins (14 November 1991)—came up with the same expression to capture what ailed George Bush and John Major as chief executives. Rockman characterized Bush as a "pastel political personality." He asserted further that Bush had made himself a sort of chief-executive chameleon. His vaunted popularity—Rockman wrote before the collapse of Bush's approval ratings in fall 1991—derived from his blending into the political context of the moment. America was catching its breath from the headier Reagan years. Bush's radical determination not to lead gave the country space for deciding where it wanted to go.

Jenkins, writing in fall 1991 as Britons were developing concerns about Major's seeming lack of direction, believed that his "pastel hue" had begun to clash against the political realities of the "broad-brush" of the run up to the 1992 election. Like Bush, Major had made a virtue of appearing visionless. Jenkins, however, was arguing that the impending British election had placed Major in a situation in which he had to define his direction. Rockman anticipated a similar fate for Bush. Independent of the impending 1992 presidential election, Rockman detected a secular swing in the public mood from benign indulgence of a visionless president to rising expectations (Rockman 1991b, 23).

Early in 1993, a number of factors suggested that, indeed, pastel politics had taken a turn for the worse. That is, the Anglo-American democracies began to serve up hosts of problems which seemed to be prompting chief executives to take more sharply defined positions. Signs of immense stress on infrastructure due to budget cuts seemed to have aroused public concern. The media could summon any number of accounts of the unintended consequences of major deregulation or privatization initiatives. Generally, electorates seemed to have twigged on the deleterious effects of trimming and dismantling social safety nets.

Importantly, the backdrop to pastel politics had changed. During the Cold War, Anglo-American leaders—especially U. S. presidents and British prime ministers—could wrap themselves in their respective flags when the public was wanting broad strokes. Through astute use of "crisis inflation" they could present the illusion of leadership while in fact simply distracting public attention (Campbell 1986, 10–13). With the collapse of the Soviet Union, the foreground suddenly became the backdrop. Not even George Bush could camouflage his failure to treat domestic ills with smoke and mirror effects. The fact that he lost his reelection bid so soon after his triumph in the Persian Gulf drove this point home emphatically.

The intervening years since this early-1993 prognosis provide at best mixed evidence of a return to broad-brush politics. Bill Clinton appeared capable of broad-brush leadership. However, his first attempt at a masterpiece, the health reform package, suggested that he did not have a clue about composition. His administration retreated to least-common-denominator positions. Its studious observance of its "triangulation" strategy would make the backgrounds for the TV series *Miami Vice* look broad-brush. Newt Gingrich and his Contract with America certainly satisfied all the requirements of a broad-brush approach. However, the fact that the Republican zealots actually meant what they said finally sunk in and scared the American public. Major made a profession of re-pressing the broad-brush tendencies of his party. Meanwhile, a subli-mator par excellence, Tony Blair, waited in the wings. Canada's Liber-als ran in 1993 on a platform called the "Red Book." They had adroitly identified the hot button issues which suggested that the electorate might be moving into a broad-brush phase. In government, they became pas-tel whenever they encountered resistance. The Australians flirted with broad-brush politics when John Hewson led the Liberals in the 1993 election. At the last minute, they scurried back to Labor. But Paul Keat-ing, Mr. Arrogant, could not make himself as nonoffensive as John Howard, Mr. Pastel, in the 1996 election.

In 1993, when Bill Clinton was seen carrying around a biography of FDR, it still did not appear as if chief executives would find the way open toward "new order" politics. The prevailing public moods in Anglo-American systems would not sustain brave new ventures in pos-itive statecraft. However, clusters of social ills had developed which ap-peared to stem from the build-down of the state. The public reflex seemed less willing than before to excuse even benign neglect of these problems on the part of chief executives. Further, some signs developed indicating that voters might recognize the need for bitter medicine: for instance, that only tax increases and cuts of favorite programs could lead to appreciable deficit reduction.

Clinton's clutching of FDR's biography signaled, thus, an opportu-nity for leaders to take slightly more dramatic steps toward a more pos-itive view of the state. To be sure, voters still remained profoundly trau-matized by the 1970s bursting of the bubble that had sustained candy-store politics during much of the 1950s and 1960s. Chief execu-tives still could not pursue "new order" approaches. However, they could at least attempt "executive" or "let's deal" styles which sharpened the parameters of governance without expanding the role of government. That is, within the limited art of the possible, they could lift their game by leading publics to decisions which could make the best of difficult circumstances. Such challenges could promote adoption of realistic fis-cal policies—both regarding revenue and spending. They could also introduce thoroughgoing assessment of the consequences and outcomes of government policies including decisions to circumscribe the role of the state.

TOWARD A RECASTING OF EXECUTIVE LEADERSHIP

The dawning of the new millennium might tempt us to think grand thoughts about the types of executive leaders we will require in Anglo-American societies in the twenty-first century. This book will discipline itself by sticking to the more modest task at hand: How do we get these aging democracies on a footing which will allow them to think creatively about their missions in the twenty-first century?

In the first and second thirds of the twentieth century the Anglo-American nations galvanized as bulwarks of democracy. Notwithstanding the preoccupation of the Anglo-Saxon political mind with individual rights, our countries also became places in which attaining equality of opportunity served as a centerpiece of statecraft. Since the early 1970s, technology—through electronics—has served up leaders poorly qualified for statecraft of any kind. Further, globalization has clipped the wings of our countries' economies. The demise of the Keynesian world of steady growth, low inflation and high employment has put paid to the candy-store possibilities of the interventionist state. To many in our nations, equality of opportunity as a democratic goal became the carry-on baggage which passengers leave behind if their plane crashes.

We find ourselves in a trend toward improvement. Experience seems to count more in the selection of chief executives. This phenomenon might mean that electorates have become more cautious about electronic appeals which blithely skate over political and economic realities. The economies of our four countries appear as well to have stabilized. All have experienced considerable slippage in the definition of full employment. That is, all now tolerate higher levels of unemployment before adopting special measures for those without work. As well, concerns have emerged in each nation about whether the economy has left completely behind substantial numbers of young and middle-aged workers who lack the skills required to find work. Yet our systems seem to have gotten themselves out of wild gyrations in unemployment. Our economies also remain recession-prone. The bond markets have become neuralgic about any hint of inflation. And all of our systems have encountered problems with perceptual lags whereby voters believe they still suffer from episodes of recession when the economy has actually recovered and their personal circumstances have improved. Yet confidence seems to increase as each passing year lightens the memory of the late 1970s and stagflation.

Thus, we might well be moving into an epoch which invites chief executives to pursue more positive statecraft than we have seen since the early 1980s. As Bill Clinton discovered with his failed health care reform, the new environment probably will not sustain major and/or intricate attempts to redefine the role of the state. However, such attempts will go beyond the smile-with-a-name-tag on the status quo which characterized John Major's Citizens' Charter.

The emergence of a renewed vision of statecraft will call, initially, for hard-nosed assessment of the unintended consequences of the build-down of government. The renewal will then look to pressure points. Where can government make a difference? What essential functions have gone into free fall and need rescuing? What new, unaddressed problems have emerged from the age of minimalist government which urgently require attention? Many chief executives and the cabinet officers and officials upon whom they rely might prove temperamentally ill-disposed to this type of statecraft. That is, they will bring to office either nostalgia for the interventionist era or inertia from the age of contraction. We really are looking here for pilots and first officers who do not choke just because their 767 has run out of fuel yet recognize that they will not be able to soar.

As well, the new breed of chief executive must center his or her appeals much more than before upon palpable economic benefit. We have given a great deal of attention to the degree to which Anglo-American peoples eschew organic views of society. On occasion, individuals in these nations will give assent to policies not based on narrow self-interest. However, such situations have become relatively rare. The expansive programs of the 1960s and 1970s strained the capacity of our political cultures for governance beyond managing the interface between the state and the market. This reality poses daunting difficulties for those trying to capture segments of the population who still harbor high expectations for governance. No matter how much their hearts bleed in the right place, chief executives heading traditional left-of-center parties have encountered backlashes whenever they have tried to move their appeals rightward.

Bill Clinton's encounter with health care reform has become almost emblematic of the obstacles faced by leaders trying to inch forward the social welfare. The cost of health insurance became a central concern of corporations in the early 1990s. As well, the sizable constituency for efficiency and effectiveness could point to some embarrassing facts about American, market-style health care. For instance, it consumed a greater proportion of GNP than any other health care system and cost much more to manage. An opportunity presented itself whereby an astute leader could wed concern about costs with social concerns. The system did provide Cadillac coverage to a portion of the population. But it offered nothing to huge categories of individuals. Most troubling here were those whose treatment costs had exhausted existing coverage and those without insurance due to unemployment or a change of job.

Clinton tried to form a grand coalition around health care reform but failed. His concept, managed competition, would have expanded coverage by regulating the insurance market and limiting costs. Much of the insurance and care provision establishment saw this new government role as threatening. Those concerned about the uncovered did not receive sufficient assurance of universality. Middle-income Americans with coverage saw the specter of an immensely complicated system which seemed bent upon forcing them into managed care.

As we saw in Chapter 3, Clinton himself eventually acknowledged that he bit off too much in trying to bring about comprehensive reform with a shaky coalition. However, even incremental changes had encountered difficulty. In the final days of the Reagan administration, Congress passed legislation providing protection for the elderly who fell victim to catastrophic illnesses which threatened their life savings. The Bush administration got Congress to rescind the legislation. It could not take the flak from wealthy elderly taxpayers reacting to the additional levy against their income designed to pay for the new coverage. Therefore, any attempt to meld economic and social justification must consist of one part pragmatism and the other courage under fire.

SOME BEARINGS FOR FUTURE PRESIDENTS

Late in 1995, an American Airlines 757 smashed into a mountainside while on approach to Cali, Colombia. The pilots had become distracted in conversation. They could have taken over the controls at the first sign of confusion over their course. Instead, they made a succession of adjustments to the automatic pilot the cumulative effect of which spelled disaster. A few months later, American Airlines acknowledged that it had to revamp training so pilots would become less deferential to the computers which nowadays do most of the routine work in flying. They recognized that they had to take a leaf from Northwest Airlines' emergency manual whose cover emblazons in red letters the obvious exhortation "FLY THE AIRCRAFT."

Presidents have not done well at flying the aircraft these days. Many have been lulled into overconfidence when approval ratings seem to allow them to sustain leadership without actually engaging the machinery of government. George Bush captured the phenomenon perfectly in fall 1990 when he defied Congress by saying that he found it easier to deal with Saddam Hussein than with Congress. A year later, Bush had put Hussein out of Americans' minds. And the fact that he did not know how to relate to Congress became palpable.

This book has focused on the presidency as related to executive leadership elsewhere in the Anglo-American world. Along the way, it has looked for ideas about how presidents might better attain policy competence. This involves achieving a blend of responsive and neutral competence which would allow leaders to modulate their reliance on direct appeals to the public and engagement of the standing apparatus for government. Creative blending of these emphases would allow leaders to achieve their ends with fuller utilization of the permanent machinery available for governance. It would also provide greater immunity against mishaps resulting from overreliance on the "automatic pilot" of governance in the electronic era—that is, focusing only on what the polls are saying.

The experiences of presidents and prime ministers in our four countries suggest many specific areas in which the former might attain a greater degree of policy competence. These fall, of course, under the two headings which we have employed in this book, namely gearbox-I and gearbox-II. The first concerns the relationship between an administration and the permanent bureaucracy; the second, how a president relates to his team, including the cabinet and personal advisory staff.

In the 1960s, political scientists generally viewed presidents as huge beneficiaries of the emergence of electronics as a leadership tool. Now presidents appear most susceptible to the hobbling effects of what we might term multiple electronic advocacy. More than just the president can make media appeals. The resulting cacophony has jaded the public. What seems to alarm the public most is the emergence of a governability gap. The combination of multiple electronic advocacy with the separation of powers has presented the image of hopelessly gridlocked government. Bill Clinton failed at bridging the gap even though he was the first president in twelve years to have a Congress controlled by his own party. Newt Gingrich thought he could close the gap by turning a Republican-controlled Congress into the de facto government. We should not dismiss the possibility of the eventual development of such a competing steering capacity in Congress. Indeed, the United States might gradually drift toward French-style cohabitation in times when the presidency and Congress are controlled by different parties. That is, the congressional leadership might compete cogently over the agenda-setting function.

If presidents want to steer better they will have to pay a great deal more attention to the two gearboxes. The first, in fact, will probably require the cumulative efforts of successive presidents. Incumbents must see the importance of making the gearbox between an administration and the career public service governance by collaboration between political appointees and permanent bureaucrats who otherwise would be strangers.

Presidents must cut back on the levels of political appointees between the heads of departments and agencies and the first layer of career civil servants. My Japanese students who come to the Graduate Public Policy Institute in their late twenties have already encountered more opportunities to work directly with their top political authorities, ministers, than many permanent U. S. officials in their fifties would experience with their cabinet secretaries. Increasingly, administrations keep top officials from the big executive-bureaucratic contest. This exclusion exacerbates the tendency for bureaucrats to leverage themselves through contacts with congressional staff and interest groups. Either that, or they hunker down within their specialized areas and do research work with only marginal utility to governance, much less the administration of the day. Whichever, the disconnect between appointees and permanent bureaucrats carries with it immense costs. Presidents would gain a much more engaged public service if they eliminated appointees as much as possible from the deputy-assistant-secretary level (that is, five layers down in departments). They also should greatly reduce the staffing of policy research (as contrasted with analysis) units in departments. They should encourage the links between appointees and career officials to be tight. However, they should pursue lean and mean policy units. Gone are the days when bureaucratic organizations can provide havens for researchers who see work with immediate policy salience as something to avoid.

Management reform in the public service presents a formidable challenge to future presidents. The United States lacks a unified civil service culture, making comprehensive change immensely difficult to achieve. Administrations have not helped by narrowly construing what reform might involve. Even Vice President Al Gore failed to set the right tone. Most of his anecdotes about what ails the public service focused on the activities of what the French call *petits bureaucrates* and on the foolishness of relatively isolated actors. Someday an administration must come up with a view of the public service which amounts to more than the sum of all its parts. Relatedly, it has to provide the infrastructure for thinking about the public service in more than departmental terms. The Office of Personnel Management might have proven a vehicle for this task had Reagan not gutted it. Ironically, the Clinton administration dismantled much of the Office of Management and Budget's management policy capability as part of its efforts at "reinvention."

Task forces working close to the president or the vice president can provide a great deal of energy to change. However, administrations have to connect the zealots to the permanent apparatus if reform efforts are to go beyond the ephemeral. Usually, the department responsible for the budget keeps the lines out to the entire bureaucracy necessary for dissemination of best practices. Administrations will, of course, encounter the difficulty of budget examiners not thinking management amounts to that much as administrative costs only comprise a small part of what they review. But they do not resolve the problem by yielding to the budget agency's distaste for management. Ultimately, cultural change will occur only in pockets of the public service unless management reform relates to budgeting. That is, only budget agencies keep lines out to the totality of the public service. Only they can introduce and enforce systems which require departments and the line bureaucrats within them to use innovative management to optimize available resources.

The second gearbox presents even more daunting challenges for presidents. First, few U. S. cabinets have functioned as teams. Presidents who want to base collegiality on group dynamics find little support for this in constitutional conventions. Those who have achieved some success have, therefore, pressed the instrumental utility of such approaches. Here Reagan during the first term stands out. He had become convinced of the need for cabinet consultation while governor of California. By reflex, he would remind cabinet secretaries who lobbied him privately that he had to "roundtable" issues before reaching decisions. The Reagan II, Bush, and Clinton administrations all saw considerable retreats from this principle. In these instances, presidents attended meetings only sporadically. When cabinet secretaries conclude that the president probably will not be at a meeting, they more likely than not will send a delegate. Ultimately, cabinet-level bodies effectively become deputies' committees. Once again the opportunity to create group dynamics which can buttress cabinet teamwork slips through the president's fingers. The temptation of some deputies' groups to save time by meeting electronically further exacerbated problems associated with developing teamwork in administrations.

The configuration of the White House staff has posed especially severe problems for presidents. The experience of Republican incumbents since WWII suggests that they frequently fall victim to chiefs of staff bent on arrogating to themselves too many prerogatives of the president. On the other hand, Democratic presidents tend to run relatively chaotic White Houses. The art of the possible for each type of president no doubt relates to the foibles of their respective parties.

Regardless, the modified-spokes-in-a-wheel (MSIAW) format as pursued by Reagan in his first term presents itself as highly worth emulating regardless of the partisan culture from which the president comes. We might expect Republican presidents to develop relatively disciplined variants. They might even lean somewhat toward a chief of staff approach. If so, they must recognize much earlier than historically when they have grown the chief of staff too large. No White House can run effectively if the chief of staff's ego starts to eclipse the president's. On the other hand, Democratic presidents have to exert a great deal more care in the selection of the "spokes" in the White House wheel. They should restrict these to three or four people each of whom serves as a hub for a significant cluster of White House activities. Democrats represent an exceedingly diverse group. Presidents face no small challenge in selecting staff members who embody the diversity of the party while at the same time being able to work together. Democratic presidents have to weigh more carefully the degree to which diversity might come at the cost of teamwork or vice versa. The impression that Bill Clinton did not learn how to do the presidency until after November 1994 stems to no small degree from the fact that the mid-term election defeat forced him to achieve a modicum of MSIAW.

References

SCHOLARLY AND OFFICIAL PUBLICATIONS

Aberbach, Joel D. 1991."The President and the Executive Branch." In *The Bush Administration: First Appraisals*, eds. Colin Campbell and Bert A. Rockman. Chatham, NJ: Chatham House.

Aberbach, Joel D. 1996. "The Federal Executive Under Clinton." In *The Clinton Presidency: First Appraisals*, eds. Colin Campbell and Bert A. Rockman. Chatham, NJ: Chatham House.

Aitkin, Don. 1985. "The New Electorate." In *Government, Politics and Power in Australia*, eds. Dennis Woodward, Andrew Parkin, and John Summers. Melbourne: Longman Cheshire.

Arndt, Heinz W. 1978. *The Rise and Fall of Economic Growth*. London: Longman.

Aucoin, Peter. 1990. "Comment: Assessing Managerial Reforms." *Governance* 3:197–204.

Baker, Ross K. 1993. "Sorting Out and Suiting Up: The Presidential Nominations." In *The Election of 1992*, ed. Gerald M. Pomper. Chatham, NJ: Chatham House.

Barber, James David. 1972. *The Presidential Character: Predicting Performance in the White House*. Englewood Cliffs, NJ: Prentice-Hall.

Barber, James David. 1977. "Comment: Qualls' Nonsensical Analysis of Nonexistent Works." *American Political Science Review* 71:212–225.

Bartlett, C. J. 1992. *"The Special Relationship: A Political History of Anglo-American Relations Since 1945."* New York: Longman.

Berman, Larry. 1979. *The Office of Management and Budget and the Presidency, 1921–1979*. Princeton: Princeton University Press.

Berman, Larry and Bruce W. Jentleson. 1991. "Bush and the Cold-War Worlds: New Challenges for American Leadership." In *The Bush Administration: First Appraisals*, eds. Colin Campbell and Bert A. Rockman. Chatham, NJ: Chatham House.

Blackstone, Tessa and William Plowden. 1988. *Inside the Think Tank: Advising the Cabinet 1971–83*. London: Heinemann.

Blais, Andre and Stephane Dion, eds. 1991. *The Budget-Maximizing Bureaucrat: Appraisals and Evidence*. Pittsburgh: University of Pittsburgh Press.

Bothwell, Robert, Ian Drummond, and John English. 1981. *Canada since 1945: Power, Politics and Provincialism*. Toronto: University of Toronto Press.

Bradley, A. W. 1989. "The Sovereignty of Parliament—in Perpetuity?" In *The Changing Constitution*, eds. Jeffrey Jowell and Dawn Oliver. Oxford: Oxford University Press.

Brennan, Frank, S.J. 1995. *One Land, One Nation*. St. Lucia: University of Queensland Press.

Buchanan, James M. and Gordon Tullock. 1962. *The Calculus of Consent: Logical Foundations of Constitutional Democracy*. Ann Arbor: University of Michigan Press.

Bureau of Industry Economics. 1994. *International Performance Indicators: Overview*. Research Report 53, Feb. 1994. Canberra: Bureau of Industry Economics.

Burnham, Walter Dean. 1996. "Realignment Lives: The 1994 Earthquake and Its Implications." In *The Clinton Presidency: First Appraisals*, eds. Colin Campbell and Bert A. Rockman. Chatham, NJ: Chatham House.

Burns, James MacGregor. 1963. *The Deadlock of Democracy: Four-Party Politics in America*. Englewood Cliffs, NJ: Prentice-Hall.

Butler, David and Dennis Kavanagh. 1992. *The British General Election of 1992*. New York: St. Martin's Press.

Campbell, Colin. 1983. *Governments Under Stress: Political Executives and Key Bureaucrats in Washington, London and Ottawa*. Toronto: University of Toronto Press.

Campbell, Colin. 1985. "Cabinet Committees in Canada: Pressures and Dysfunctions Stemming from the Representational Imperative." In *Unlocking the Cabinet: Cabinet Structures in Comparative Perspectives*, eds. Thomas T. Mackie and Brian Hogwood. London: Sage.

Campbell, Colin. 1986. *Managing the Presidency*. Pittsburgh: University of Pittsburgh Press.

Campbell, Colin. 1988. "The Search for Coordination and Control: When and How Are Central Agencies the Answer?" In *Organizing Governance: Governing Organizations*, eds. Colin Campbell and B. Guy Peters. Pittsburgh: University of Pittsburgh Press.

Campbell, Colin. 1991. "The White House and Presidency Under the 'Let's

Deal' President." In *The Bush Administration: First Appraisals*, eds. Colin Campbell and Bert A. Rockman. Chatham, NJ: Chatham House.

Campbell, Colin. 1993. "Political Executives and Their Officials." In *The State of the Discipline II*, ed. Ada W. Finifter. Washington, DC: American Political Science Association.

Campbell, Colin and John Halligan. 1992. *Leadership in an Age of Constraint: The Australian Experience*. Sydney: Allen & Unwin.

Campbell, Colin and Donald Naulls. 1991. "The Limits of the Budget-Maximizing Theory: Some Evidence from Officials' Views of Their Roles and Careers." In *The Budget-Maximizing Bureaucrat: Appraisals and Evidence*, eds. Andre Blais and Stephane Dion. Pittsburgh: University of Pittsburgh Press.

Campbell, Colin and George Szablowski. 1979. *The Superbureaucrats: Structure and Behavior in Central Agencies*. Toronto: Macmillan.

Campbell, Colin and Graham Wilson. 1995. *The End of Whitehall: Death of a Paradigm*. Oxford: Blackwell.

Campbell, Colin and Bert Rockman, eds. 1996. *The Clinton Presidency: First Appraisals*. Chatham, NJ: Chatham House.

Carmichael, Edward. 1988. "The Mulroney Government and the Deficit." In *Canada Under Mulroney*, eds. Andrew Gollner and Daniel Salee. Montreal: Vehicle Press.

Castles, Francis G. and Deborah Mitchell. 1992. "Identifying Welfare State Regimes: The Links Between Politics, Instruments and Outcomes." *Governance* 5:1–26.

Chartrand, P. J. and K. L. Pond. 1970. *A Study of Executive Leadership Paths in the Public Service of Canada*. Chicago: Public Personnel Association.

Commonwealth of Australia. 1983. *Reforming the Australian Public Service: A Statement of the Government's Intention*. Canberra: Australian Government Publishing Service.

Commonwealth of Australia. 1984. *Reforming the Australian Public Service: A Statement of the Government's Intention*. Canberra: Australian Government Publishing Service.

Considine, Mark. 1988. "The Corporate Management Framework as Administrative Science: A Critique." *Australian Journal of Public Administration* 47:4–17.

Cooper, John Milton, Jr. 1983. *The Warrior and the Priest: Woodrow Wilson and Theodore Roosevelt*. Cambridge, MA: Harvard University Press.

Dahl, Robert. 1971. *Polyarchy: Participation and Opposition*. New Haven: Yale University Press.

Department of Finance. 1988. *FMIP and Program Budgeting: A Study of Implementation in Selected Agencies*. Canberra: Australian Government Publishing Service.

Derlien, Hans-Ulrich. 1993. "German Unification and Bureaucratic Transformation." *International Political Science Review* 14:319–334.

Destler, I. M. 1982. "National Security II: The Rise of the Assistant (1961–81)." In *The Illusion of Presidential Government*, eds. Hugh Heclo and Lester M. Salamon. Boulder, CO: Westview.

Diamond, Martin. 1975. "The Revolution of Sober Expectations." In *The American Revolution: Three Views*. New York: American Brands.

Dimbleby, David and David Reynolds. 1989. *An Ocean Apart: The Relationship between Britain and America in the Twentieth Century*. New York: Vintage.

Dobbin, Murray. 1993. *The Politics of Kim Campbell: From School Trustee to Prime Minister*. Toronto: Lorimer.

Doern, G. Bruce and Brian W. Tomlin. 1991. *The Free Trade Story: Faith and Fear*. Toronto: Stoddard.

Doern, G. Bruce. 1971. "The Budgetary Process and the Policy Role of the Federal Bureaucracy." In *The Structures of Policy-making in Canada*, eds. G. Bruce Doern and Peter Aucoin. Toronto: Macmillan.

Donahue, John D. 1989. *The Privatization Decision: Public Ends, Private Means*. New York: Basic Books.

Drew, Elizabeth. 1996. *Showdown: The Struggle between the Gingrich Congress and the Clinton White House*. New York: Simon & Schuster.

Durant, Robert F. 1992. *The Administrative Presidency Revisited: Public Lands, the BLM, and the Reagan Revolution*. Albany: State University of New York Press.

Edwards, George C., III. 1991. "George Bush and the Public Presidency: The Politics of Inclusion." In *The Bush Administration: First Appraisals*, eds. Colin Campbell and Bert A. Rockman. Chatham, NJ: Chatham House.

Edwards, George C., III. John H. Kessel, and Bert A. Rockman. 1993. "Introduction." In *Researching the Presidency: Vital Questions, New Approaches*, eds. Authors. Pittsburgh: University of Pittsburgh Press.

Esping-Andersen, Gosta. 1990. *The Three Worlds of Welfare Capitalism*. Cambridge: Polity.

Feigenbaum, Harvey B. 1985. *The Politics of Public Enterprise: Oil and the French State*. Princeton: Princeton University Press.

Feigenbaum, Harvey, Richard Samuels, and R. Kent Weaver. 1993. "Innovation, Coordination, and Implementation in Energy Policy." In *Do Institutions Matter? Government Capabilities in the United States and Abroad*, eds. R. Kent Weaver and Bert A. Rockman. Washington, DC: Brookings.

Fenno, Richard F., Jr. 1959. *The President's Cabinet: Analysis in the Period from Wilson to Eisenhower*. Cambridge, MA: Harvard University Press.

Finn, Paul. 1993. "The Law and Officials." In *Ethics in Public Service*, ed. Richard A. Chapman. Ottawa: Carleton University Press.

Fisher, Nigel. 1982. *Harold Macmillan*. New York: St. Martin's Press.

Franks Report. 1983. *Falkland Islands Review, Report of a Committee of Privy Councillors*. London: Her Majesty's Stationery Office.

Freedman, Lawrence. 1988. *Britain and the Falklands War*. Oxford: Blackwell.

George, Alexander. 1974. "Assessing Presidential Character." *World Politics* 26:234–282.

George, Alexander. 1980. *Presidential Decisionmaking in Foreign Policy: The Effective Use of Information and Advice*. Boulder, CO: Westview.

Glassco Commission. 1962. *Report for the Royal Commission on Government Reorganization,* abridged ed. Ottawa: Queen's Printer.

Goldenberg, Susan. 1994. *Troubled Skies: Crisis, Competition and Control in Canada's Airline Industry*. Whitby, Ontario: McGraw-Hill.

Gordon, Michael R. and General Bernard E. Trainor. 1995. *The General's War: The Inside Story of the Conflict in the Gulf War*. Boston: Little, Brown.

Graetz, Brian and Ian McAllister. 1987. "Popular Evaluations of Party Leaders. In the Anglo-American Democracies." In *Political Elites in Anglo-American Democracies*, eds. Harold D. Clarke and Moshe M. Czudnowski. DeKalb, IL: Northern Illinois University Press.

Granatstein, J. Y. L. 1982. *The Ottawa Men: The Civil Service Mandarins, 1935–37*. Toronto: Oxford.

Granatstein, J. L. and Robert Bothwell. 1990. *Pirouette: Pierre Trudeau and Canadian Foreign Policy*. Toronto: University of Toronto Press.

Green, Donald P. and Ian Shapiro. 1994. *Pathologies and Rational Choice Theory: A Critique of Applications in Political Science*. New Haven: Yale University Press.

Greenstein, Fred I. 1982. *The Hidden-Hand Agenda: Eisenhower as Leader*. New York: Basic Books.

Gwyn, Richard. 1980. *The Northern Magus: Pierre Elliott Trudeau and Canadians*. Toronto: McClelland and Stewart.

Halligan, John. 1987. "Reorganizing Australian Government Departments, 1987." *Canberra Bulletin of Public Administration* 52:40–47.

Halligan, John and J. Power. 1990. "Development Stages in the Reform of Australian Public Sectors." In *Dynamics in Australian Public Management*, eds. A. Kouzmin and N. Scott. Melbourne: Macmillan.

Hansen, Michael and Charles H. Levine. 1988. "The Centralization-Decentralization Tug-of-War in the New Executive Branch." In *Organizing Governance: Governing Organizations*, eds. Colin Campbell and B. Guy Peters. Pittsburgh: University of Pittsburgh Press.

Hargrove, Erwin C. 1992. "Presidential Personality and Leadership Style." In *Researching the Presidency*, eds. George C. Edwards III, John H. Kessel, and Bert A. Rockman. Pittsburgh: University of Pittsburgh Press.

Hawke, Bob. 1994. *The Hawke Memoirs*. Port Melbourne: Heinemann.

Heclo, Hugh. 1977. *A Government of Strangers*. Washington, DC: Brookings.

244 *The U.S. Presidency in Crisis*

Heclo, Hugh. 1981. "Introduction: The Presidential Illusion." In *The Illusion of Presidential Government*, eds. Hugh Heclo and Lester M. Salamon. Boulder, CO: Westview.

Heclo, Hugh and Aaron Wildavsky. 1974. *The Private Government of Public Money*. London: Macmillan.

Henderson, Alan. 1990. "The Commonwealth-State Dimension." In *The Cabinet & Budget Processes*, eds. Brian Galligan, J. R. Nethercote, and Cliff Walsh. Canberra: Centre for Research on Federal Financial Relations and Royal Australian Institute of Public Administration (ACT Division).

Henig, Jeffrey R. 1994. *Rethinking School Choice: Limits of the Market Metaphor*. Princeton: University of Princeton Press.

Hennessey, Peter. 1986. *Cabinet*. Oxford: Basil Blackwell.

Hennessy, Peter. 1992. *Never Again: Britain 1945–1951*. London: Jonathan Cape.

Hess, Stephen. 1988. *Organizing the Presidency*. Washington, DC: Brookings.

Hockin, Thomas A. 1971. *Apex of Power: The Prime Minister and Political Leadership in Canada*. Scarborough: Prentice-Hall.

Hood, Christopher. 1990. "De-Sir Humphreyfying the Westminister Model of Bureaucracy: A New Style of Governance?" *Governance* 3:205–214.

Jeffrey, Brooke. 1992. *Breaking Faith: The Mulroney Legacy of Deceit, Destruction and Disunity*. Toronto: Key Porter.

Jentleson, Bruce. 1994. *With Friends Like These: Reagan, Bush and Saddam, 1982–1990*. New York: Norton.

Johnson, Haynes and David S. Broder. 1996. *The System: The American Way of Politics at the Breaking Point*. Boston: Little, Brown.

Jones, Charles O. 1996. "Campaigning to Govern: The Clinton Style." In *The Clinton Presidency: First Appraisals*, eds. Colin Campbell and Bert A. Rockman. Chatham, NJ: Chatham House.

Jones, Charles O. 1994. *The Presidency in a Separated System*. Washington, DC: Brookings.

Jones, George W. 1983. "Prime Ministers' Departments Really Create Problems: A Rejoinder to Patrick Weller." *Public Administration* 61: 79–84.

Jones, George W. 1991. "Presidentialization in a Parliamentary System?" In *Executive Leadership in Anglo-American Systems*, eds. Colin Campbell and Margaret Jane Wyszomirski. Pittsburgh: University of Pittsburgh Press.

Jowell, Jeffrey. 1989. "The Rule of Law Today." In *The Changing Constitution*, eds. Jeffrey Jowell and Dawn Oliver. Oxford: Oxford University Press.

Kaufmann, William F. 1964. *The McNamara Strategy*. New York: Harper & Row.

Keating, M. 1988. "Managing Change in the Public Sector." *Canberra Bulletin of Public Administration* 55:59–63.

Keating, M. and Geoff Dixon. 1989. *Making Economic Policy in Australia 1983–1988*. Melbourne: Longman Cheshire.

Keating M. and M. Holmes. 1990. "Australia's Budgetary and Financial Management Reforms." *Governance* 3:168–185.

Keegan, William. 1984. *Mrs Thatcher's Economic Experiment*. Harmondsworth: Penguin.

Keegan, William. 1989. *Mr. Lawson's Gamble*. London: Hodder & Stoughton.

Keegan, William. 1992. *The Spectre of Capitalism: The Future of the World Economy After the Fall of Communism*. London: Radius.

Kellner, Peter and Lord Crowther-Hunt. 1980. *The Civil Servants: An Inquiry into Britain's Ruling Class*. London: MacDonald.

Kelly, Paul. 1984. *The Hawke Ascendancy: A Definitive Account of its Origins and Climax 1975–1983*. Sydney: Angus and Robertson.

Kelly, Paul. 1994. *The End of Certainty: Power, Politics and Business in Australia*. Sydney: Allen and Unwin.

Kernell, Samuel. 1986. *Going Public: New Strategies of Presidential Leadership*. Washington, DC: Congressional Quarterly Press.

Ketcham, Ralph. 1984. *Presidents Above Party: The First American Presidency, 1789–1829*. Chapel Hill: University of North Carolina Press.

King, Anthony, ed. 1975. *Why Is Britain Becoming Harder to Govern?* London: BBC Books.

King, Roger. 1986. *The State in Modern Society: New Directions in Political Sociology*. London: Macmillan.

Light, Paul. 1985. *Artful Work: The Politics of Social Security Reform*. New York: Random House.

Lijphart, Arend. 1977. *Democracy in Plural Societies: A Comparative Exploration*. New Haven: Yale University Press.

Lijphart, Arend, Roger Rogowski, and R. Kent Weaver. 1993. "Separation of Powers and Cleavage Management." In *Do Institutions Matter? Government Capabilities in the United States and Abroad*, eds. R. Kent Weaver and Bert A. Rockman. Washington, DC: Brookings.

Lind, Michael. 1995. *The Next American Nation: The New Nationalism and the Fourth American Revolution*. New York: Free Press.

Lindblom, Charles E. 1965. *The Intelligence of Democracy: Decision-Making Through Mutual Adjustment*. New York: Free Press.

Little, Graham. 1983. "Hawke in Place: Evaluating Narcissism." *Meanjin* 42:431–444.

Lowi, Theodore J. 1969. *The End of Liberalism: Ideology, Policy, and the Crisis of Public Authority*. New York: Norton.

Lynn, Lawrence E., Jr., and David deF. Whitman. 1981. *The President as Policymaker: Jimmy Carter and Welfare Reform*. Philadelphia: Temple University Press.

Mackintosh, John P. 1977. *The British Cabinet*. London: Stevens.

Marmor, Theodore R., Jerry L. Mashaw, and Philip L. Harvey. 1990. *America's Misunderstood Welfare State: Persistent Myths, Enduring Realities.* New York: Basic Books.

Martin, Lawrence. 1993. *Pledge of Allegiance: The Americanization of Canada in the Mulroney Years.* Toronto: McClelland & Stewart.

Martin, Lawrence. 1995. *Chrétien: The Will to Win.* Toronto: Lester.

Mayhew, David R. 1991. *Divided We Govern.* New Haven: Yale University Press.

Mayntz, Renate. 1980. "Executive Leadership in Germany: Dispersion of Power or 'Kanzlerdemokratie.' " In *Presidents and Prime Ministers*, eds. Richard Rose and Ezra N. Suleiman. Washington, DC: American Enterprise Institute.

McDonald, Forrest. 1985. *Novus Ordo Seclorum: The Intellectual Origins of the Constitution.* Lawrence: University Press of Kansas.

McRoberts, Kenneth and Dale Posgate. 1980. *Quebec: Social Change and Political Crisis*, 2nd. ed. Toronto: McClelland & Stewart.

McWilliams, Wilson Carey. 1993. "The Meaning of the Election." In *The Election of 1992*, ed. Gerald M. Pomper. Chatham, NJ: Chatham House.

Miller, Gary J. 1993. "Formal Theory and the Presidency." In *Researching the Presidency: Vital Questions, New Approaches*, eds. George C. Edwards, John H. Kessel, Bert A. Rockman. Pittsburgh: University of Pittsburgh Press.

Moe, Terry M. 1985. "The Politicized Presidency." In *The New Direction in American Politics*, eds. John E. Chubb and Paul E. Peterson. Washington, DC: Brookings.

Moe, Terry M. 1993. "Presidents, Institutions and Theory." In *Researching the Presidency: Vital Questions, New Approaches*, eds. George Edwards, John Kessel, and Bert A. Rockman. Pittsburgh: University of Pittsburgh Press.

Morton, W. L. 1955. "The Formation of the First Federal Government." *Canadian Historical Review* 36:113–25.

Munnell, Alicia, ed. 1991. *Is There a Shortfall in Public Capital Investment?* Boston: Federal Reserve Bank of Boston.

Nathan, Richard. 1975. *The Plot That Failed: Nixon and the Administrative Presidency.* New York: Wiley.

Nathan, R. P. 1983. *The Administrative Presidency.* New York: Wiley.

Nelson, Anna Kasten. 1981. "National Security I: Inventing A Process (1945–1960)." In *The Illusion of Presidential Government*, eds. Hugh Heclo and Lester M. Salamon. Boulder, CO: Westview.

Neustadt, Richard E. 1976. *Presidential Power: The Politics of Leadership.* New York: Wiley.

Neustadt, Richard E.1990. *Presidential Power and Modern Presidents: The Politics of Leadership from Roosevelt to Reagan.* New York: Free Press.

Newland, Chester. 1983. "The Reagan Presidency: Limited Government and Political Administration." *Public Administration* 43:1–21.

Newton, Kenneth. 1993. "Caring and Competence: The Long, Long Campaign." In *Britain at the Polls 1992*, ed. Anthony King. Chatham, NJ: Chatham House.

Niskanen, William A. 1971. *Bureaucracy and Representative Government*. New York: Aldine and Atherton.

Niskanen, William A. 1973a. *Structural Reform of the Federal Budget Process*. Washington, DC: American Enterprise Institute.

Niskanen, William A. 1973b. *Bureaucracy: Servant or Master? Lessons from America*. London: Institute of Economic Affairs.

Olsen, Johan P. 1983. *Organized Democracy: Political Institutions in a Welfare State: The Case of Norway*. Oslo: Universitetsforlaget.

Olson, Mancur. 1982. *The Rise and Decline of Nations: Economic Growth, Stagflation, and Social Rigidities*. New Haven: Yale University Press.

Parliamentary Labor Party. 1983. *Labor and the Quality of Government* (A Report Issued on 9 February). Canberra: Australian Labour Party.

Pearson, Lester B. 1975. *Mike: The Memoirs of the Right Honourable Lester B. Pearson*, v. 3 [1957–1968], eds. John Munro and Alex Linglis. Toronto: University of Toronto Press.

Pempel, T. J. 1982. *Policy and Politics in Japan: Creative Conservatism*. Philadelphia: Temple University Press.

Peters, B. Guy. 1991. "Executive Leadership in an Age of Entrenchment." In *Executive Leadershiop in Anglo-American Systems*, eds. Colin Campbell and Margaret Wyszomirski. Pittsburgh: University of Pittsburgh Press.

Peterson, Paul E. and Mark Rom. 1988. "Lower Taxes, More Spending, and Budget Deficits." In *The Reagan Legacy: Promise and Performance*, ed. Charles O. Jones. Chatham, NJ: Chatham House.

Phillips, Kevin. 1990. *The Politics of the Rich and Poor: Wealth in the American Electorate in the Reagan Aftermath*. New York: Random House.

Pierson, Christopher. 1991. *Beyond the Welfare State? The New Political Economy of Welfare*. University Park: Pennsylvania State University Press.

Pierson, Paul. 1994. *Dismantling the Welfare State? Reagan, Thatcher, and the Politics of Retrenchment*. Cambridge: Cambridge University Press.

Pilger, John. 1992. *A Secret Country*. London: Vintage.

Pomper, Gerald M. 1993. "The Presidential Election." In *The Election of 1992*, ed. Gerald M. Pomper. Chatham, NJ: Chatham House.

Porter, John. 1965. *The Vertical Mosaic: An Analysis of Social Class and Power in Canada*. Toronto: University of Toronto Press.

Porter, Roger B. 1980. *Presidential Decision Making*. Cambridge: Cambridge University Press.

Porter, Roger B. 1991. "Council of Economic Advisors" In *Executive Leader-*

ship in Anglo-American Systems, eds. Colin Campbell and Margaret Wyszomirski. Pittsburgh: University of Pittsburgh Press.

Pressman, Jeffrey L. and Aaron Wildavsky. 1973. *Implementation*. Berkeley: University of California Press.

Pruitt, Dean. 1982. *Negotiating Behavior*. New York: Academic Press.

Public Service Commissioner. 1988. *Public Service 2000: The Australian Public Service Workforce of the Future*. Canberra: Public Service Commission.

Pusey, Michael. 1988. "Our Top Canberra Public Servants Under Hawke." *Australian Quarterly* 60:109–22.

Pusey, Michael. 1991. *Economic Rationalism in Canberra: A Nation Building State Changes Its Mind*. Cambridge: Cambridge University Press.

Qualls, James H. 1977. "Barber's Typological Analysis of Political Leaders." *American Political Science Review* 71:182–211.

Quirk, Paul J. 1991. "Domestic Policy: Divided Government and Cooperative Presidential Leadership." In *The Bush Administration: First Appraisals*, eds. Colin Campbell and Bert A. Rockman. Chatham, NJ: Chatham House.

Quirk, Paul J. and Joseph Hinchliffe. 1996. "Domestic Policy: The Trials of a Centrist Democrat." In *The Clinton Presidency: First Appraisals*, eds. Colin Campbell and Bert A. Rockman. Chatham, NJ: Chatham House.

Radwanski, George. 1978. *Trudeau*. Toronto: Macmillan.

(RIPA). Royal Institute for Public Administration. 1987. *Top Jobs in Whitehall: Report of a Working Group*. London: RIPA.

Roberts, Paul Craig. 1984. *The Supply-Side Revolution: An Insider's Account of Policymaking in Washington*. Cambridge: Harvard University Press.

Rockman, Bert A. 1984. *The Leadership Question*. New York: Praeger.

Rockman, Bert A. 1991a. "The Leadership Style of George Bush." In *The Bush Administration: First Appraisals*, eds. Colin Campbell and Bert A. Rockman. Chatham, NJ: Chatham House.

Rockman, Bert A. 1991b. "The Leadership Question: Is There an Answer?" In *Executive Leadership In Anglo-American Systems*, eds. Colin Campbell and Margaret Jane Wyszomirski. Pittsburgh: University of Pittsburgh Press.

Rockman, Bert A. 1996. "Leadership Style and the Clinton Presidency." In *The Clinton Presidency: First Appraisals*, eds. Colin Campbell and Bert A. Rockman. Chatham, NJ: Chatham House.

Rose, Richard. 1976. *Managing Presidential Objectives*. New York: Free Press.

Rose, Richard. 1991. *The Postmodern President: George Bush Meets the World*, 2nd ed. Chatham, NJ: Chatham House.

Rose, Richard and Guy Peters. 1978. *Can Government Go Bankrupt?* New York: Basic Books.

Russell, Peter H. 1993. *Constitutional Odyssey: Can Canadians Become a Sovereign People?* Toronto: University of Toronto Press.

Savoie, Donald T. 1994. *Thatcher, Reagan, Mulroney: In Search of a New Bu-reaucracy.* Pittsburgh: University of Pittsburgh Press.

Schick, Allen. 1981. "The Problem of Presidential Budgeting." In *The Illusion of Presidential Government,* eds. Hugh Heclo and Lester M. Salamon. Boulder, CO: Westview.

Scott, Graham and Peter Gorringe. 1989. "Reform of the Core Public Sector: The New Zealand Experience." *Governance* 3:138–67.

Self, Peter. 1993. *Government by the Market?: The Politics of Public Choice.* Boulder, CO: Westview.

Seymour-Ure, Colin. 1991. "The Role of Press Secretaries on Chief Executive Staffs in Anglo-American Systems." In *Executive Leadership in Anglo-American Systems,* eds. Colin Campbell and Margaret Wyszomirski. Pittsburgh: University of Pittsburgh Press.

Shoemaker, Christopher C. 1991. *The NSC Staff.* Boulder, CO: Westview.

Simeon, Richard. 1972. *Federal-Provincial Diplomacy: The Making of Recent Policy in Canada.* Toronto: University of Toronto Press.

Sinclair, Barbara. 1991. "Governing Unheroically (and Sometimes Unappetiz-ingly): Bush and the 101st Congress." In *The Bush Administration: First Appraisals,* eds. Colin Campbell and Bert A. Rockman. Chatham, NJ: Chatham House.

Sinclair, Barbara. 1996. "Trying to Govern Positively in a Negative Era." In *The Clinton Presidency: First Appraisals.* Chatham, NJ: Chatham House.

Skene, Wayne. 1994. *Turbulence: How Deregulation Destroyed Canada's Air-lines.* Vancouver: Douglas and McIntyre.

Stanley, Harold W. 1996. "The Parties, the President, and the 1994 Midterm Elections." In *The Clinton Presidency: First Appraisals,* eds. Colin Campbell and Bert A. Rockman. Chatham, NJ: Chatham House.

Stewart, Walter. 1972. *Shrug: Trudeau in Power.* Toronto: New Press.

Stewart, Walter. 1973. *Divide and Con: Canadian Politics at Work.* Toronto: New Press.

Stockman, David. 1986. *The Triumph of Politics: How the Reagan Revolution Failed.* New York: Harper & Row.

Suleiman, Ezra. 1978. *Elites in French Society.* Princeton, NJ: Princeton University Press.

Sundquist, James L. 1986. *Constitutional Reform and Effective Government.* Washington, DC: Brookings.

Sundquist, James L. 1988–89. "Needed: A Political Theory for the New Era of Coalition Government in the United States." *Political Science Quarterly* 103: 613–35.

Szanton, Peter. 1981. *Federal Reorganization: What Have We Learned?* Chatham, NJ: Chatham House.

Tarnopolsky, Walter S. 1983. "The Constitution and Human Rights." In *And No One Cheered,* eds. Keith Banting and Richard Simeon. Ontario: Methuen.

Taylor, Peter. 1990. *Britain and the Cold War: 1945 as a Geopolitical Transition*. London: Pinter.

Thatcher, Margaret. 1993. *The Downing Street Years*. New York: HarperCollins.

Thompson, Elaine. 1994. *Fair Enough: Egalitarianism in Australia*. Sydney: University of New South Wales Press.

Trudeau, Pierre. 1993. *Memoirs*. Toronto: McClelland and Stewart.

Turpin, Colin. 1989. "Ministerial Responsibility: Myth or Reality?" In *The Changing Constitution*, eds. Jeffrey Jowell and Dawn Oliver. Oxford: Oxford University Press.

Van Loon, Richard. 1985. "A Revisionist History of Planning Processes in Ottawa? An Open Letter to Colin Campbell." *Canadian Public Administration* 28:307–318.

Walker, Jack L. 1966. "A Critique of the Elitist Theory of Democracy." *American Political Science Review* 60:285–295.

Walker, Jack L. 1969. "The Diffusion of Innovations Among the America States." *American Political Science Review* 63:880–890.

Wattenberg, Martin P. 1991. *The Rise of Candidate-Centered Politics*. Cambridge, MA: Harvard University Press.

Weaver, Kent. 1986. "The Politics of Blame Avoidance." *Journal of Public Policy* 6:371–398.

Webley, Simon. 1985. *Stiffening the Sinews of the Nations: Economic Infrastructure in the United States, United Kingdom and Canada*. London: British-North American Committee.

Weller, Patrick. 1983. "Do Prime Ministers' Departments Really Create Problems?" *Public Administration* 61:59–78.

Weller, Patrick. 1985. *First Among Equals: Prime Ministers in Westminster Systems*. London: Allen and Unwin.

Wettenhall, Roger. 1989. "Recent Restructuring in Canberra: A Report on Machinery-of-Government Changes in Australia." *Governance* 2:95–106.

White, Joseph. 1995. *Competing Solutions: American Health Care Proposals and International Experience*. Washington, DC: Brookings.

Wildavsky, Aaron. 1974. *The Politics of the Budgetary Process*, 2nd ed. Boston: Little, Brown.

Wildavsky, Aaron. 1983. "From Chaos Comes Opportunity: Movement Toward Spending Limits in American and Canadian Budgeting," *Canadian Public Administration* 26:163–81.

Wood, Gordon. 1969 and 1983. *The Creation of the American Republic, 1776–1787*. Chapel Hill: University of North Carolina Press.

Woodward, Bob. 1994. *Agenda: Inside the Clinton White House*. New York: Simon & Schuster.

Yeatman, Anna. 1987. "The Concept of Public Management and the Australian State in the 1980s." *Australian Journal of Public Management* 46:339–356.

NEWSPAPERS

Apple, R. W., Jr. "Clinton's Refocusing," *New York Times*, 6 May 1993.

Apple, R. W., Jr. "Clinton at Work: Is Motion the Same as Action," *New York Times*, 30 October 1993.

Baker, Russell. "The Flexible Goodbye," *New York Times*, 26 July 1994.

Balz, Dan. "For Clinton, Here Comes the Hard Part," *International Herald Tribune*, 18 January 1993.

Balz, Dan. "Health Plan Was Albatross for Democrats: Big Government Label Hurt Party, Poll Finds," *Washington Post*, 18 November 1994.

Balz, Dan and John E. Yang. "Gingrich to Lower His Public Profile," *Washington Post*, 2 December 1995.

Barr, Stephen and Al Kamen. "Transition Momentum Bogs Down at Sub-Cabinet Level," *Washington Post*, 11 January 1993.

Batchelor, Charles and George Parker. "Rail Privatisation Boosted as First Three Franchises Are Sold," *Financial Times*, 20 December 1995.

Bates, Stephen. "Portillo Bid to Hijack the Agenda," *Guardian*, 15 January 1994.

Berke, Richard L. "Centrists Are Wary of Clinton Tilting," *New York Times*, 3 December 1993.

Berke, Richard L. "The Good Son," *New York Times*, 20 February 1994.

Bevins, Anthony. "Cabinet Warning to PM," *Independent*, 17 November 1990.

Bevins, Anthony. "Patten Emerges as the Guiding Intelligence," *Independent*, 13 March 1991.

Bevins, Anthony. "Major's Farewell to Confrontation," *Independent*, 7 May 1991.

Bevins, Anthony and Nicholas Timmins. "Cabinet Dismay on Referendum," *Independent*, 19 November 1990.

Blumenthal, Sidney. "Rendez-vous with Destiny," *New Yorker*, 8 March 1993.

Bradsher, Keith. "Administration Rift Reported over Course of Trade Policy," *New York Times*, 23 April 1993.

Bradsher, Keith. "Clinton's Shopping List for Votes Has Ring of Grocery Buyer's List," *New York Times*, 17 November 1993.

Brindle, David. "Treasury Plan to Curb Youth Hardship Bill," *Guardian*, 2 June 1994.

Broder, David S. "The Clinton Generation Brings Its Own Scars," *International Herald Tribune*, 11 February 1993.

Broder, David S. "He Can't Go It Alone," *Washington Post*, 19 May 1993.

Broder, David S. "Clinton's Approval Ratings Weaken," *Washington Post*, 16 November 1993.

Broder, David S. "NAFTAmath," *Washington Post*, 19 November 1993.

Broder, David S. "Bipartisanship Forged by Crime," *Washington Post*, 15 August 1994.

Broder, David S. "Does Clinton Want to Govern," *Washington Post*, 4 February 1996.

Brown, Colin. "Happy Days Are Here Again," *Independent*, 17 December 1990.

Brown, Maggie. "Tory Leadership Contest: Weekend Attacks May Backfire on Prime Minister," *Independent*, 20 November 1990.

Burns, Jimmy and John Kampfner, "Government 'Inept' says Ex-Ambassador," *Financial Times*, 10 February 1996.

Cohen, Richard. "The Battle Over Gays," *Washington Post*, 26 March 1993.

Colebatch, Tim. "Time for a Kinder Keating to Take a Tougher Stage," *Age*, 6 October 1994.

Dawkins, William. "Tokyo Finance Ministry Under Threat" *Financial Times*, 8 February 1996.

Delacourt, Susan. "PM Promises Political Stability," *Globe and Mail*, 2 November 1995.

Delacourt, Susan. "PM's Star Rises Among Premiers," *Globe and Mail*, 22 December 1993.

Delacourt, Susan and Rheal Seguin. "Mulroney Attempts to Reassure Wells," *Globe and Mail*, 13 June 1990.

DeParle, Jason. "Clinton Social Policy Camps: Bill's vs. Hillary's," *New York Times*, 20 December 1992.

Devroy, Ann. "Understanding McLarty, a Second-Tier Contest," *Washington Post*, 14 December 1992.

Devroy, Ann. "A Bonding Experience at Camp David," *Washington Post*, 5 February 1993.

Devroy, Ann. "Clinton Shuffles Staff to Return to 'Basics'," *Washington Post*, 7 May 1993.

Devroy, Ann. "Post Vacation Clinton Swims Toward Mainstream," *Washington Post*, 6 September 1993.

Devroy, Ann. "How the White House Runs and Stumbles," *Washington Post*, 9 November 1993.

Devroy, Ann. "Another Miserable White House August," *Washington Post*, 10 August 1994.

Devroy, Ann. "For Clinton, Crime and Health Equaled Another Bad Day at the Office," *Washington Post*, 12 August 1994.

Devroy, Ann. "GOP and White House Confront an Era of New Relations: Reasserting Presidency Means Rethinking Almost Everything," *Washington Post*, 14 November 1994.

Devroy, Ann. "President Struggling to Stake Out Strategy and Take the Offensive," *Washington Post*, 30 November 1994.

Devroy, Ann. "Panetta Holds Gingrich's Words Against Him—and His Party," *Washington Post*, 6 December 1994.

Devroy Ann. "Another Attempt to Begin Again," *Washington Post*, 15 December 1994.

Devroy, Ann. "Tax-Cut Plan Is Geared to Families: President Vows to Put Aside Politics," *Washington Post*, 16 December 1994.

Devroy, Ann. "Republican Advisor Stages a Quiet White House Coup," *Washington Post*, 18 June 1995.

Devroy, Ann. "After Series of Moves to the Center, Clinton Stakes Out Traditional Position," *Washington Post*, 20 July 1995.

Devroy Ann. "Clinton's Shifts Show Influence of Consultant," *Washington Post*, 3 November 1995.

Devroy, Ann and Ruth Marcus. "White House Needs 'Tighter Coordination,' Clinton Concedes," *Washington Post*, 5 May 1993.

Devroy, Ann and Ruth Marcus. "Panetta Claims 'Authority' to Make Changes," *Washington Post*, 1 July 1994.

Devroy, Ann and David S. Broder. "Democrats Plan Longer Phase-in to Full Coverage," *Washington Post*, 22 July 1994.

Devroy, Ann and John F. Harris. "Clinton Says His Record Shows Remarkable Consistency," *Washington Post*, 31 January 1996.

Dionne, E. J., Jr. "Anatomy of a Feud," *Washington Post*, 7 December 1993.

Dowd, Maureen. "New Role, New Troubles," *New York Times*, 6 March 1994.

Dowd, Maureen. "Amid a Debate on White House Women, Hillary Clinton Tries to Push On," *New York Times*, 29 September 1994.

Dwyer, Michael. "Keating Dismisses Pressure for Action on Deficit," *Financial Review*, 11 October 1994.

Editorial. "It Is a Tough Country to Govern," *Globe and Mail*, 20 June 1990.

Editorial. *Independent*, 4 January 1992.

Editorial. "Win Who May, He Will Be Waiting," *Independent*, 7 March 1992.

Edley, Christopher, Jr. "The Road to Clinton's Big Speech," *Washington Post*, 23 July 1995.

Edsall, Thomas B. "Split Over NAFTA May Strengthen Force of Disaffected Voter," *Washington Post*, 19 November 1993.

Federal News Service, "President Accepts Share of Responsibility for the Democrats' Shellacking," *Washington Post*, 10 November 1994.

Friedman, Thomas L. "Change of Tone for Clinton: High Energy to Low Profile," *New York Times*, 11 November 1992.

Friedman, Thomas L. "Democratic Leader and Clinton Friend Gain Major Posts," *New York Times*, 13 December 1992.

Friedman, Thomas L. "Judge Rules Military's Ban on Homosexuals Is Void," *New York Times*, 29 January 1993.

Friedman, Thomas L. "For Clinton, Foreign Policy Comes Afterward," *International Herald Tribune*, 9 February 1993.

Friedman, Thomas L. "Clinton's Foreign Policy: Top Adviser Speaks Up," *New York Times*, 31 October 1993.

Friedman, Thomas L. and Elaine Sciolino. "Clinton and Foreign Issues: Spasms of Attention," *New York Times*, 22 March 1993.

Friedman, Thomas L. and Maureen Dowd. "Amid Setbacks, Clinton Team Seeks to Shake off the Blues," *New York Times*, 25 April 1993.

Gelb, Leslie H. "Avoiding Carter's Mistakes," *New York Times*, 28 January 1993.

Gelb, Leslie H. "Where's Bill," *New York Times*, 11 March 1993.

Gellman, Barton. "Service Moving to Protect Turf, Powell to Rebuff Call to Streamline," *Washington Post*, 28 January 1993.

Gellman, Barton. "Pentagon Deadlock as a Deal Collapses, How Powell's Switch on Cuts Scuttled a Capitol Scenario," *International Herald Tribune*, 30–31 January 1993.

Gherson, Giles. "Never Mind the Approval Ratings, What Really Counts Is a Solid Start," *Globe and Mail*, 4 November 1993.

Gherson, Giles. "Nagging Doubts that the Government Really Has a Quebec Strategy," *Globe and Mail*, 25 January 1995.

Goodwin, Stephen. "Parliament and Politics: Howe Tells of 'Tragic' Conflict of Loyalties," *Independent*, 14 November 1990.

Gordon, Michael. "Inside Keating's Creative Nation," *Weekend Australian*, 22 October 1994.

Greenhouse, Steven. "Resignations at Treasury Raise the Question:Is Bentsen Next?" *New York Times*, 25 August 1993.

Greenspon, Edward. "Chrétien Strives to Get the Plumbing Right," *Globe and Mail*, 25 October 1994.

Gugliotta, Guy. "97 Budget Casts No Shadows," *Washington Post*, 5 February 1996.

Ha, Tu Thanh. "Ottawa to Serve Unity Aim at Dinner," *Globe and Mail*, 12 September 1995.

Helprin, Mark. "School of Scandal," *Wall Street Journal*, 25 March 1994.

Hencke, David. "Cabinet Plans U-turn on Bill to Cut Red Tape," *Guardian*, 24 November 1993.

Hencke, David. "PM Stands by His Role in Dam Aid," *Guardian*, 19 January 1994.

Hencke, David. "More Quit Whitehall to Be Consultants," *Guardian*, 13 February 1995.

Hennessy, Peter. "Whitehall Watch: War Gives Major a New Gravitas," *Independent*, 21 January 1991.

Hoagland, Jim, "Candidate Against Change," *Washington Post*, 16 February 1995.

Hutton, Kelly, and White "Clarke Lays Out His Centrist Stall," *Guardian*, 5 May 1994.

Ifill, Gwen. "Economic Plan Grew Slowly Out of Marathon Debate," *New York Times*, 21 February 1993.

Ifill, Gwen. "The Economic Czar Behind the Economic Czars," *New York Times*, 7 March 1993.

Ifill, Gwen. "Off-the Books Advisors Giving Clinton a Big Lift," *New York Times*, 1 April 1993.

Jehl, Douglas. "Hinting at More Changes, Panetta Takes the Reins," *New York Times*, 28 June 1994.

Jehl, Douglas. "New Chief of Staff Gets a Lesson on Who's the Boss," *New York Times*, 30 June 1994.

Jenkins, Peter. "Market-Driven, Socially-Aware," *Independent*, 14 February 1991.

Jenkins, Peter. "The Shift of Key to Major May Not Be Enough," *Independent*, 14 November 1991.

Kampfner, John. "Probe Urged into Regulator after Flight's Admission," *Financial Times*, 13 December 1995.

Kelly, Michael. "Furor Appears to Doom Cabinet Contender," *New York Times*, 17 December 1992.

Kelly, Michael. "Bill Clinton: The President's Past," *New York Times*, 31 July 1994.

Kolbert, Elizabeth. "The Stealth Strategist Refocusing Clinton," *New York Times*, 1 July 1995.

Kurtz, Howard. "Gingrich Plans to End Daily News Briefings," *Washington Post*, 3 May 1995.

Linton, Martin. "Labour Winning Over Voters on Taxation," *Guardian*, 16 March 1994.

Marcus, Ruth. "Vote Victory Was Vital Boost for Clinton's Beleaguered Chief," *Washington Post*, 29 May 1993.

Marcus, Ruth. "Clinton Reiterates How to Pursue New Democratic Agenda," *Washington Post*, 11 November 1994.

Meikle, James. "Major Taps Tory Anger on Schools," *Guardian*, 1 January 1994.

Meikle, James. "Tension Over Values and 'Nannyism'," *Guardian*, 11 January 1994.

Meikle, James. "Major Moves Aid to Lost Generation," *Guardian*, 26 July 1994.

Mitchell, Alison. "New Strategy Puts Clinton on His Own," *New York Times*, 15 June 1995.

Norton-Taylor, Richard. "Civil Servants Call for Code to Stop Ministers' Passing Buck," *Guardian*, 16 November 1993.

Pear, Robert. "First Lady Gets Office and Job in West Wing," *New York Times*, 22 January 1993.

Pear, Robert. "A White House Fight," *New York Times*, 25 May 1993.

Pear, Robert. "Health Planners at White House Consider Lid on Medicare Costs," *New York Times*, 30 August 1993.

Pear, Robert. "High Level Dispute on Who Will Redo Health Care Policy," *New York Times*, 13 October 1994.

Peston, Robert. "Sale of State Railroad Company Hits Serious Obstacle," *Financial Times*, 14 February 1996.

Peston, Robert. "Escape After the Storm," *Financial Times*, February 1996.

Pianin, Eric and John F. Harris. "Hill Republican Leaders See Compromise as Possible While Some Administration Allies See a Blunder," *Washington Post*, 15 June 1995.

Priest, Dana. "Putting Health Care Under Microscope," *Washington Post*, 16 April 1993.

Priest, Dana and Ruth Marcus. "Key Clinton Health Ideas Face Major Opposition," *Washington Post*, 20 February 1994.

Purdum, Todd. "Clinton Turns to Gore's Proposal for Faster, Cheaper Government," *New York Times*, 19 December 1994.

Raspberry, William. "Developing Human Capital," *Washington Post*, 26 December 1994.

Redburn, Tom. "U. S. Aims to Inject Life into G-7," *International Herald Tribune*, 21 June 1993.

Robinson, Peter. "Government by Thuggery," *Sunday Morning Herald*, 20 March 1994.

Rosenbaum, David E. "On Economics, White House Is Steering Clear of Bickering," *New York Times*, 27 May 1994.

Rosenbaum, David E. "Starting Point for Talks," *New York Times*, 14 June 1995.

Rosenbaum, David E. "Both Sides of the Aisle Sense Capital's Unrest," *New York Times*, 21 October 1995.

Rowen, Hobart. "Invitation to a Trade War," *Washington Post*, 3 March 1994.

Samuelson, Robert, ". . . And He Isn't FDR," *Washington Post*, 19 May 1993.

Seelye, Katherine. "As a Model, Gingrich Takes Presidents, Not Predecessor," *New York Times*, 11 April 1995.

Sherrill, Martha. "Hillary Clinton's Inner Politics," *Washington Post*, 6 May 1993.

Staff. "And Now, Paying for the Promises: Tax Rises and Spending Cuts Loom," *International Herald Tribune*, 15 January 1993.

Staff. "Mrs. Clinton to Head Health Task Force," *International Herald Tribune*, 26 January 1993.

Staff. "A Too-Frank Aide and Balky Congress," *International Herald Tribune*, 28 April 1993.

Toner, Robin. "How Much Health-Care Reform Will the Patient Go Along With?" *New York Times*, 7 March 1993.

Toner, Robin. "Clinton's Health-Care Plan," *New York Times*, 7 April 1993.

Travis, Alan. "Howard Plans Boot Camps," *Guardian*, 2 June 1994.

Von Drehle, David and Ann Devroy. "White House Plans Broad Staff Shifts," *Washington Post*, 29 May 1993.

Waterford, Jack. "All is not Well Behind the Facade." *Canberra Times*, 25 March 1994.

White, Michael. "Major Sets Agenda to Attack Blair," *Guardian*, 28 July 1994.

White, Michael, Ian Black, and Richard Norton-Taylor. "Major Gave Go-ahead for Pergau Buy-out," *Guardian*, 12 November 1994.

White, Michael and Patrick Wintour. "Clarke Keen to 'Protect' Single Mothers," *Guardian*, 16 November 1993.

Williams, Juan. "Clinton's Morning in America," *Washington Post*, 12 November 1995.

Wines, Michael. "A 'Bazaar' Method of Dealing for Votes," *New York Times*, 11 November 1993.

Wines, Michael. "First Lady's Health Strategy: Accept Less or Gamble It All?" *New York Times*, 5 July 1994.

Wines, Michael. "The Health Care Debate: The Campaign," *New York Times*, 2 August 1994.

Wines, Michael. "Cramming: So Many Minds to Be Changed, So Little Time," *New York Times*, 11 September 1994.

Wines, Michael. "White House Regrouping for Round Two on Health Care," *New York Times*, 28 September 1994.

Wines, Michael. "In Defeat, Clinton Aides Find Their Silver Lining," *New York Times*, 12 November 1994.

Wines, Michael. "White House in Struggle to Take Back the Agenda," *New York Times*, 17 November 1994.

Winsor, Hugh. "Liberal Cabinet Designed for Comfort," *Globe and Mail*, 5 November 1993.

Winsor, Hugh, "Bourgon Key Woman in Ottawa," *Globe and Mail*, 25 February 1994.

Winsor, Hugh. "Chrétien's Approval Ratings Soar in Recent Polls," *Globe and Mail*, 17 November 1994.

Winsor, Hugh. "Ottawa Sticks to Game Plan in Vote Fight," *Globe and Mail*, 8 September 1995.

Wintour, Patrick. "Portillo in New Benefit Crackdown," *Guardian*, 30 May 1994.

Wintour, Patrick. "Let the Yobbos Knock Blair about a Bit," *Guardian*, 22 November 1994,

Wintour, Patrick. "Blair Cool on Thatcher Praise," *Guardian*, 29 May 1995.

Wood, Alan. "Labor's 10-Year Hoodoo," *Weekend Australian*, 5 March 1994.

Woodward, Bob. "Clinton Felt Blindsided over Slashed Initiatives," *Washington Post*, 5 June 1994.

Woodward, Bob. "A War among Advisors for the President's Soul," *Washington Post*, 6 June 1994.

Zapor, Patricia. "Text Clinton," *Catholic News*, 27 October 1992.

Author Index

Subject Index

Adams, Sherman, 61, 68, 69
age of constraint, 44; restraint of "big government", 45; and neo-liberalism, 46; George Bush's presidency in, 65
Air Canada, 22, 223
Albright, Madeleine, 78
Altman, Roger, 90
American Political Science Association (APSA), 39
Aspin, Les, 78
Australia, and adaptability, 3, 10; effects of globalization on, 20; federalism, 14, 25–27; and economic rationalism, 17, 18, 181; reform of public service, 184, 185, 189; comparison of ERC and UK Star Chamber, 177; PM leadership styles, 22, 180; and the ACTU
Australian Council of Trade Unions (ACTU), and Bob Hawke as head, 30, 194
Axworthy, Lloyd, 178

Baker, James A., as head of Legislative Strategy Group, 52; as Ronald Reagan's Chief of Staff, 61, 92,
Begala, Paul, 82
Bentsen, Lloyd, 78, 90
big government. *See* age of constraint
Black, Conrad, 133, 203
Blair, Tony, 127, 230
Bloc Québécois. *See* political parties
Blumenthal, W. Michael, 52
Board of Economic Development Ministers, created by Pierre Trudeau, 155
Bouchard, Lucien, 163, 174
Bourgon, Jocelyn, 175
Bureau of the Budget (BOB) (US), as part of development of economic strategy, 54, 56; creation by Congress, 57; Richard Nixon's reform of, 59
Burney, Derek, 166
Burns, Terry, 108; as Margaret Thatcher's Chief Economic Advisor, 115
Bush, George, in aftermath of Iraqi invasion, 8, 66, 223; vision of "kinder and gentler America", 18, 65; relations with Congress, 37, 69; loss of mandate, 40, 73–75; and divided government, 46; leadership style, 48, 67, 87, 102; relationship with the NSC, 52, 67, 89; relations with Chief of Staff, 53, 68, 82,

93; creation and management of economic policy agencies, 55, 58; foreign policy, 67, 79, 224; negotiation of NAFTA, 75; comparison with John Major, 122, 123
Butler, Robin, 121, 127, 132, 134

cabinet consultation, under Margaret Thatcher, 108, 117, 118, 237
cabinet government, 50; under Jimmy Carter 62; under Ronald Reagan, 63; as backlash to Richard Nixon, 87; Margaret Thatcher's approach to, 117, 119; as element of Margaret Thatcher's downfall, 124; John Major's approach to, 140; Pierre Trudeau's approach to, 159, 228; Jean Chrétien's approach to, 176; Michael Keating's approach to, 201; 228
Cabinet Office (UK), role of, 106–9
Callaghan, James, 107, 112, 119; role in the Winter of Discontent, 141
Campbell, Kim, role in PC defeat, 17, 170; ministerial experience, 24, 30; leadership style, 35; as a transitional figure, 144; rise to PM, 168; failures of, 169–70; public service reform, 170; compared to Jean Chrétien, 176
Campbellmania, 168
Carter, Jimmy, leadership style, 48; domestic policy, 51; creation and use of domestic policy agencies, 52, 55–59; compared with Ronald Reagan, 60,185; compared with Bill Clinton 82; pursuit of cabinet government, 87; compared with George Bush, 123
Canada, constitution of, 6, 148, 219; and Charter of Rights and Freedoms, 7, 15; and FTA, 9, 166; as federal system, 14, 26, 37, 42; and neo-liberalism, 16; leadership styles in, 22, 144, 221; under Kim Campbell, 24; under Jean Chrétien, 172, 176, 230; under Brian Mulroney, 3, 16, 17, 100, 160, 163; under Pierre Trudeau, 150; and Quebec issue, 144, 151, 156–58; class background of ministers, 146; and divided government, 46
Carville, James, 82
Council of Economic Advisors (CEA) (US), 54–56